CYBERCRIME

A Reference Handbook

Other Titles in ABC-CLIO's
CONTEMPORARY WORLD ISSUES
Series

Courts and Trials, Christopher E. Smith
Dating and Sexuality in America, Jeffrey Scott Turner
Drug Use, Richard Isralowitz
Environmental Activism, Jacqueline Vaughn Switzer
Families in America, Jeffrey Scott Turner
Gay and Lesbian Issues, Chuck Stewart
Healthcare Reform in America, Jeannie Jacobs Kronenfeld and Michael R. Kronenfeld
Media and American Courts, S. L. Alexander
Media and Politics in America, Guido H. Stempel III
Nuclear Weapons and Nonproliferation, Sarah J. Diehl and James Clay Moltz
Police Misconduct in America, Dean J. Champion
Racial and Ethnic Diversity in America, Adalberto Aguirre, Jr.
Racial Justice in America, David B. Mustard
Reproductive Issues in America, Janna C. Merrick and Robert H. Blank
U.S. Immigration, Michael C. LeMay
Voting in America, Robert E. DiClerico
Women and Equality in the Workplace, Janet Z. Giele and Leslie F. Stebbins
Women in Prison, Cyndi Banks

Books in the Contemporary World Issues series address vital issues in today's society such as genetic engineering, pollution, and biodiversity. Written by professional writers, scholars, and nonacademic experts, these books are authoritative, clearly written, up-to-date, and objective. They provide a good starting point for research by high school and college students, scholars, and general readers as well as by legislators, businesspeople, activists, and others.

Each book, carefully organized and easy to use, contains an overview of the subject, a detailed chronology, biographical sketches, facts and data and/or documents and other primary-source material, a directory of organizations and agencies, annotated lists of print and nonprint resources, and an index.

Readers of books in the Contemporary World Issues series will find the information they need in order to have a better understanding of the social, political, environmental, and economic issues facing the world today.

CYBERCRIME

A Reference Handbook

Bernadette H. Schell
and
Clemens Martin

CONTEMPORARY WORLD ISSUES

Santa Barbara, California Denver, Colorado Oxford, England

Library of Congress Cataloging-in-Publication Data

Schell, Bernadette H. (Bernadette Hlubik), 1952–
Cybercrime : a reference handbook / Bernadette H. Schell and Clemens Martin.
p. cm—(Contemporary world issues)
Includes bibliographical references and index.
ISBN 1-85109-683-3 (hardcover : alk. paper)
ISBN 1-85109-688-4 (e-book)
1. Computer crimes. 2. Cyberterrorism. I. Martin, Clemens. II. Title. III. Series.
HV6773.S3547 2004
364.16'8—dc22

2004013960

07 06 10 9 8 7 6 5 4 3

This book is also available on the World Wide Web as an e-book.
Visit http://www.abc-clio.com for details.

ABC-CLIO, Inc.
130 Cremona Drive, P.O. Box 1911
Santa Barbara, California 93116–1911

This book is printed on acid-free paper ♾.
Manufactured in the United States of America

Contents

Preface

Cybercrime: A Reference Handbook examines many forms of computer exploits—some positively motivated and some negatively motivated—from the Hacking Prehistory Era before 1969 through the present.

The good side of hacking, known as the White Hat variety, includes creative exploits into the cyberworld motivated by the perpetrator's quest for knowledge. White Hats tend to hack into systems with authorization to find flaws in the computer network that could be invaded by unwanted cyberintruders.

The bad side of hacking, known as the Black Hat or cybercrime variety, includes destructive computer exploits prompted by the invader's desire for revenge, sabotage, blackmail, or pure personal gain. Like crimes that are not of a cybernature, Black Hat exploits can result in harm to property and/or to people.

Experts now fear that death or devastation to multitudes of cybertargets could occur as a result of an apocalyptic cyberattack—one utilizing a computer or a network of computers—in the very near future. In fact, some cyberexperts believe that an "Internet Chernobyl" could occur as early as 2005.

According to recent estimates, the cost to victims of malicious computer attacks (more appropriately called cracks) has totaled about $10 billion over the past 5 years, including recent cell phone fraud exploits (IBM Research, 2004).

Malicious computer exploits can be far-ranging. Files containing critical government security information or medical records can be destroyed. Companies' trade secrets can be stolen or threatened by blackmailers, and banks' so-called secure systems can be tampered with. Moreover, with the growing popularity of e-mail, the Internet, and Web sites, computer crimes will likely continue to escalate.

For these reasons, it is important for citizens in the private and public sectors around the world to understand not only how the White Hat hackers can find creative solutions to fighting cybercrime, but also how the Black Hat crackers and cyberterrorists perform their exploits so that people can better protect themselves and their property from harm.

In a recently released 2003 CSI/FBI (Computer Security Institute/Federal Bureau of Investigation) survey on computer crime completed by 530 computer security practitioners in U.S. corporations, government agencies, financial institutions, medical institutions, and universities, more than half of the respondents said that their enterprises had experienced some kind of unauthorized computer use or intrusion in the previous year. Although this finding may seem to be a somewhat positive sign in that not all computer systems were adversely impacted, it should be noted that an overwhelming 99 percent of the companies surveyed had thought that they had adequate protection against cyberintruders because their systems had antivirus software, firewalls, access controls, and other security measures. Such findings indicate that better intrusion protection measures are needed (Richardson, 2003).

Furthermore, these computer intrusions were costly. In the 2003 CSI/FBI survey, the total estimated costs of these computer system intrusions were reported to be nearly $202 million. Other key findings of this survey include the following (Richardson, 2003):

- As in previous years, theft of proprietary information caused the greatest reported financial loss to the enterprises (in the $70–71 million range).
- In a shift from previous years, the second most expensive computer crime, reported at a cost of more than $65 million, was denial-of-service (DoS). Denial-of-service attacks render corporate Web sites inaccessible, causing a loss in revenues.
- As in previous years, virus incidents (82 percent) and "insider" abuse of network access by employees (80 percent) were the most cited forms of computer system attack or abuse.

- Compared to internal systems and remote dial-in, the Internet connection was cited as a frequent point of attack (78 percent).
- The percentage of respondents who reported unauthorized intruder attacks to law enforcement officers was low (30 percent).

As will be discussed in this book, for Black Hats wanting to conduct malicious exploits, talent is not necessarily required. Even neophyte crackers, called scriptkiddies or newbies in the computer underground, can easily find and exploit help on the World Wide Web. In fact, some 1,900 Web sites offer computer system intrusion tips and tools. So, terrorists intent on destroying property or people in targeted countries or states could either learn the cracking trade themselves or hire talented Black Hats. By the way, the reported "black market" price for a simple break-in to a computer system is only in the $8,000–$10,000 range (Fischetti, 1997).

This book will help readers better understand how the present-day anxieties about an imminent cyberapocalypse developed, and how to best protect their property and their persons from harm inflicted through the computer. The chapters are as follows:

- Chapter 1 describes the history of cybercrime in the United States and elsewhere, citing critical events from the 1960s to the present. The chapter also discusses the various categories of cybercrime and the growth in anxiety about a cyberapocalypse that has occurred over the past five years.
- Chapter 2 discusses in everyday language the problems and controversies associated with program security, operation system and database security, and computer networking and networked applications. Some technical and legislative solutions for curbing intrusions are discussed.
- Chapter 3 summarizes the chronology of the "wired world" and places cybercrimes in a timeline of telephony services, computing, and Internet workings.
- Chapter 4 gives biographical sketches of key headline makers (both White Hat and Black Hat) in the wired world, with a focus on those from the 1960s to the present.

- Chapter 5 provides reliable facts and data on important cybercrime cases investigated in the United States over the past 5 years.
- Chapter 6 lists pertinent agencies and organizations devoted to curbing cybercrime.
- Chapter 7 cites selected print and nonprint resources and products devoted to fighting cybercrime.
- The glossary defines some of the major computer, cracking, and cybercrime terms.

Resources

Fischetti, M. 1997. "Helpful Hacking." http://domino.research.ibm.com/comm/wwwr_thinkresearch.nsf/pages/hacking397.html (cited January 27, 2004). Originally published in *IBM Think Research Magazine,* vol. 35, 1997.

IBM Research. "Global Security Analysis Lab." http://domino.research.ibm.com/Comm/bios.nsf/pages/gsal.html (cited January 27, 2004).

Richardson, R. 2003. "2003 CSI/FBI Computer Crime and Security Survey." http://i.cmpnet.com/gocsi/db_area/pdfs/fbi/FBI2003.pdf (cited January 27, 2004).

1

History and Types of Cybercrime

This chapter provides a history of cybercrime in the United States and elsewhere and details critical real-world events that have provoked anxieties about cyberterrorism. The chapter also discusses how cybercriminals select their targets, identify the systems to be attacked, gain access into the computer systems, acquire privileges that they should not have, avoid detection, and realize their goals. The legal criteria for cybercrime and the most common categories of cybercrime are also described in this chapter.

Basic Cybercrime Terms

Hacker and Cracker

Previously, the word *hacker* in Yiddish meant an inept furniture maker. In present-day terminology, and particularly in media reports, the word *hacker* has now taken on numerous meanings, from a person who enjoys learning the details of computer systems and how to stretch their capabilities to a malicious or inquisitive meddler who tries to discover information by deceptive or illegal means. A cracker is someone who breaks security on a system. The term was coined in 1985 by hackers angered at the journalistic misuse of the word hacker.

In recent years, the boundary between the meanings of the terms *hacking* and *cracking* has become blurred. In fact, most media pieces reporting computer system intrusions today typically use the word hacker when the more correct term would be *cracker.* To White Hat hackers—the "good guys" in the computer underground—the Black Hats, or crackers, are the cybercriminals. The White Hats maintain that they are motivated by creative exploits into the cyberworld, including the quest for knowledge or the need to find intrusion flaws by breaking into a computer system with authorization. The Black Hat crackers, on the other hand, commit crimes using a computer. Their motives vary: getting revenge, sabotaging competitors' computer systems, stealing information or identities from others, and terrorizing selected targets.

A White Hat Case in Point

Computer-savvy White Hat hackers are employed by companies, governments, and financial institutions to find flaws in systems that can be attacked. For example, in a seventeenth-floor corner office in Toronto, Canada, a group of computer hackers are feverishly attacking computer systems in Canadian corporations and getting paid for it.

"If you have a system on-line, you will be a target. You are either a target of choice or a target of opportunity," says Simon Tang, manager of Deloitte & Touche LLP's Internet security team. Simon oversees a busy computer lab of ten "ethical hackers." Simon's team of information technology security experts probes the computer systems of corporate clients, searching for vulnerabilities and weaknesses. Ethical hacking, or "penetration testing," is a niche business spun out of the corporate world's increasing dependence on the Internet to stay connected with clients and to move products and services worldwide. Unfortunately, as a firm's online presence grows, so does the risk of attack from ill-motivated crackers (Damsell, 2003a).

Cybercrime

By definition, cybercrime is a crime related to technology, computers, and the Internet. The majority of publicized cybercrimes that concern governments, industry officials, and citizens worldwide include:

- Cracking: gaining unauthorized access to computer systems to commit a crime, such as digging into the code to make a copy-protected program run without a password or a valid license string, flooding Internet sites and thus denying service to legitimate users, erasing information, corrupting information, and deliberately defacing Web sites

- Piracy: copying protected software without authorization
- Phreaking: obtaining free telephone calls or having calls charged to a different account by using a computer or another device to manipulate a phone system
- Cyberstalking: harassing and terrorizing selected human and institutional targets using the computer, causing them to fear injury or harm
- Cyberpornography: producing and/or distributing pornography using a computer
- Cyberterrorism: unlawful attacks and threats of attack by terrorists against computers, networks, and the information stored therein to intimidate or coerce a government or its people to further the perpetrator's political or social objectives

A Black Hat Case in Point

A cybercrime case prominent in the media was the 1988 Internet worm of Robert Morris.

The son of the chief scientist at the National Computer Security Center (part of the National Security Agency, or NSA), this Cornell University graduate student first encountered a computer when his father brought home one of the original Enigma cryptographic machines from the NSA. Robert Morris, now an associate professor at MIT, was a gifted adolescent. As a teenager, he had an account on Bell Lab's (an international research and development community and a subsidiary of Lucent Technologies, one of the market leaders in telecommunication and network products) computer network, where his early hacking forays gave him "super-user" status with administrative privileges on the system (Slatella, 1997a).

After crashing 6,000 Internet-linked UNIX-based computers with his 1988 worm (simply called the "Internet worm"), Morris became the first person to be charged and convicted under the Comprehensive Crime Control Act, computer fraud and abuse statute, in the United States. Passed during the early 1980s to curb cracking-related activities, this piece of legislation gave the United States Secret Service jurisdiction over credit card and computer fraud, among other activities. Mr. Morris got a $10,000 fine for his cracking exploits and was sentenced to 400 hours of community service.

History of Cybercrime

The White Hats

The opportunity for creative computer hardware and software invention became available in the 1960s and 1970s through the academic explorations at the all-male Massachusetts Institute of Technology (MIT) Tech Model Railroad Club (TMRC). The TMRC was formed in 1946 and continues to this day as an actual model railroad club. The original members used their skills learned at MIT to employ advanced control systems and became the first White Hat hackers.

During this period, the word hacker began to represent a technologically focused individual and the term was applied to those who spent time crawling under the railroad tracks at the Railroad Club facility with the primary objective of connecting switches to relays with cables. Back in the early 1960s and 1970s, a "hack" meant a prank of the kind that the students and the MIT faculty played on their school or on their rivals. A hack would be an "out-of-the-box" prank such as wrapping the entire roof in tinfoil. A "good hack" would have been some creative exploit that would have impressed observers to remark, "How in the [heck] did they do that?!" (Walleij, 1999a). Eventually, the term evolved from meaning any prank to a computer prank as the students worked more closely with computer systems.

Famous White Hats (a term borrowed from black-and-white early western movies that indicated the heroes, or good guys, of the story) at MIT included Alan Kotok, Stewart Nelson, Richard Greenblatt, Tom Knight, and Bill Gosper. These early hackers were known to work in the lab for 30-hour-plus shifts and found the primitive computers so fascinating that they forgot about everything else while they were working on them. Put simply, they were enthralled with and perhaps addicted to what they were doing. They even taught themselves to pick locks in the MIT computer science building to gain access to the computers after hours. From the White Hats' perspective, this lock-picking was not criminal activity because they felt they were simply putting all available equipment to its best use. In short, the White Hats believed that computers should not be locked and should be available 24 hours a day, 7 days a week.

These early hackers were not criminals, but highly talented programmers committed to finding novel solutions to difficult problems. If the type of software or hardware they wanted was not available, these hackers would develop it. The search for new solutions created a hacker community of people who began to share computer code while building an open and freely accessible body of knowledge among peers. It was the sort of intellectual environment that is afforded to academics and is protected by academic freedom and tenure.

Some would likely argue that it was this same creative White Hat spirit that was the driving force behind the announcement by MIT on April 4, 2001, that over the next 10 years, materials for nearly all courses offered would be freely available on the Internet (MIT News, 2001).

After the 1960s and 1970s, the cyberfrontier blew wide open, with White Hat hackers across the United States exploring and figuring out how the wired world worked—and paving the way for incredible growth along the information superhighway.

The White Hat Ethic

The White Hat Hacker Ethic, perhaps best expressed now in Steven Levy's 1984 book *Hackers: Heroes of the Computer Revolution,* was the guiding light for positively motivated White Hat hackers back in the 1960s. In fact, the Hacker Ethic is said to still be the backbone of creative hacking today. The Hacker Ethic includes two key principles formulated in the early days of the MIT hacker escapades (Levy, 1984):

1. Access to computers—and anything that might teach individuals something about the way the world works—should be free.
2. All information should be free.

In the context in which these two principles were formulated, the computers were "research machines" and the information was "software and systems information." The cautionary theme behind the White Hat Hacker's Ethic is that information hoarding by government and other authorities is not only inefficient, but it also retards the evolution of technology and the growth of the information economy.

Four other tenets described by Levy are also referred to by present-day White Hats as being integral to the motivations behind their positively predisposed behaviors. These include the ideas that (Levy, 1984):

1. Authority should be mistrusted, and decentralization of information should be promoted.
2. Hackers' status in their community should be judged by their hacking prowess, skill sets, and outcomes—and not by irrelevant criteria such as formal educational degrees, age, race, or societal position.
3. Both art and beauty can be created on a computer.
4. Computers can, indeed, change one's life for the better.

Richard Stallman, an elite and highly recognized hacker in the computer community who worked at the MIT Artificial Intelligence (AI) Laboratory during the 1970s and who was the founder of the Free Software Foundation, speaks to the notion of the Hacker Ethic (Schell, Dodge, and Moutsatsos, 2002, p. 45):

> I don't know if there actually is a hacker's ethic as such, but there sure was an MIT Artificial Intelligence Lab ethic. This was that bureaucracy should not be allowed to get in the way of doing anything useful. Rules did not matter—results mattered. Rules, in the form of computer security or locks on doors, were held in total, absolute disrespect. We would be proud of how quickly we would sweep away whatever little piece of bureaucracy was getting in the way, how little time it forced you to waste. Anyone who dared to lock a terminal in his office, say because he was a professor and thought he was more important than other people, would likely find his door left open the next morning. I would just climb over the ceiling or under the floor, move the terminal out, or leave the door open with a note saying what a big inconvenience it is to have to go under the floor, "so please do not inconvenience people by locking the door any longer." Even

now, there is a big wrench at the AI Lab titled, "the seventh-floor master key" to be used in case anyone dares to lock up one of the more fancy terminals.

The Black Hats

Black Hats in the United States

Like the White Hats, the term Black Hats also originated in the United States from black-and-white western movies and was meant to represent the villians, or bad guys. Though White Hat hackers generally place the Hacker's Ethic on a rather high intellectual plane, honor it, and expect it to be honored by others in the computer underground, Black Hat hackers are typically not committed to or behaviorally ruled by the Ethic. Though there is considerable debate about when the term *Black Hat,* or *cybercriminal,* was actually coined, reports seem to indicate that John Draper (a.k.a. Cap'n Crunch), user of a cereal box whistle that generated a 2,600-Hz tone when blown, was likely the first alleged "criminal" cracker to come to the attention of the popular North American media.

The year was 1971, and the stimulus was journalist Ron Rosenbaum's article in *Esquire* magazine on Draper's amazing whistle-blowing phreaking exploits, which not only allowed Draper to make free telephone calls but also eventually landed him in prison. By covering one of its holes and blowing through the Cap'n Crunch whistle (a trick he had learned from some friends who were blind), Draper could produce a tone with the frequency of exactly 2,600 Hz. This happened to be the tone that American Telephone and Telegraph (AT&T) and other long-distance phone companies used at that time to indicate that long-distance phone lines were available. If either phone that was party to a call emitted this tone, the switch controlling the call would be fooled into thinking that the call had ended, and all billing for the call would stop. In short, the whistle enabled Draper and some of his friends to call each other long-distance for free.

While incarcerated, Draper was approached by Mafia members wanting to utilize his unique skill set. After Draper refused to cooperate with them, he was severely beaten. Upon his release from prison, Draper was approached by an old friend, Steve Wozniak, developer of the Apple II computer. Wozniak asked Draper to stop phreaking in favor of computer programming, and there began a more positive era in Draper's life. It was John Draper who wrote Easy Writer, the word-processing program sold in 1981 by IBM with their personal computers (PCs). This story has a happy ending in that "Cap'n Crunch" eventually became one of the first high-tech millionaires. A little-known fact about this once-criminal phreaker is that he was honorably discharged from the United States Air Force in 1968 after serving in Vietnam (Slatella, 1997).

Since Draper's time, there have been countless young, creative crackers who are generally self-taught or who are taught by colleagues in the computer underground. These crackers exploit various computer systems. Sometimes they get caught and are imprisoned; other times, however, they commit their exploits without being caught. Often, note researchers Schell, Dodge, and Moutsatsos (2002), after age 30, these crackers begin to embrace the Hacker's Ethic and to contribute positively to society.

Many times, cracking and phreaking exploits become a means by which troubled and often talented young minds act out their anger and frustration. Rather than working through their issues, perhaps with mental health experts, troubled young crackers often turn to their computer as a means of escaping reality. Unfortunately, they may use their computers to commit crimes. According to Garry Jenkins of the United States Secret Service (Mulhall, 1997b, p. 292):

> Recently, we have witnessed an alarming number of young people who for a variety of sociological and psychological reasons have become attached to their computers and are exploiting their potential in a criminal manner. Often, a progression of criminal activity occurs which involves telecommunications fraud (free long distance phone calls), unauthorized access to other computers (whether for profit, fascination, ego, or the intellectual challenge), credit card fraud (cash advances and unauthorized purchases of goods), and the move to other destructive activities like computer viruses. Our experience shows that many computer hacker suspects are no longer misguided teenagers mischievously playing games with their computers in their bedrooms. Some are now high tech computer operators using computers to engage in unlawful conduct.

In 2001, Josef Chamberlin, a 34-year-old, self-taught hacker—who, at age 12, had also made free long-distance calls by cracking into the telephone system using the Cap'n Crunch cereal whistle—was hard at work at EDS, an international electronic data management company in California. Chamberlin was trying to track down the worm dubbed Code Red, which twice in two weeks during 2001 had threatened to bring the Internet to its knees. The worm hijacked Web sites that used certain Microsoft server software, slowing server traffic while it tied up resources searching for other servers to infect.

Chamberlin's specialty is security and intrusion detection, and today with the modern growth in cybercrime, his computer skills are in high demand. Chamberlin claims to have had his own tense "experimental" cybermoments. As a teenager in southern California, he learned programming using one of the first personal computers, a Timex Sinclair. He purportedly experimented with electronic bulletin boards and the ARPANET, the early Internet established by the United States Department of Defense. Exactly what he did as an experimental adolescent he does not say, but he remarks that he was glad he was a juvenile, giving the impression that he was likely cut from the same cloth as John Draper. Chamberlin insists, however, that he never actually got into legal trouble (Lau, 2001). Chamberlin's story illustrates that though he may have had some Black Hat tendencies in youth, he eventually realized that his talents could be better utilized as a White Hat.

Black Hats in Great Britain

Elsewhere around the globe, the term *cybercriminal* took a bit longer than it did in the United States to find its way into the press limelight. In Great Britain in April 1986, for example, the term *criminal hacker* was alluded to, triggering the public's fears about cybercrimes, with the convictions of Robert Schifreen and Steven Gold, highly profiled crackers of the BT Prestel service.

In 1984, BT Prestel operated a text information retrieval system that was accessible over the public switched telephone system by means of a modem. The electronic mailbox information could be retrieved and viewed on a personal computer or on a television screen. Although some of the information was available to users at no charge, other information required a fee. To access the information system, users were each given a unique personal identification number (PIN), much like those used by customers today to access funds from automated banking machines.

The cybercrime of Schifreen and Gold was cracking into the system and leaving a greeting for His Royal Highness the Duke of Edinburgh on his British Telecom Prestel mailbox (an early phone voicemail system). The two were convicted on a number of criminal charges under the British Forgery and Counterfeiting Act of 1981. However, in April 1988, their convictions were set aside through an appeal to the House of Lords. The reasoning of the judges hearing the case was that the spirit of the Forgery and Counterfeiting Act was being stretched to an unacceptable limit and the Act was considered to be inappropriate for application in cracking-related circumstances.

Shortly thereafter, in July 1988, the British press reported the cybercrime exploits of Nicholas Whiteley, known as the Mad Hacker. In May 1990, he was one of the first crackers in Britain to be convicted under the Criminal Damage Act of 1971. Whiteley was given a custodial sentence for cracking into the computer systems at the universities of London, Bath, and Hull, causing them to crash (Mulhall, 1997a).

The cases of Schifreen, Gold, and Whiteley were instrumental in bringing cybercrime into the public arena in Britain. Moreover, they were instrumental in prompting the passing of legislation specifically geared to computer hacking. Michael Colvin, a member of Parliament, worked with the Department of Trade and Industry to get a bill through the British Parliament that eventually translated into the Computer Misuse Act of 1990 (Mulhall, 1997a).

Emerging Fears about Cyberterrorism

From 1971 through 1998, both White Hat hackers and Black Hat crackers received media air time for a variety of cyberexploits, some of which will be described throughout this book. Then in 1999, a new cyber-related fear emerged. Two professional soldiers in China's People's Liberation Army proposed a new way of waging war by using terrorist attacks and cyberattacks on critical infrastructure as a way to keep a superpower adversary reeling. But it was unclear whether this threat was an emerging real one or just fiction.

In a foreshadowing media story that appeared in February 2000, John Serabian, the CIA's information issue manager, said in written testimony to the United States Joint Economic Committee, "We are detecting, with increasing frequency, the appearance of doctrine dedicated cyber warfare programs in other countries.

We have identified several, based on all-source intelligence information, that are pursuing government-sponsored offensive cyber programs" (McCarthy, 2000).

Dorothy Denning's Testimony

In a May 23, 2000, testimony on cyberterrorism before the Special Oversight Panel on Terrorism (part of the Committee on Armed Services in the U.S. House of Representatives), Dr. Dorothy Denning, a cybercrime expert who was then at Georgetown University, commented early on in her submissions that cyberspace was indeed constantly under assault, making it fertile ground for cyberattacks against targeted individuals, companies, and governments—a point repeated often by the White Hat hackers over the past 20 years. "Cyber spies, thieves, saboteurs, and thrill seekers," noted Denning, "break into computer systems, steal personal data and trade secrets, vandalize Web sites, disrupt service, sabotage data and systems, launch computer viruses and worms, conduct fraudulent transactions, and harass individuals and companies. These attacks are facilitated with increasingly powerful and easy-to-use software tools, which are readily available for free from thousands of Web sites on the Internet" (Schell, Dodge, and Moutsatsos, 2002, p. 188).

Moreover, affirmed Denning, many of these attacks were serious and costly. (The ILOVEYOU virus and many of its variants, for example, have been estimated to have targeted tens of millions of users and to have cost billions of dollars in damage and service disruption.) Dr. Denning went on to say in her testimony that two key factors must be considered when trying to understand the real threat of cyberterrorism—which can result in harm or death to many citizens. One factor is whether there are targets vulnerable to attacks that could lead to violence or severe harm. The other factor is whether there are actors with the capability and the motivation to carry out cyberterrorism.

Denning then noted that several studies in the late 1990s had shown that critical computerized infrastructures were potentially vulnerable to cyberterrorist attacks. For example, Eligible Receiver, a no-notice computer exercise conducted by the Department of Defense in 1997, found that the power grid and emergency 911 systems in the United States had weaknesses that could be exploited by an adversary using only tools that were publicly available on the Internet. Although neither of these critical systems was actually attacked during the computer exercise, the study concluded that service on these systems could be severely disrupted (Schell, Dodge, and Moutsatsos, 2002).

Dr. Denning continued her testimony by citing the findings of the 1997 President's Commission on Critical Infrastructure Protection. The Commission's report warned that through mutual dependencies and interconnectedness, critical infrastructures could be vulnerable in new ways. The report also noted that while these vulnerabilities had been steadily increasing, the costs of mounting an attack had been steadily decreasing—a point important to underscore. And she affirmed (Schell, Dodge, and Moutsatsos, 2002, pp. 189–190):

> Although many of the weaknesses in computerized systems can be corrected, it is effectively impossible to eliminate all of them. Even if the technology itself offers good security, it is frequently configured or used in ways that make it open to attack. In addition, there is always the possibility of insiders, acting alone or in concert with other terrorists, misusing their access capabilities.

This expert noted that if one accepts that critical infrastructures are vulnerable to a cyberterrorist attack, then the next major factor becomes whether there are actors with the capability and the motivation to carry out such an operation. "While many hackers have the knowledge, skills, and tools to attack [critical] computer systems," posited Denning, "they generally lack the motivation to cause violence or severe economic or social harm. Conversely, terrorists who are motivated to cause violence seem to lack the capability or motivation to cause that degree of damage in cyberspace" (Schell, Dodge, and Moutsatsos, 2002, p. 190).

In further testimony, Dr. Denning conceded that present-day terrorists do use cyberspace to facilitate traditional forms of terrorism, such as bombings. For example, they construct Web sites to spread their messages and to recruit supporters, and they use the Internet to communicate and to coordinate actions. She then cited the 1999 findings of the Center for the Study of Terrorism and Irregular Warfare at the Naval Postgraduate School in Monterey, California. In their report entitled *Cyberterror: Prospects and Implications,* the Center stated their investigation goal as assessing the prospects of terror organizations pursuing cyberterrorism. Briefly, the study examined five potential terrorist group types—religious, New Age, ethno-nationalist separatist, revolutionary, and far-right extremists. Their conclusion was that only the religious groups—fifty known groups were studied—were likely to seek the most damaging capability level, as it was consistent with their indiscriminate application of violence, an aspect that has distinguished much of their activity. The roots of religious extremism go back 2,000 years. For most of the twentieth century, motivations based on Marxist or nationalist revolutionary issues have been prevalent. For the religiously motivated terrorist, violence appears to have an inspired, god-driven aspect. Thus, contrary to the revolutionary terrorists' tendency to focus violence on social issues, religious extremists not only engage in more indiscriminate acts of violence directed against a wider category of targets, but they declare as enemies anyone who does not share their religious beliefs. Moreover, some of these religiously motivated acts of terrorism have been designed to require a supreme sacrifice—the perpetrator's life (Schell, Dodge, and Moutsatsos, 2002).

Denning affirmed that this study estimated that it would take 6–10 years for a terrorist group to reach a complex, coordinated level at which they would be able to create sophisticated hacking tools and to cause mass disruption against integrated, heterogeneous computer network defenses. Though the report concluded that the barrier to entry for anything beyond annoying hacks is quite high and that terrorists generally lack the wherewithal and human capital needed to mount a meaningful operation, Denning argued that some terrorist groups might reach that more advanced and highly destructive complex coordinated level in just a few years—especially if they turned to outsourcing or to government sponsorship. Thus, suggested Denning (Schell, Dodge, and Moutsatsos, 2002, p. 191):

> At this time, cyberterrorism does not seem to pose an imminent threat. This could change. For a terrorist, it would have some advantages over physical methods. It could be conducted remotely and anonymously, and it would not require the handling of explosives or a suicide mission. It would likely garner extensive media coverage, as journalists and the public alike are fascinated by practically any kind of computer attack. Indeed, cyberterrorism could be immensely appealing precisely because of the tremendous attention given to it by the government and media.

Dr. Denning finished her presentation before the Special Oversight Panel on Terrorism by positing that the next generation of terrorists will grow up in a digital world with ever more powerful and easy-to-use hacking tools at their disposal. They might see a greater potential for cyberterrorism than the bomb-related terrorism of today, and their level of skill relating to computer hacking will be greater. Skilled outsider hackers as well as insiders, she proposed, might even be recruited by terrorist groups—or might themselves become self-recruiting cyberterrorists. This expert warned that unless critical computer systems are secured, conducting an operation that physically harms individuals or societies may become as easy as penetrating a Web site is today. She concluded by saying (Schell, Dodge, and Moutsatsos, 2002, p. 191):

> [T]he violent pursuit of political goals using exclusively electronic methods is likely to be at least a few years into the future. However, the more general threat of cybercrime is very much a part of the digital landscape today. In addition to cyberattacks against digital data and systems, many people are terrorized on the Internet today with threats of physical violence. Online stalking, death threats, and hate messages are abundant. The Florida teen who threatened violence at Columbine High School in an electronic chat room is but one example. These crimes are serious and must be addressed. In so doing, we will be in a better position to prevent and respond to cyberterrorism if and when the threat becomes more serious.

An Internet Chernobyl?

As affirmed by Dr. Denning, the foundation of daily life in Western society in this new millennium—banking, stock exchanges, transportation controls, utility grids, medical facilities, and nuclear power stations—depends on a vast, networked information infrastructure. Therefore, the potential for destabilizing a civilized society through cyberattacks against banking or telecommunications systems, for example, becomes increasingly large.

If we use Dr. Denning's estimates, is it likely that a massive destructive cyberattack, which some scientists have called the Internet Chernobyl or Internet Apocalypse, will occur as early as 2005.

In a piece published in *The New Yorker* on May 28, 2001, Peter G. Neumann, a principal scientist at the technological consulting firm SRI International and a consultant to the navy, Harvard University, and the National Security Agency, underscored his concerns about the deadly cybercriminal arm. What worried Neumann was "the big one." Malicious hackers could get into the country's important systems in minutes or in seconds, he said, and wipe out one-third of the computer drives in the United States in a single day, or shut down the power grids and emergency response systems of twenty states. Neumann affirmed that the Internet is waiting for its Chernobyl, and he does not think that we will be waiting much longer—we are, he says, already running too close to the edge (Specter, 2001).

Code Red and NIMDA

On July 19, 2001, the Code Red worm infected hundreds of thousands of computers worldwide in less than 14 hours, overloading the Internet's capacity. It struck again in August 2001, exacerbating fears of cyberterrorism.

In the October issue of *Scientific American,* computer security expert Carolyn Meinel labeled the worm a "computer disease" that has computer security researchers more worried than ever about the integrity of the Internet—and about the likelihood of imminent cyberterrorist attacks. She noted that the Code Red worm was like an electronic ailment, akin to computerized snake bites that infected Microsoft Internet Information Servers (IIS)—the lifeline to many of the most popular Web sites around the world. It produced repair costs worldwide of about $2.6 billion (Meinel, 2001).

What really disturbed system administrators and other experts about Code Red was the possibility that it was the harbinger of more virulent Internet plagues. In the past, said Meinel in this article, Web defacements were perpetrated by people breaking into sites individually, a type of cyberwarfare equivalent to the dropping of propaganda leaflets on targets. However, since the appearance of Code Red, computer researchers have dreaded the arrival of better-designed automated attack worms that could degrade or demolish the World Wide Web. In fact, some researchers in 2001 worried that Code Red was merely a test of the type of computer programs that any government or terrorists could use to crash the Internet in times of war (Meinel, 2001).

"This past spring's online skirmishes over the U.S. spy plane incident with China," affirmed Meinel, "emphasize the dangers. Full-scale cyberwarfare could cause untold damage to the industrialized world. These assaults could enlist your PC [personal computer] as a pawn, making it a 'zombie' that participates in the next round of computerized carnage" (Meinel, 2001, p. 42).

Two months after Code Red was contained, a "relative" by the name of NIMDA (ADMIN spelled backward) arrived. Though NIMDA did not create a catastrophic disruption to the critical infrastructure of the United States, it was a good example of the increasing technical sophistication showing up in cyberattacks. Moreover, it demonstrated that the weapons available to organized and technically savvy attackers have the capability to learn and adapt to their local environment. NIMDA was an automated cyberattack—a blend of a computer worm and a computer virus. A computer worm is a self-replicating computer program. It is self-contained and does not need to be part of another program to propagate. A virus, in contrast, attaches itself to and becomes part of another executable program. NIMDA made its way across the United States with enormous speed and tried several ways to infect the computer systems it invaded until it gained access and destroyed files. As it moved across the country, it went from being nonexistent to being a nationwide monster in just 1 hour. It lasted for days and attacked an estimated 86,000 computers ("The National Strategy," 2003).

September 11, 2001

The autumn of 2001 was especially memorable in terms both of cyberattacks by viruses and worms and of conventional attacks on United States soil. On September 11, 2001, at around 9 A.M. and within a span of 18 minutes, one U.S. passenger jet was deliberately crashed into each of the twin towers of the World Trade Center in Manhattan, bringing down one of the most powerful symbols of capitalism in the world. The crashes killed thousands of innocent civilians and rescue workers and changed the course of history. By 9:45 A.M., a third U.S. passenger jet had been deliberately crashed on a helicopter landing pad beside the Pentagon in Washington, D.C., causing one side of the five-sided structure to collapse, killing everyone aboard the plane, and killing hundreds within the building (Campbell, 2001).

Within minutes of the Pentagon crash, the U.S. Capitol was evacuated. The U.S. Federal Aviation Administration moved quickly, grounding all flights scheduled to depart from U.S. airports. But the trauma did not end there. At about 9:58 that same morning, a man called an emergency dispatcher in Pennsylvania, saying that he was a passenger aboard United Airlines Flight 93. He shouted, "We are being hijacked! We are being hijacked!" Ten minutes later, Flight 93 crashed in rural Sunset County (about 120 kilometers, or 75 miles, southeast of Pittsburgh, Pennsylvania). All forty-five people on board were killed. Authorities believed that the intended target of Flight 93 had been the White House, with the hijackers intending to kill the president of the United States in the crash (Campbell, 2001).

This tragic set of events was not the apocalyptic work of cyberterrorists, but rather the work of about nineteen hijackers who "social-engineered" their way into North American mainstream society and onto four U.S. jets, to execute a mission of mass murder. United States officials linked the terrorists to Osama bin Laden, who is reportedly worth more than an estimated $300 million and who is known for setting up terrorist training camps in Afghanistan. He was connected to the then-ruling Taliban in Afghanistan and as of this writing remains at large (Yost, 2001)

Though it is difficult to pinpoint when fears of a cyberapocalypse and those of terrorist attacks became meshed, paranoia regarding a potential cyberapocalypse was already evident on July 21, 2001. On that date, crackers commandeered 200,000 computer servers worldwide to attack the White House Web site. Quick action by the government deflected the cyberassault. The cyberassault came one day before the Bush administration went on the offensive against cybercriminals. Attorney General John Ashcroft announced the formation of ten new special units to prosecute cyberattackers. As a result of this July 21, 2001, attack, government officials worried that cyberterrorists would shut down vital services and create chaos by crashing power, banking, and telecommunication networks. The events of September 11, 2001, increased the paranoia of terrorist attacks, especially those combining traditional terrorist measures—such as bombs or airline crashes—along with cyberattacks (Yang 2001).

The United States Counterattack on Afghanistan

The U.S. military struck back within a month of the September 11 airborne attacks—this time utilizing high-tech weapons. On October 8, 2001, waves of cruise missiles, satellite-guided bombs, and food packages (intended for the civilian population) rained down on Afghanistan, as the United States and Great Britain launched their first offensive in a war that President George W. Bush warned could bring sacrifices at home and abroad. Long-range bombers and fighter jets struck targets in every major city across Afghanistan after dark on this day, hitting military installations of the Taliban in the middle of the night.

Two days later, Osama bin Laden's terrorist network called for a global holy war (or jihad) against the United States and praised the September 11 terrorist attacks for being "a good deed." A spokesman for bin Laden's al-Qaeda network issued a videotaped statement saying that legions of suicide bombers were prepared to wage war against the United States. "The Americans must know that the storm of [hijacked] airplanes will not stop," Sulaiman Abu Ghaith said, speaking in Arabic. "There are thousands of young people who are as keen about death as Americans are about life" (Stackhouse, 2001, p. A1)

Countering Cyberterrorists: The Homeland Security Act

On November 25, 2002, the United States government publicly acknowledged the possibility of an apocalyptic cyberattack on the United States and its allies, as well as the possibility of terrorist attacks of the conventional type, using suicide bombs and other means of mass destruction. President George W. Bush signed a piece of legislation called the Homeland Security Act of 2002. Section 225, known as the Cyber Security Enhancement Act of 2002, created the Department of Homeland Security (DHS). This new cabinet-level department united twenty-two federal entities for the common purpose of improving U.S. homeland security (*Homeland Security Act H.R. 5005,* 2002).

The DHS secretary's responsibilities in the area of cyberspace security included the following ("The National Strategy," 2003):

1. Developing a comprehensive national plan for securing the key resources and critical infrastructure of the United States
2. Providing crisis management in response to attacks on critical information systems
3. Providing technical assistance to the private sector and various government bodies regarding emergency recovery plans for failures of critical information systems

4. Coordinating with other agencies of the federal government to provide specific warning information and advice about appropriate protective measures and countermeasures to state, local, and nongovernmental organizations, including the private sector, academic, and the public
5. Performing and funding research and development along with other bodies and agencies, leading to new scientific understandings and technologies in support of homeland security

The case for action was simply stated by the White House in "The National Strategy to Secure Cyberspace" (2003a, p. 5):

> The terrorist attacks against the United States that took place on September 11, 2001, had a profound impact on our nation. The federal government and society as a whole have been forced to reexamine conceptions of security on our home soil, with many understanding only for the first time the lengths to which self-designated enemies of our country are willing to go to inflict debilitating damage.
>
> We must move forward with the understanding that there are enemies who seek to inflict damage on our way of life. They are ready to attack us on our own soil, and they have shown a willingness to use unconventional means to execute those attacks. While the attacks of September 11 were physical attacks, we are facing increasing threats from hostile adversaries in the realm of cyberspace as well.

On January 24, 2003, President Bush swore in Tom Ridge as the secretary of Homeland Security to safeguard the property and the people of the United States against terrorists and cyberterrorists.

2003: Exacerbating Cyberterrorism Anxieties

The War Against Terror

In March 2003, President Bush and Tony Blair, the prime minister of the United Kingdom, declared war in principle against

Iraq's allegedly terrorist-supporting leader Saddam Hussein, any state or anyone who aided and abetted terrorists (dubbed by President Bush as the Axis of Evil), and an alleged arsenal of chemical and biological weapons of mass destruction stored in Iraq. On Wednesday night, March 19, 2003, the United States–United Kingdom "war against terror" began. The United States commenced Operation Iraqi Freedom with a barrage of Tomahawk missiles and laser-guided bombs against what the Pentagon termed "targets of military opportunity" in Iraq ("War on Iraq," 2003)

In his address to the people about the war, President George W. Bush said ("Operation Iraqi Freedom," 2003c, pp. 1–2):

> Our nation enters this conflict reluctantly—yet, our purpose is sure. The people of the United States and our friends and allies will not live at the mercy of an outlaw regime that threatens the peace with weapons of mass murder. We will meet that threat now, with our Army, Air Force, Navy, Coast Guard and Marines, so that we do not have to meet it later with armies of fire fighters and police and doctors on the streets of our cities. Now that conflict has come, the only way to limit its duration is to apply decisive force. And I assure you, this will not be a campaign of half measures, and we will accept no outcome but victory.

By the summer of 2003, the "tide of war" in Iraq had turned to a "tide of peacekeeping efforts" by soldiers from the United States and United Kingdom. Saddam Hussein's sons were dead, and many of his scientific and intelligence officers were captured or found dead by the soldiers, but as of that time, Saddam Hussein was nowhere to be found. And although Osama bin Laden was allegedly also still in hiding, his mastermind colleague in the September 11 attacks—Khalid Shaikh Mohammed, was captured in Pakistan in March 2003 and was being interrogated by United States intelligence officers about the successful plots, including potential cyberattacks, of al-Qaeda and about those not yet launched.

SoBigF, Blaster, and Welchia

In late August 2003, three crippling worms and viruses were invading home and office computers in the United States and elsewhere, causing considerable cyberdamage and increasing the stress levels of business leaders and citizens alike. The most damaging of these was the e-mail-borne SoBigF virus, the fifth variant of a bug that had initially invaded computers in January 2003 and now resurfaced with a vengeance on August 18, 2003 (Symantec Security Response, 2003).

In addition to SoBigF, there was a worm called Blaster that surfaced on August 11, 2003, and exploited security holes found in Microsoft Windows XP. Finally, the so-called Welchia worm also surfaced on August 11, 2003. Targeting active computers, Welchia went to Microsoft's Web site, downloaded a program that fixes Windows security holes, and then deleted itself (Symantec Security Response, 2003). The latter, sometimes called a "do-gooder" worm because it fixed the problem it detected, also had a major down side, for it continued to clog servers. The do-gooder name is misleading, as these worms are designed by Black Hats to run on computers without authorization. Computers running the "do-gooder" worms are prone to crash.

The SoBigF virus arrived in e-mails (with subjects such as "Your Details") that appeared to be sent from someone with whom the recipient had already corresponded. Thus, the recipient would be tricked into believing that the attachment was coming from a "trusted" source. Security experts maintain that SoBigF was designed so that its author could update the software in the future, leaving the door open for a virus writer to concoct a version of SoBigF that could erase data or steal sensitive data. Furthermore, the e-mail sparked many companies' systems to send an automatic reply saying that the message was blocked. That, in turn, increased exponentially the amount of junk e-mail traveling over the Internet. As a result, numerous company servers were severely slowed, or were halted altogether (Bloom, 2003).

The damages in lost production and other economic losses caused by these worms and viruses have been estimated to be about $2 billion for the 8-day period of August 11–18, 2003. Moreover, a burning question loomed worldwide: Were any of these viruses or worms generated by cyberterrorists? It is difficult to tell at this point, but most experts think they were probably not. Vincent Gullotto, vice president of Network Associates Inc.'s Anti-Virus Emergency Response Team (AVERT), said that the summer worms of 2003 were not nearly as lethal as some predecessors, particularly 2001's Code Red virus (Damsell, 2003b).

On August 14, 2003, the U.S. Department of Homeland Security issued specific advice for protection against the Blaster worm ("Homeland Security Provides Advice," 2003d). By the autumn of 2003, the only suspected developer of any of these pests was a Minneapolis, Minnesota, 18-year-old high school senior named Jeffrey Lee Parson. Believed to be the developer of a variant of the Blaster worm (but likely not of the original), Parson was arrested on August 29, 2003, on one count in violation of Title 18 of the United States Code; namely, intentionally causing and attempting to cause damage to a protected computer. If convicted, Parson would face a maximum sentence of 10 years in federal prison and a $250,000 fine ("Minneapolis, Minnesota 18 Year Old," 2003e).

Parson told the FBI that he had built into his version of the worm a method for reconnecting to victim computers at a later date. Investigators said the worm allowed him to access individual computers and users' personal communications and finances. It was not immediately clear, however, how Parson might have used that personal information (Bakst, 2003).

In a press release from the White House, Attorney General John Ashcroft remarked that the Blaster computer worm and its variants wreaked havoc on the Internet and cost businesses and computer users substantial time and money. Cybercracking, said Ashcroft, is not mere joy riding, as it disrupts people's lives, victimizing innocent people across the nation. The Department of Justice, he said, takes these crimes very seriously, and it will devote every resource possible to tracking down those who seek to attack the technological infrastructure of the United States. Ashcroft congratulated the U.S. Attorney's offices in the western district of Washington and Minnesota, the Computer Crime and Intellectual Property Section of the Criminal Division, the Federal Bureau of Investigation, the Department of Homeland Security, and the United States Secret Service for their excellent work on the Parson case—noting that Parson's arrest was a prime example of how federal agencies can work together to combat computer crime ("Minneapolis, Minnesota 18 Year Old," 2003e).

The U.S. East Coast Power Blackout

As if the nuisance and economic losses affiliated with the Blaster, Welchia, and SoBigF bugs were not enough for Americans to cope with that summer, on or about August 14, 2003, the citizens on the East Coast of the United States and in Ontario, Canada, found themselves without electricity. This electrical blackout, said to be the biggest ever affecting the United States, lasted from hours to days, depending on the geographical location. Citizens in Manhattan were especially nervous, thinking that they were once again being targeted by terrorists.

In early September 2003, Joe Weiss, a utility control system expert at Kema Consulting in Cupertino, California, said that the two events—the computer worm invasions and the blackout—might have been linked. The Blaster worm had crippled or slowed an estimated one-half million computers around the world, and it therefore might have exacerbated utilities' problems during the blackout, bringing down—or perhaps blocking communications on—computers used to monitor the grid. The Ohio utility that was the chief focus of the blackout investigation, FirstEnergy Corporation, was investigating whether the Blaster worm might have caused a computer problem described on the company's telephone transcripts as hampering its response to multiple power line failures. Back in January 2003, the Slammer Internet worm had taken down monitoring computers at FirstEnergy's idled Davis-Besse nuclear plant, and a follow-up report by the North American Electric Reliability Council said that the worm had also blocked commands that operated other power utilities, though it caused no outages at that time (Associated Press, 2003a, p. 3)

In 1998, the power grid's electromechanical switches and analogue technology had made it more or less impervious to computer maladies, but the United States National Security Agency had begun to warn of the power grid's growing vulnerabilities as it became a more computerized system. But by the time of the 2003 Northeast blackout, the technology was such that switches and monitoring gear could be upgraded and programmed remotely with software, requiring a "vulnerable" connection to a computer network. And for networks that ran on Microsoft Corporation operating systems—which virus writers seem to favor as a target—the vulnerabilities became increasingly sharpened. According to news releases following the 2003 blackout, researchers working for the United States, Canadian, and British governments warned that, given these vulnerabilities, Black Hat hackers could with a few focused keystrokes shut down the computer gear or change settings in ways that might trigger cascading blackouts, thus wreaking considerable havoc on society.

For example, Eric Byres, a cybersecurity researcher for critical infrastructures at the British Columbia Institute of Technology (BCIT) in Vancouver, Canada, said that because his team knew where "the holes" were, even they could shut down the grid—not the whole North American grid, but a state's grid, for sure. Byres further said that the holes noted in the power grid system even back in 1998 had largely gone unpatched (i.e., unrepaired), and with an expected spate of post–August 2003 upgrades, the computer-heavy grid would become even more vulnerable to terrorist and Black Hat attacks (Associated Press, 2003a, p. 3)

In recent years, security researchers have determined how to crack into a device known as a remote terminal unit and then to command it to trip and reset a breaker. This would incapacitate a substation (the electricity distribution point for a town and neighborhood where high-voltage electricity is transformed for local use). In fact, a typically feared apocalyptic cracking scenario involves a cyberterrorist's changing the settings on substations' programmable circuit breakers. For example, a cyberterrorist could lower settings from, say, 500 amperes to 200 amperes on some breakers while raising others to 900 amperes. Normal power usage could trip the 200-amp breakers and take those lines out of service by diverting power and thereby overloading neighboring lines, and for the breakers set at 900 amperes—too high to trip—the resulting overloads would cause transformers and other critical equipment to "melt down." Moreover, the time required for repairs would prolong a power blackout.

"We have a plethora of intelligent electrical devices going into substations and power stations all over the United States," said Gary Seifert, a researcher with the Energy Department's Idaho National Engineering and Environmental Laboratory. "What's to keep somebody from accessing those devices and changing the settings? Hackers have very little trouble cracking an eight-digit password." (Associated Press, 2003a, p. 3). Substation phone lines that connect to these relays can be found with so-called war dialers—simple personal computer programs that dial consecutive phone numbers looking for modems. Thus, Seifert warns, manufacturers need to take countermeasures such as programming their control devices to accept calls only from certain phone numbers, or simply disconnecting idle modems. Like anyone dependent on networked computers for crucial operations, posits Seifert, grid operators will be vulnerable to Black Hat exploits. "We're still going to have back doors no matter how hard we try," he says. "You can't keep them out, but you hope to slow them down" (Associated Press, 2003a, p. 3).

Americans' Growing Cyberattack Concerns, and the New Terror Threats

It is little wonder that, with all the worries associated with the September 11, 2001, terrorist attacks and their traumatic aftermath, Americans might feel somewhat concerned about cyberattacks in the near future.

In a poll of 1,001 adults taken in the United States before the power blackout and the plague of Internet viruses and worms in the summer of 2003, the Pew Internet and American Life Project found that one in two adults polled expressed concern about the vulnerability of the national infrastructure to terrorist hackers. Moreover, the study found that although 58 percent of the women polled feared an imminent attack, only 47 percent of the men feared such an attack. On the positive side, 71 percent of those polled were fairly confident that the United States federal government would provide them with sufficient information in the event of another terrorist attack ("Americans Concerned," 2003).

Technology experts say citizens' fears are grounded in reality. "I think there is an 80 percent probability we could see an attack in the next two years," says Paul Henry, vice president of CyberGuard Corporation, a Florida Internet security firm. "We know the expertise is out there among hackers and terrorists. It's simply a question of the will of terrorists to attack" ("Americans Concerned," 2003, p. 1). He further suggests that terrorists could launch a double-barreled assault, combining physical destruction, such as a bomb blast on a building, with a computer attack, such as sabotaging the control system for a nearby drawbridge, making it difficult for emergency officials to raise the bridge and respond. And although the risks of cyberterrorism are substantial, he says that growing awareness of the problem could help avert disaster.

Winn Schwartu, author of *Information Warfare: Chaos on the Electronic Superhighway* (1999), agrees with Henry that the U.S. infrastructure is so interconnected that a harmful cyberattack is a real possibility. He said that several years ago in Brooklyn, New York, a fire in a wastebasket triggered a shutdown at a power company substation. When the substation could not be brought back online, a telephone outage developed, because most current phones need electrical power, leading to a major tie-up with air traffic controllers—and several hours later, a national air gridlock nearly developed, showing how much such systems can depend on each other. Finally, Richard Ford, a research professor at the Center for Information Assurance in Florida, maintains that a potentially catastrophic cyberattack is simply a matter of when, not if. He says that the levels of preparedness for cyberattacks in the United States and other nations are low—as demonstrated by the recent Blaster worm, which attacked e-mail systems globally, despite numerous warnings from computer security experts to businesses and instutions about the need to fix, or patch, their computer systems ("Americans Concerned," 2003 p. 1).

The good news is that the U.S. government appears to be listening. Although most Americans now rely on television and radio for notification of an emergency, the August 2003 blackout showed that these two communication lines are vulnerable to a loss of power, making alternative warning systems vital. Kenneth B. Allen, executive director of the Partnership for Public Warning (a Washington-based nonprofit group founded in the wake of September 11), is promoting an alternative warning system idea with Congress and with the Department of Homeland Security. "We are trying to create tech standards for a communications backbone and also do an educational program to make people aware of where to go for information," he says. Some integral parts of a warning system would be personal digital assistants, cell phones, and pagers, making use of text messaging to deliver information. Other elements would include warning people of emergencies by using fire sirens, church bells, and phone calls with a reverse 911 system ("Americans Concerned," 2003 p. 2).

On September 10, 2003, chilling new threats of even more spectacular terrorist attacks emerged from Osama bin Laden. In a taped message broadcast on the eve of the second anniversary of the suicide hijackings that destroyed New York's World Trade Center towers, and as Americans prepared to mourn the thousands killed in the attacks, al-Qaeda's new message warned: "What you saw until now are only the first skirmishes . . . the real epic [struggle] has not begun." Upon its release, U.S. intelligence experts were closely examining the tape, which showed bin Laden and one of his top lieutenants walking through unidentified mountainous terrain. They also studied the tape's separately recorded soundtrack to determine whether the tape and soundtrack combined contained hidden or coded signals (known as steganography) ordering positioned al-Qaeda cells to launch attacks. "Devour the Americans just like lions devour their prey," said the voice on the tape. "Bury them in the Iraqi graveyard" (Koring, 2003, p. A1).

After September 11, 2003, newspaper articles appeared featuring assertions by Khalid Shaikh Mohammed—the so-called mastermind of the September 11, 2001, attacks—that he had first discussed his plot with Osama bin Laden in 1996, five years before its occurrence. Also, he said that the original plan had called for hijacking five commercial jets on each U.S. coast but that this original plan had to be modified several times because it just was not feasible. For example, when two of the four original operatives assigned by Osama bin Laden to the September 11 plot failed to get U.S. visas because they were Yemenis, bin Laden changed course and asked the two to study the possibility of hijacking planes in Asia. Before the September 11, 2001, terrorist attacks, screening of Saudis and Yemenis requesting visas was designed to filter out those who might try to settle in the United States after their work visa expired. If they did not appear on criminal or terrorist watch lists they were granted a visa (United Press International, 2003).

Apparently, the operatives' mission in eastern Asia was to fly commercial airliners to gain familiarity with how jets operated in that region. Bin Laden then chose additional participants for the September 11 United States East Coast plan, offering a member of his personal security detail as well as a large group of young Saudi men who ultimately made it onto the ill-fated jetliners. Throughout its various permutations, Mohammed affirmed that Osama bin Laden was the individual in charge who made the final decisions (Solomon, 2003).

Yet another event, this one on September 24, 2003, further raised distress levels and added to the cyberterrorist threat potential: The media spread the suspicion that al-Qaeda may have penetrated the United States military. Senior Airman Ahmad al-Halabi, a 24-year-old Arabic-speaking translator who had spent almost a year working at the heavily guarded, razor-wired compound where alleged al-Qaeda and Taliban members are held in Guantanamo Bay, Cuba, was arrested and charged with four counts of espionage and more than twenty other criminal violations, including bank fraud. Moreover, the Pentagon disclosed that 35-year-old Islamic chaplain Captain Yousef Yee, a Muslim convert who ministered to many of the camp's 660 inmates and who had graduated from West Point military academy, has been detained in a military prison in South Carolina since September 10, 2003, on suspicion of espionage. U.S. officials said that although the two suspects knew each other, their relationship was unclear (Appleby, 2003).

The Symantec Report

On October 1, 2003, Symantec Corporation, a California security threat monitoring company, added to the cybercrime concern by reporting that Internet surfers in the United States and around the globe needed to brace themselves for a growing number of sophisticated and contagious cyberspace bugs. "The frequency of the attacks, whether it be malicious code or direct hacker attacks, is increasing. The complexity is increasing and actually the capabilities of the attacks are changing and getting a little more sophisticated," said Michael Murphy, general manager of the company's Canadian operations. The report further stated that the rate of network-based Internet attacks rose by 19 percent in the first 6 months of 2003, as compared with the same period in 2002. On average, companies reportedly experienced about thirty-eight attacks per week in the first half of 2003, up from thirty-two per week just a year before. Even more frightening, so-called blended threats—complex attacks combining the characteristics of computer worms and viruses—rose nearly 20 percent in the first 6 months of 2003. Moreover, the blended threats were reportedly being released at a faster rate than the associated software flaws were being identified (Damsell, 2003b, p. B5).

Types of Cybercrime

Social Engineering

Before this chapter discusses the legalities and types of cybercrimes that exist, it is important to note that some deliberate attacks on computer systems originate in nontechnical ways and use "social engineering" techniques that take advantage of naïve or inadequately trained employees. In other words, some cybercrimes are committed without much sophistication. The perpetrators simply capitalize on the "weakest links" in the system.

Social engineering describes the deceptive process whereby crackers "engineer" a social situation to allow them to obtain access to an otherwise closed network. Typically, the objective of this exercise is to get others—the weakest links—to reveal information that can be used to copy or steal data. For example, a cracker could talk a computer help desk employee into resetting the password on a stolen account. Once a password was obtained, access to the system by the cracker could be either permanent or temporary.

One of the most notorious social engineers in the computer underground went by the pseudonym of Susan Thunder. Susan Thunder was reportedly mistreated as a child and became a prostitute in her teens. In her spare time, Susan Thunder fraternized with various rock bands. She discovered how easy it was to get backstage passes for concerts just by calling the appropriate people and pretending to be, for example, a secretary at a record company—a form of social engineering. Susan eventually became an active phone phreaker, and, with the now-famous cracker team of Kevin and Ron Mitnick, she broke into the telephone lines in the 1970s. Susan Thunder exploded the then-popular myth that only men could enjoy the "pleasures" of cracking. Eventually, the team of three cracked into U.S. Leasing's systems, deleted all of the information off one computer, filled the computer with messages like "F— YOU F— YOU F—YOU," and programmed the printers to continuously spit out similar insults. Interestingly, among all the profanities were planted the names of Kevin and Ron (Walleij, 1999b).

This incident led to the first conviction of Kevin Mitnick, the winner of the DefCon 2003 contest, an annual hacker trivia competition, and a present-day system security consultant. Rumor had it that Susan Thunder was angry with Ron, with whom she was romantically involved, for finding a more socially acceptable girlfriend elsewhere (recall that Susan was a prostitute). When Ron and Kevin were arrested, Susan was given immunity from prosecution in return for testifying against them. Later, she referred to herself as a security expert and conspicuously demonstrated how she could break into military computers, using her well-honed social engineering techniques (Walleij, 1999b).

Categories of Cybercrime

Cybercrime is a crime committed against a computer or by means of a computer. Harm resulting from such crimes can be to property, to persons, or to both. There are also politically motivated crimes, controversial crimes, and technical "nonoffenses" in the cybercrime world (Brenner, 2001a,b).

Cybercrimes Resulting in Harm to Property

Cybercrime resulting in property harm is generally carried out using cracking techniques and includes such common variations as:

1. Flooding—a form of cyberspace vandalism resulting in denial-of-service (DoS) to authorized users of a site or system
2. Virus and worm production and release—a form of cyberspace vandalism causing corruption, and possibly erasing, of data
3. Spoofing—the cyberspace appropriation of an authentic user's identity by nonauthentic users, causing fraud or attempted fraud in some cases, and critical infrastructure breakdowns in other cases
4. Phreaking—a form of cyberspace theft and/or fraud consisting of using technology to make free telephone calls
5. Infringing intellectual property rights and copyright—a form of cyberspace theft involving the copying of a target's information or software without consent

Cybercrimes Resulting in Harm to Persons

Cybercrime resulting in harm to persons is generally classified as:

1. Cyberstalking—using cyberspace to control, harass, or terrorize a target to the point that he or she fears harm or death, either to self or to others close to him or her
2. Cyberpornography—using cyberspace to possess, create, import, display, publish, or distribute pornography (especially child pornography) or other obscene materials

Technical Nonoffenses

Politically motivated, controversial, and technical nonoffenses in the cybercrime world include:

1. Hacktivism—hacker activists, or hacktivists, pairing their activism interests with their hacker skills to promote their platforms and missions
2. Cybervigilantism—the convergence of cyberspace and vigilantism

Cyberterrorism and terrorism were also in this nonoffense category before the United States Congress hastily passed the antiterrorist USA PATRIOT Act in 2001. The Act was passed within 7 weeks of the September 11 terrorist attack on the World Trade Center and during a time when the United States was under siege by a bioterrorist anthrax attack. Formerly, terrorists and cyberterrorists who caused harm to persons or property were charged under other applicable laws, such as homicide, assault, and property destruction. If the United States passes the proposed PATRIOT II Act, it is likely that Black Hat hacktivism and cybervigilantism will become crimes.

On January 10, 2003, Attorney General John Ashcroft sent around to some of his colleagues a draft of the PATRIOT II Act, also known as the Domestic Security Enhancement Act of 2003. This proposed Act would have more than 100 new provisions that would fill in the holes of the USA PATRIOT Act. Some of the more controversial provisions in the draft include the following (Welch, 2003):

- Americans could have their citizenship revoked if they are found to have contributed "material support" to organizations deemed by the government—even retroactively—to be "terrorist."
- Legal permanent residents could be deported instantaneously, without a criminal charge or evidence, if the attorney general considers them to be a threat to national security.
- The government would be instructed to build a database of citizens' DNA information aimed at detecting, investigating, prosecuting, preventing, or responding to terrorist activities.
- Authorities could wiretap anyone for 15 days and monitor that person's Internet usage (including chat rooms and e-mail) without obtaining a warrant.
- The government would be specifically instructed not to release any information about detainees held on

suspicion of terrorist activities until they are actually charged with a crime.

- American citizens could be subject to secret surveillance by their own government on behalf of foreign countries, including dictatorships.
- The death penalty would be expanded to cover fifteen new offenses.
- Many of PATRIOT I's sunset provisions—meaning that they expire on December 31, 2005— for the expanded new enforcement powers to be rescinded in 2005 would be erased from the books, cementing Ashcroft's rushed legislation in the law books.

Criminal Liability: Four Elements

Conventional Crimes and the Four Elements

For "old-fashioned" or conventional crimes to occur, Anglo-American law bases criminal liability on the coincidence of four elements (Brenner, 2003):

1. A culpable mental state (the *mens rea*).
2. A criminal action or a failure to act when one is under a duty to do so (the *actus reus*).
3. The existence of certain necessary conditions or "attendant circumstances." With some crimes, it must be proven that certain events occurred, or certain facts are true, in order for a person to be found guilty of a crime.
4. A prohibited result, or harm.

The conventional crime of bigamy, for example, illustrates how all these elements must combine for the imposition of liability. To commit bigamy, an individual must enter into a marriage knowing either that he or she is already married, or that the person whom he or she is marrying is already married. The prohibited act, then, is the redundant marriage (the *actus reus*). The culpable mental state (the *mens rea*) is the perpetrator's knowledge that he or she is entering into a redundant marriage. The attendant circumstance is the existence of previous marriage still in force. Finally, the prohibited result, or harm, is the threat that bigamous marriages pose to the stability of family life. Simply stated, both conventional crimes and cybercrimes involve conduct unacceptable by society's standards. Society, through its laws, therefore imposes criminal liability on both.

Cybercrimes and the Four Elements

According to Brenner (2001), the following is an illustration of the coincidence of the four elements for a property cybercrime involving (1) criminal trespass, defined as entering unlawfully into an area for the purpose of committing an offense, and (2) theft of information or software—the intended offense to be done upon entry.

To begin, a cyberperpetrator enters the computer or computer system and unlawfully takes, or exercises unlawful control over, the property—the information or the software of another (*actus reus*). He or she enters with the purpose of committing an offense once inside and acts with the purpose of depriving the lawful owner of software or information (*mens rea*). By society's standards, the cyberperpetrator has no legal right to enter the computer or computer system in question, or to take or exercise control over the software or information (attendant circumstances). The cybercriminal is, therefore, liable for his or her acts. The perpetrator unlawfully entered the computer or computer system (i.e., criminal trespass) in order to commit an offense (i.e., theft) once inside, and as a result, the target is deprived of his or her software or information (harm).

Except for bigamy and sexual assault—which technically cannot be committed in cyberspace because they are truly real-world acts, says Brenner—other conventional crimes seem to be able to make a smooth transition into the virtual world. This is not to suggest, however, that there has been an absence of controversy around virtual "sexual assault" cases.

A Case of Cybercrime Controversy

A series of events occurring in the late 1990s in a text-based online virtual community known as LambdaMOO provoked extensive controversial discussion about whether "virtual rape" is or should be a criminal offense. These events also provoked discussion about whether cyberstalking or cyberpornography occurred in this instance.

In 1998, Julian Dibbell described the cyber "complaints" that emerged in LambdaMOO (Dibbell, 1998, p. 1):

> They say he raped them at night. They say he did it with a cunning little doll, fashioned in their image and imbued with the power to make them do whatever he desired. They say that by manipulating the doll, he forced them to have sex with him, and with each other, and to do horrible, brutal things to their own bodies. And though I wasn't there that night, I think I can assure you that what they say is true, because it all happened right in the living room—right there amid the well-stocked bookcases and the sofas and the fireplace—of a house I came later to think of as my second home.

LambdaMOO was a Black Hat equivalent of the present-day popular online game, Sims Online. Or to be more precise, it was a subspecies of MUD (a multiuser dungeon) known as a MOO, which is short for "MUD, object-oriented." In short, it was a kind of database designed to give users the vivid impression of moving through a physical space. When users dialed into LambdaMOO, the program immediately presented them with a brief textual description of one of the database's fictional rooms in a fictional mansion. The rooms, the things in them, and the characters were allowed to interact according to rules very roughly mimicking the laws of the physical world. In general, LambdaMOOers were allowed a broad freedom to create. They could describe their characters any way they liked, they could decorate the rooms any way they saw fit, and they could build new objects almost at will. Though the combination of all of this user activity with the physics of the database could induce a lucid illusion of presence, what the user really saw when he or she visited LambdaMoo was a kind of slow-moving script, lines of dialogue, and stage direction creeping steadily up the computer screen (Dibbell, 1998).

On the night of the cybercrime in question, the cyberperpetrator was a LambdaMOO individual known as Mr. Bungle, who, with an online voodoo doll and a piece of programming code, could spoof other players by appropriating their identities. In the context of LambdaMOO, this meant that by typing actions into the virtual voodoo doll, Bungle could make it appear as if another player in LambdaMOO were performing certain actions. One evening, Mr. Bungle logged into LambdaMOO and used the voodoo doll to make it appear that a number of the female participants were engaging in various forms of sexually humiliating activities. One player who used the codename Moonfire saw on her screen the words, "As if against her will, Moonfire jabs a steak knife up her ass, causing immense joy. You hear Mr. Bungle laughing evilly in the distance" (Brenner, 2001, p. 27).

The targets of Mr. Bungle's attention—Mr. Bungle's real-life puppeteer was a New York University computer user—were shocked and traumatized by how he had manipulated their characters and by how powerless they had been to stop him. Outraged by their suffering, some LambdaMOO participants demanded "capital punishment" for Mr. Bungle, insisting that his character be annihilated. Others disagreed, claiming freedom of speech and the like. Before the issue was formally resolved, one member of the computer community eliminated Mr. Bungle's persona and the corresponding user account in the system. It was clear, however, says Brenner (2001), that what Mr. Bungle did could not be prosecuted under extant rape laws, as he did not commit the rape crime—that requires a physical assault.

Moreover, Mr. Bungle did not commit an act of pornography, as he did not engage in or depict others having sexual activities without consent. Instead, it was the victims themselves—or, actually, their virtual selves—who were engaging in sexual activity against their will. Finally, Mr. Bungle did not commit a cyberstalking crime, because stalking consists of a persistent pattern of harassment or terrorism that causes the target to fear harm or death. Again, Mr. Bungle's targets were forced to engage in sexual activity against their will—activities that they felt were abhorrent, but that were not perpetrated by Mr. Bungle. Though the LambdaMOO example also had elements of identity theft—the malicious misuse of someone's identity—participants in the cyber community did not allege any such infractions, concludes Brenner (2001).

Today, however, identity theft, both in the real world and in the virtual world, is one of the most troubling and increasing crimes. Sometimes, identity theft is committed using a computer (and is thus a cybercrime), and sometimes no computer is used. In 2002, the Federal Trade Commission in the United States received 380,000 identity fraud complaints for that year alone—and the number keeps growing ("Identity Theft," 2003).

With identity theft, victims suddenly find that someone has stolen their identities, cleaned out their bank accounts, "maxed out" their credit cards, and left them with a huge debt. Worse, sometimes the impostor has committed a serious crime under the victim's identity, leaving him or her with an undeserved criminal record. And although identity theft is often viewed as a high-tech crime perpetrated by crackers, the thief is often a real-life family member, a trusted friend, or a coworker who has knowledge of the target's personal information, including passwords to bank accounts (Hammond, 2003).

Cyberthieves glean the information needed to steal someone's identity—name, social security number, driver's license number, mother's maiden name, and bank information—through electronic methods. A target's good credit history is then used by the thief to secure a line of credit that is then used up to the limit—and the Black Hat cracker then disappears (Pipkin, 2003).

Targets have reported spending significant amounts of time trying to resolve the harm resulting from identity theft—bounced checks, loan denials, credit card application rejections, and debt collection harassment. Some targets even experience criminal investigation, false arrest, or conviction. A significant number of targets report losses and/or out-of-pocket expenses as a result of identity theft to be in the $5,000 to $10,000 range (United States General Accounting Office, 2002).

Property Cybercrime

Increasingly, property cybercriminals are becoming highly creative in their exploits by combining a number of cyber and "old-fashioned" acts. For example, a 19-year-old was accused on October 9, 2003, of dumping worthless securities on an unwitting online trader, in what U.S. authorities called a uniquely sophisticated combination of cracking, identity theft, mail and wire fraud, and securities-related offenses. The alleged perpetrator, a student by the name of Van Dinh from Pennsylvania, allegedly used a keystroke logging, or monitoring program, to capture the user inputs (usually key presses and mouse clicks) to reconstruct the activities of the user. In this manner he obtained the password information on the TD Waterhouse account of a Massachusetts man. He then used that account to sell options for Cisco Systems, Inc., stock that were about to expire and "cost" the cyberthief nearly $100,000. That is, Van Dinh attempted to create a market that did not exist (Associated Press, 2003b).

Van Dinh then created a "buyer" for some of his worthless

options by using a Trojan Horse program—a destructive program that masquerades as a benign application—to get the login and password of a real-life target. The real-life target thought that he was testing a new stock-charting tool on his computer when the cybercriminal Van Dinh arrived. The cybercriminal virtually "cleaned out" the target's stock account, using the nearly $47,000 in it toward "buy" orders in Cisco options. Authorities were called in when the target realized his account had been emptied (Associated Press, 2003b).

The Internet Fraud Complaint Center

To deal with cyberincidents resulting in fraud, identity theft, or combinations thereof, the Internet Fraud Complaint Center (IFCC) was set up in the United States in May 2000 by the FBI and the National White Collar Crime Center. The IFCC deals with complaints about online fraud and provides victims with resources for protecting themselves. To date, the IFCC has received complaints about crimes including online auction frauds, nondeliverable goods, credit card fraud, identity theft, and nonpayment for services. Since its inception, the IFCC site has averaged about 1,000 complaints each week (Karp, 2002).

In 2002, the total dollar losses from all referred fraud cases were $54 million, up from $17 million in 2001. In cases in which the perpetrator was identified, nearly four in five of these perpetrators were male. For the third consecutive year, Internet auction fraud was the most-reported offense (46 percent of complaints), followed by nondelivery of merchandise (31 percent of complaints), followed by credit and debit card fraud (12 percent of complaints). Investment fraud, business fraud, confidence fraud, and identity theft contained the balance of complaints referred to law enforcement. In recent years, California, New York, Florida, Texas, and Illinois were the five states having the most reported cases of Internet fraud ("Dramatic Increase," 2003).

The Role of Legislation

Recently, a number of U.S. states (as well as other jurisdictions) with high fraud complaint records have been fighting cyberfraud through improved legislation. For example, a new California law, known as California Senate Bill 1386 and signed into law on September 25, 2002, amended the California Civil Code to require notice be given to the Department of Defense regarding security breaches involving unencrypted (i.e., unprotected) personal information ("California," 2003).

And, on April 2, 2003, the Texas senate passed a comprehensive bill that would protect consumers against identity theft and give the attorney general authority to prosecute ID thieves. Under the measure, the state attorney general has authority to assess hefty civil penalties for individuals convicted of identity theft, and the measure allows the target to recover attorney's fees from the identity thief. Also under the bill, a business that accepts a debit or credit card from a customer cannot print a receipt that shows more than the last four digits of the cardholder's debit or credit card account number ("Texas," 2003).

Dealing with Identity Theft

There is little question that identity theft and other property cybercrime can cause substantial harm, emotional as well as economic, to the lives of targets. Even though financial institutions may not hold victims liable for fraudulent debts, victims often feel personally violated when they are informed that an identity theft problem exists. However, not all financial institutions are happy about informing their consumers of identity thefts, for fear of losing consumer confidence. John Brady, vice president of merchant fraud control at Mastercard International, for example, maintains that it may not be appropriate to release information about a security breach in every circumstance. "The message I want to get out is: Let's not create a panic here" ("Identity Theft," 2003, p. 3).

However, there are a number of companies and financial institutions that believe in improving system security to prevent unwanted property cybercrime such as identity theft. David McIntyre, president of TriWest Healthcare Alliance, said that his company voluntarily spent about $1 million to correct a major security breach that occurred in December 2002. Confidential files containing the names and personal data of military personnel and their families were stolen from the Phoenix office of TriWest, the central region's contractor for the Department of Defense's TRICARE health system. "First and foremost," said McIntyre, "we believed it was necessary to alert DOD [Department of Defense], as well as the affected individuals, so that they could take action to protect themselves, should the thieves choose to misuse the personal information they illegally obtained" ("Identity Theft," 2003, p. 3)

Cybercrimes against Persons

Cyberstalking

Cyberstalkers, like their nonvirtual counterparts, tend to have poor interpersonal skills, mental health issues, and a lifetime history of interpersonal rejection (Schell and Lanteigne, 2000). Motivated by a desire to exert control over their targets, the majority of cyberstalkers are men, and the majority of targets are women. Cyberstalking often begins when the target either rejects advances to begin a relationship or tries to end a previous relationship (U.S. Attorney General, 1999). Though no clear-cut number regarding the prevalence of cyberstalking is available, the CyberAngels, a not-for-profit organization assisting the victims of cybercrimes, estimates that there are more than 60,000 Internet stalkers and more than 450,000 targets worldwide (CyberAngels, 2001).

Since 1990, the United States, Canada, the United Kingdom, and Australia have passed legislation to stop stalkers in their tracks. Some states, such as Alabama, Arizona, Connecticut, Hawaii, Illinois, New Hampshire, and New York have added language into their antiharassment legislation specifically dealing with the electronic transmission of threatening communications. Alaska, Oklahoma, Wyoming, and California have designated electronically delivered statements as conduct constituting stalking for the purpose of applying antistalking laws.

In April 1999, the first successful prosecution under California's cyberstalking law occurred. Prosecutors obtained a guilty plea from a 50-year-old former security guard who had used the Internet to encourage the sexual assault of a 28-year-old woman who rejected his romantic advances. The charges were one count of stalking and three counts of solicitation of sexual assault. The security guard terrorized this woman by impersonating her in various Internet chat rooms and online BBs (bulletin boards), where he posted her telephone number, address, and messages saying that she fantasized about being sexually assaulted. On at least six occasions, sometimes in the middle of the night, men knocked on the target's door saying they were there to fulfill her fantasies (National Center for Victims of Crime, 2001).

In addition to the laws, a number of other cyberstalking resources exist online to help targets to manage their situations and to get protection and prevention advice. These include CyberAngels, GetNetWise, International Association of Computer

Investigative Specialists, National Center for Victims of Crime, National Cybercrime Training Partnership, Privacy Rights Clearinghouse, and Search Group, Inc. (Posey, 2003).

Cyberpornography and Child Cyberpornography

There is little question that cyberpornography, particularly that directed toward children, is alive and well, but there are White Hats who are fighting back. A German Web site (with English translation available) dedicated to the regulations of cyberpornography can be found at http://www2.fmg.uva.nl/sociosite/websoc/indexE.html. This site is dedicated to the moral and technological filters, social control, and criminal prosecution of cyberpornography. It has been designed from a global point of view, giving users access to the worldwide findings of social science research regarding cyberpornography.

In 1995, the so-called anticriminal activist segment of the hacker community, known as the CyberAngels, started to appear online. Today, the group has more than 6,000 volunteers residing in seventy countries. Their job is to patrol the Web around the clock in the battle against child pornography and cyberstalking. In 1999, the organization helped Japanese authorities locate child pornography sites, resulting in the first-ever set of arrests in Japan of Internet child pornographers (Karp, 2000).

Child pornography can consist of depictions of a child or children engaged in sexual behavior alone or with one or more adults, or it can involve two or more children performing sexual acts, with or without adults being involved or being visible. Such imagery can range from sexualized photographs of a single child or multiple children, or sexualized images of their genitals, to pictures of brutal anal or vaginal rape, bondage, oral sex, bestiality, or other forms of degradation. Sometimes very young children or babies are involved (Posey, 2003).

At least 80 percent of those who purchase child pornography are active child molesters. Moreover, 36 percent of child pornographers who used the U.S. mail to exploit a child have been found to be actual child molesters. Child pornographers range in age from 10 to 65. Child pornography is a $2–3 billion per year industry (Posey, 2003).

One of the biggest roundups of child pornography perpetrators was launched in May 2002—called Operation Ore—after the FBI accessed the credit card details, e-mail addresses, and home addresses of 7,300 alleged British pedophiles using the Internet.

The identities of the alleged pedophiles were then given to the British police for investigation. The arrest of a computer consultant in Texas led to an international investigation that jailed Thomas Reedy for 1,335 years for running the pornography ring. About 1,300 other perpetrators were also arrested, including teachers, childcare workers, social workers, soldiers, surgeons, and fifty police officers. As a result, forty children, twenty-eight of them in London, were placed under protective care. Police say that many child pornography sites are run from eastern Europe; Britain's high-tech crime unit has therefore been working with police in countries such as Romania to shut them down (BBC News, 2003).

The United States and other countries have very specific laws against possession, distribution, and manufacturing of child pornography. In recent years, a number of tough pieces of legislation fighting child pornography have been introduced in certain countries. For example, on March 14, 2001, Canada introduced an omnibus bill in the context of amendments to the Canadian criminal code, creating a new offense targeting Internet luring, or the act of communicating with children via the Internet with the intent of committing a sexual offense, and child pornography on the Internet. The bill allowed Internet service providers (ISPs) to remove from their servers any material that could reasonably be found to be child pornography, allowed a judge to order the forfeiture of any materials or equipment used in the commission of a child pornography offense, and strengthened sentencing provisions for convictions related to child pornography and Internet luring (Department of Justice, 2001).

Many countries do not have laws pertaining to child pornography, or the laws are not strictly enforced. Areas such as eastern Europe and Asia, where child sex rings, child sex tourism, and child prostitution are widespread, are the sources for most of the new child pornography material in huge demand (Posey, 2003).

The Nonoffenses of Cybervigilantism and Hacktivism

Two activities that often give rise to criminal prosecutions but do not themselves constitute cybercrimes are cybervigilantism and hacktivism. In the conventional world, a vigilante is someone who enforces others' obedience to the law without having the legal authority to do so. The law has never recognized a crime called vigilantism; instead, vigilantes are prosecuted for other recognized offenses that they commit in the course of their efforts to enforce obedience to the law—such as homicide or assault. An example of cybervigilantism would be cracking into a child pornography site and wiping out its hard drives. Likewise, the law has never recognized such a crime as activism, in which perpetrators have as their primary objective the advancing of a social or political agenda. Instead, activists can be prosecuted for other crimes that they commit in the course of their acts, including harm to property or harm to persons. An example of hacktivism would be using cyberspace to sabotage sites conducting activities or advocating philosophies that hacktivists find unacceptable. For these reasons, cybervigilantism and hacktivism—the cyberspace versions of these activities—are also technically not designated as crimes (Brenner, 2001).

Using Anonymity to Conceal Cybercrimes

Cybercriminals wanting to conceal their identities while committing their exploits tend to use some of these popular techniques (Schell, Dodge, and Moutsatsos, 2002):

1. Anonymous remailers—sending an electronic mail message without the receiver knowing the sender's identity. Typically a remailer, a computer service that privatizes e-mail, contains the sender's identity. (During his term in office, President Clinton reportedly received e-mail death threats routed through anonymous remailers.)
2. Anonymous digital cash—combined with encryption and/or anonymous remailers, digital cash allows criminals to make transactions with complete anonymity. Digital cash is a system that allows a person to pay for goods or services by transmitting a number from one computer to another. Like the serial numbers on real dollar bills, the digital cash numbers are unique.
3. Computer penetrations and looping—a technique allowing cybercriminals to break into someone's computer account and issue commands from that account, thus allowing the perpetrator of the act to hide behind the account holder's identity.

4. Cloned cellular phones—buying cloned cellular phones in bulk and discarding them after the crime is completed. Cellular fraud is defined as the unauthorized use, tampering, or manipulation of a cellular phone or service. Previously, the cloning of cellular phones accounted for a large portion of cell fraud. As a result, the Wireless Telephone Protection Act of 1998 expanded prior United States law to criminalize the use, possession, manufacture, or sale of cloning hardware or software. Today, the primary type of cell fraud is subscriber fraud—when someone signs up for service with fraudulently obtained customer information or false identification.
5. Cellular phone cards—anonymously purchasing prepaid cards, with an available amount of air time, to commit a crime; using a telephone service without revealing one's identity.

Conclusion

This chapter provided an overview of cybercrime history, starting with the White Hat exploits at MIT in the 1960s and 1970s and then discussing the Hacker Ethic and its lack of real meaning to the Black Hat crackers. The chapter discussed John Draper, likely the first phreaker to become rich and famous, and many other troubled but talented people who have engaged in risky hacking and cracking exploits. The chapter went on to discuss the widespread anxiety that grew with the turning of the millennium and has been exacerbated since then: the fear of cyberterrorist attacks and a cyberapocalypse. The second part of this chapter focused on types of cybercrime and the "four elements" criteria. It also discussed cybervigilantism and hacktivism, noting that these are, technically, nonoffenses.

Without a doubt, in the past century, geographic isolation helped protect the United States from a direct physical invasion. But now in the new millennium, national boundaries have little meaning in cyberspace. A segment in the U.S. government's national strategy to secure cyberspace notes that information flows continuously and seamlessly across political, ethnic, and religious divides. Even the infrastructure that makes up cyberspace (software and hardware) is global in nature. Because of this global nature of cyberspace, the existing vulnerabilities are open to the world—and to anyone (White Hat or Black Hat), anywhere, who has sufficient capability to exploit them.

The only way to protect ourselves as a society is to have a sound knowledge of cybercrime and to pay heed to warnings from cybersecurity experts.

References

"Americans Concerned about Cyberattacks." *The East Carolinian*, September 5, 2003. http://www.crime-research.org/eng/news/2003/09/Mess0502.html (cited September 5, 2003).

Appleby, T. 2003. "Guantanamo Translator Charged with Spying." *The Globe and Mail*, September 24, p. A21.

Associated Press. 2003a. "The Globe and Mail Breaking News Technology: Electrical Grid Vulnerable to Hackers. Posted September 11, 3:04 PM EDT." http://www.theglobeandmail.com (cited September 11, 2003).

———. 2003b. "Hacker Case Called Unique." *The Globe and Mail*, October 10, p. B8.

Bakst, B. 2003. "FBI Arrests Suspect in Net-Virus Case." *The Globe and Mail*, August 30, p. A14.

BBC News. 2003 "Operation Ore: Can the UK Cope?" http://news.bbc.co.uk/1/hi/uk/2652465.stm (cited January 13, 2003).

Bloom, R. 2003. "Viruses Eat Away at Firms' Productivity." *The Globe and Mail*, August 21, p. B6.

Brenner, S. 2001. "Is There Such a Thing as 'Virtual Crime'?" *California Criminal Law Review*. http://www.boalt.org/CCLR/v4/v4brenner.htm (cited September 14, 2003).

"California: Legislative Priorities Set for Prevention of Identity Theft." 2003. *Cybercrime Law Report*, 3, April 21, p. 3.

Campbell, M. 2001. "Chronology of a Nightmare." *The Globe and Mail*, September 12, p. N6.

"Code Red Havoc Reported to Have Cost $2.6 Billion." 2001. *The Globe and Mail*, September 6, p. B26.

CyberAngels. 2001."Cyberstalking." http://www.cyberangels.org (cited December 9, 2001).

Damsell, K. 2003a. "Ethical Hackers' Test for Weakness." *The Globe and Mail*, August 5, pp. B1–B2.

———. 2003b. "Newer, Tougher Bugs Are Swarming Web, Study Finds." *The Globe and Mail,* October 1, p. B5.

Department of Justice. 2001. "Justice Minister Introduces Measures to Better Protect Canadians and Safeguard Children from Cybercriminals." http://www.canada.justice.gc.ca/en/news/nr/2001/doc_26058.html (cited March 14, 2001).

Dibbell, J. 1998. "A Rape in Cyberspace (Or TINYSOCIETY, and How to Make One)." http://www.juliandibbell.com/texts/bungle_print.html (cited January 20, 2004).

"Dramatic Increase in Complaints Reported," 2003. *Cybercrime Law Report,* 3, April 21, p. 11.

Hammond, R. 2003. *Identity Theft: How to Protect Your Most Valuable Asset.* Franklin Lakes, NJ: Career Press.

Homeland Security Act, H.R. 5005. 2002. http://www.whitehouse.gov/deptofhomeland/analysis (cited November 30, 2002).

"Homeland Security Provides Advice on Combating the 'Blaster' Internet Worm." 2003. http://www.whitehouse.gov/news/releases/2003/08/ (cited August 14, 2003).

"Identity Theft: FTC Hampered by Lack of Funds, Power." 2003. *Cybercrime Law Report,* 3, April 21.

Karp, H. 2000. "Angels On-Line." *Reader's Digest,* 157, pp. 50–56.

Karp, J. 2002. "Get Help Fighting Fraud Online." http://www.techtv.com/cybercrime/internetfraud/story/0,23008,3370664,00.html (cited May 7, 2002).

Koring, P. 2003. "9/11/03: He Taunts Us Still." *The Globe and Mail,* September 11, p. A1.

Lau, E. 2001. "Ex-Hacker Knows How Worm Turns: Sacbee News." http://www.pcmag.com/article2/0,4149,64189,00.asp (cited August 2, 2001).

Levy, S. 1984. *Hackers: Heroes of the Computer Revolution.* New York: Dell.

McCarthy, J. 2000. "Google News Posted at 8:52 A.M. ET." http://www.CNN.com (cited February 28, 2000).

Meinel, C. 2001. "Code Red for the Web." *Scientific American,* 285 (October), pp. 42–51.

"Minneapolis, Minnesota 18 Year Old Arrested for Developing and Releasing B Variant of Blaster Computer Worm." 2003. http://www.usdoj.gov/criminal/cybercrime/parsonArrest.htm (cited August 29, 2003).

MIT News 2001. "MIT to Make Nearly All Course Materials Available Free on the World Wide Web." http://mit.edu/newsoffice/nr/2001/ocw.html (cited April 14, 2001).

Mulhall, T. 1997a. "Where Have All the Hackers Gone? Part 1: Introduction and Methodology." *Computers and Security,* 16, pp. 277–284.

———. 1997b. "Where Have All the Hackers Gone? Part 3: Motivation and Deterrence." *Computers and Security,* 16, p. 292.

National Center for Victims of Crime. 2001. "Cyberstalking." http://www.ncvc.org/ (cited December 9, 2001).

"The National Strategy to Secure Cyberspace." 2003. http://www.whitehouse.gov/pcipb/ (cited September 19, 2003).

"Operation Iraqi Freedom: President Bush Addresses the Nation." 2003. http://www.whitehouse.gov/news/releases/2003/03/ (cited March 29, 2003).

Pipkin, D. 2003. *Halting the Hacker: A Practical Guide to Computer Security.* Upper Saddle River, NJ: Pearson Education.

Posey, J. 2003. "Child Pornography: Is It So Bad?" http://www.pedowatch.com/porn.htm (cited September 23, 2003).

Rosenbaum, R. 1971. "Secrets of the Little Box." *Esquire* (October): pp. 116–125.

Schell, B. H., J. L. Dodge, and S. Moutsatsos. 2002. *The Hacking of America: Who's Doing It, Why, and How.* Westport, CT: Quorum.

Schell, B. H., and N. M. Lanteigne. 2000. *Stalking, Harassment, and Murder in the Workplace: Guidelines for Protection and Prevention.* Westport, CT: Quorum.

Schwartu, W. 1999. *Information Warfare: Chaos on the Electronic Superhighway.* New York: Thunder's Mouth Press

Slatella, M. 1997. "Discovery Online: Hackers' Hall of Fame," http://tlc.discovery.com/convergence/hackers/bio/bio.html (cited February 2, 1997).

Solomon, J. 2003. "Mastermind Depicts Al-Qaeda Executing Plots with Fluidity." *The Globe and Mail,* September 23, p. A19.

Specter, M. 2001. "The Doomsday Click." *The New Yorker,* May 28, pp. 101–107.

Stackhouse, J. 2001. "Al-Qaeda Declares Holy War." *The Globe and Mail,* October 10, p. A1.

Symantec Security Response. 2003. "Top Virus Threats." http://www.symantec.com/avcenter/index.html (cited August 28, 2003).

"Texas: Bill Would Authorize Attorney General to Prosecute ID Thieves." 2003. *Cybercrime Law Report,* 3, April 21, p. 4.

United Press International. 2003. "Easy Visas Made Saudis Best Bet for 9/11." http://www.newsmax.com/archives/articles/2003/9/10/143556.shtml.

U.S. Attorney General. 1999. *Report on Cyberstalking: A New Challenge for Law Enforcement and Industry.* http://www.usdoj.gov/criminal/cybercrime/cyberstalking.htm (cited February 9, 2003).

U.S. General Accounting Office. 2002. *Report to Congressional Requesters: Identity Theft: Prevalence and Cost Appear to Be Growing.* GAO-02–363, March, pp. 1–70.

Walleij, Linus. 1999a. "Chapter 2: Hackers!" in *Copyright Does Not Exist.* Translated by Nirgendwo, a.k.a. Daniel Arnrup. http://home.c2i.net/nirgendwo/cdne/ch2web.htm (cited August 23, 2000).

———. 1999b. "Chapter 14: Female Hackers?" in *Copyright Does Not Exist.* Translated by Nirgendwo, a.k.a. Daniel Arnrup. http://home.c2i.net/nirgendwo/cdne/ch14web.htm (cited August 23, 2000).

"War on Iraq: The First Strike." 2003. *Time.* http://www.time.com/time/photoessays/war_firststrike (cited April 29, 2003).

Welch, M. 2003. "Get Ready for Patriot II." *http://alternet.org/print.html?StoryID=15541* (cited January 28, 2004).

Yang, J. 2001. "Government Jabs at Cyber Crime." http://abcnews.com/sections/wnt/DailyNews/cybercrime010721.html

Yost, P. 2001. "Yahoo News Posted at 7:56 A.M. ET: U.S. Flight Schools Trained Highjackers." http://www.yahoo.com (cited September 11, 2001).

2

Issues, Controversies, and Solutions

This chapter gives an overview of a number of reported incidents of computer system intrusion and discusses controversies around such cases, common methods used to commit cybercrimes, interesting and controversial cases in point, and countermeasures geared to detect or curb these crimes. Particular issues and controversies around intellectual property rights, copyright, and the 1998 Digital Millennium Copyright Act are then detailed.

This chapter also describes the issues, controversies, and solutions associated with program security, operating system and database security, and computer networking and networked applications. The discussion begins with two interesting "noncases" of cyber controversy regarding system vulnerabilities, continues with the known vulnerabilities found in system security, and closes with two forms of legislation that have been passed to counter system intruders: the 2001 Council of Europe's Draft Convention on Cyber-Crime and the U.S. Homeland Security Act of 2002. The chapter closes with the controversial topic of honeypots and the United States Federal Wiretap Act of 1998.

Computer System Intrusions

Recent Statistics on Computer Intrusions

From 1988 through 2003, the Computer Emergency Response Team (CERT) Coordination Center at Carnegie Mellon University in Pittsburgh, Pennsylvania, cited 319,992 reported incidents of computer system intrusion. An "incident," it should be noted, may involve one site, hundreds of sites, or thousands of sites. One common definition of an incident is "The act of violating an explicit or implied security policy" (Computer Emergency Response Team Coordination Center, 2004). These acts include attempts to gain unauthorized access to systems or data, unwanted disruption, or denial-of-service, unauthorized usage of systems, and changes to system hardware and software characteristics without the owner's knowledge, instruction, or consent. It is possible to accomplish these steps in as little as 45 seconds, and with automation the time to accomplish these steps decreases further. In 2003, a total of 137, 529 incidents were reported. There has been a sharp, continual rise in the number of computer intrusion incidents reported in recent years: In 1988, there were 6 intrusion incidents; in 1989, there were 132; in 1999, there were 9,859, and in 2000, there were 21,756 incidents reported, rising to 52,658 in 2001, and 82,094 in 2002. (Computer Emergency Response Team Coordination Center, 2004).

Likewise a 2003 survey of 530 computer security practitioners in United States corporations, government agencies, financial institutions, medical institutions, and universities indicated that there was no shortage of computer-related crimes in the last twelve months of 2002. A considerable 56 percent of the respondents who answered the CSI/FBI 2003 Computer Crime and Security Survey reported computer system "unauthorized use" in the workplace. And though the percentage reporting intrusions in 2003 was slightly less than the percentage of respondents reporting intrusions in 2002 (60 percent), the findings are still disturbing, because most of the respondents' companies had taken a number of varied intrusion safeguards (Richardson, 2003).

For example, notes Richardson (2003), 99 percent of the responding companies in 2003 had antivirus software (as compared to 90 percent in 2002); 98 percent of them had firewalls (as compared to 89 percent in 2002); 92 percent of them had access controls (as compared to 82 percent in 2002); and 91 percent had physical security (as compared to 84 percent in 2002). (Firewalls are used on networks to provide additional security by blocking access to certain services in the private network from the public network. Access controls are physical or logical safeguards preventing unauthorized access to information resources [Pipkin, 2003].)

Moreover, according to Richardson (2003), there was almost a tie between the number of reported likely intrusions by "outsider" crackers (82 percent of the respondents considered such an attack likely) and the number of reported likely intrusions by disgruntled employee "insiders" (80 percent of the respondents considered this type of attack likely). And although "enemy" computer invasions are increasingly on the minds of U.S. government agencies and citizens alike, the CSI/FBI 2003 findings indicate that only 28 percent of the respondents considered espionage intrusions by foreign governments to be likely (as compared to 26 percent in 2002), and only 25 percent of the respondents reported espionage intrusions by foreign corporations to be likely (as compared to 26 percent in 2002).

In terms of types of attacks or misuse detected during 2000 to 2003, viruses took the lead, with a significant 82 percent of the respondents reporting such invasions. And when the respondents were asked to place dollar values on the types of attacks or misuse experienced in 2003, of the 251 respondents specifying dollar amount losses, the top three problem areas (with estimated costs) cited were (Richardson, 2003):

1. Theft of proprietary information ($70,195,900)
2. Flooding of the system, resulting in denial-of-service, or DoS ($65,643,300)
3. Viruses and worms ($27,382,340)

Of significance is the fact that only 30 percent of the respondents said that they had reported their incidents to law enforcement officials. As would be expected, the majority of the companies, 93 percent, patched the holes to avoid future intrusions.

Interpreting Cybercrime Statistics

Surveys distributed to system administrators inquiring about computer crime and about the suspected identity of the crack attackers, the methods attackers employed, the frequency of system intrusions, the systems affected, and the dollar amounts lost tend to be used as a basis for determining organizations' system risk management strategies. That is, when system administrators try to estimate the appropriate level of investment in computer security the company should make, they tend to compare their level of "hack-attack" or intrusion risk by evaluating the experiences of other organizations with similar systems and business characteristics. However, precautions should be taken on interpretation of such data, as it is impossible for survey respondents to give completely reliable answers to such questions. First, an unknown number of crimes go undetected and therefore cannot be reported. Second, even when hack attacks are detected, it seems that few are reported (as noted by the just-cited 30 percent CSI/FBI survey figure).

Regarding the first point, in a landmark series of tests made by the United States Defense Information Systems Agency, the Agency found that very few of the penetrations it engineered against unclassified systems within the Department of Defense (DoD) were detected by the system managers. In fact, a commonly held view within the information security community is that only about one-tenth or so of all crimes committed against and using computing systems are detected (Garside, 1998).

Regarding the second point and based on the experience of security professionals who have conducted interviews on their clients' losses, only a very small percentage of known system intrusions are reported to the authorities or the public (Garside, 1998)

Again, the 2003 CSI/FBI survey findings give further insight on this issue. A significant 70 percent of the respondents said in response to the question "If your organization has experienced computer intrusion(s) within the last 12 months, which of the following actions did you take?" that they feared negative publicity, 61 percent of the respondents felt that reporting would encourage competitors to use this information to their own advantage, 53 percent of the respondents were unaware that they could report their problem somewhere, and 56 percent of the respondents felt that a civil (rather than a criminal) remedy seemed to be the better alternative (Richardson, 2003).

Moreover, says Richardson (2003), reporting cybercrimes can lead to more trouble than it is worth. The following story from 2002 makes clear the difficulties that can arise when individuals, companies, and institutions try to deal with cybercrime of a small-scale nature.

Jason Eric Smith sold his Apple Powerbook computer on www.eBay.com and was to collect his payment upon delivery. As payment, Smith received a bank cashier's check that turned out to be forged. Even though Smith tracked down the forger, he could not get federal authorities to make an arrest. Because the theft was below the FBI's $5,000 threshold and because it was not a sufficiently significant counterfeiting case for the Secret Service to pursue, these authorities were not interested in helping the victim. In the end, Jason Smith called in the local police department in the Markham, Illinois, area and got them involved in the investigation. Eventually, a criminal named Melvin Christmas was charged with defrauding over thirty victims. He was later able to get a plea bargain.

Cracking

Outside of social engineering, as described in chapter 1, most attacks on computer systems involve various degrees of technological knowledge and skill. Some methods used include cracking, flooding, erasing of information by viruses and worms, spoofing, phreaking, and piracy.

Crackers are the Black Hats who break into others' computer systems without authorization, dig into the code to circumvent copy-protected software and other digital publications, flood Internet sites, deliberately deface Web sites, and steal money or identities. Sometimes the terms *network hackers* or *net-runners* are used to describe them.

In terms of ability levels involved, cracking exploits range from the simple and automated to the highly disguised and sophisticated. From a skill set perspective, the minimum skill set needed to crack computer systems—typically ascribed to script-kiddies or newbies who rely on prefabricated software—is simply the ability to read and follow directions. After all, basic cracking tips appear on publicly accessible Web sites such as bugtraq.com, rootshell.com, and packetstorm.com.

Besides social engineering skills, crackers wanting to launch a more sophisticated attack require:

- Some knowledge of computer languages such as C, C++, Perl, and Java
- General UNIX and systems administration theory
- Theory on local area networks (i.e., networks often

contained in one or more buildings in physically close locations) and wide area networks (i.e., networks like the Internet, which connect physically distant locations)
- Access (the method by which a user is able to utilize an information resource) and common security protocol information
- Plenty of spare time

At the basic level, in order to infiltrate a system, a cracker typically needs to "social engineer" a system into thinking that he or she is a system administrator or a legitimate user. Then, the intruder needs to "communicate" with a computer system. To do this, he or she must key into the computer special identifying strings, called passwords, and an authorized "username." This two-step process is called logging in.

Crackers who are determined to infiltrate companies' systems often obtain authorized users' passwords using one or more of these common social engineering techniques (Nirgendwo, 1999):

- Glancing over an authorized user's shoulder when the user is logging in
- Recording authorized users' login keystrokes on video
- Searching for notes on or in authorized users' desks
- Calling system operators and claiming to be an employee who forgot his or her password
- "Trashing" (searching through actual garbage cans) and collecting scraps of paper with passwords on them
- Searching for authorized users' passwords by reading e-mail messages stored on company computers
- Guessing different combinations of personally meaningful initials or birth dates of authorized users

More sophisticated types of cracking involve methods of bypassing the entire security system by exploiting gaps in the systems programs (i.e., the operating systems, the drivers, or the communications protocols) that run the computer system itself. Crackers often use vulnerabilities in commands and protocols such as (Nirgendwo, 1999):

- FTP (file transfer protocol)—a protocol used to transfer files between systems over a network

- TFTP (trivial file transfer protocol)—a network protocol that allows unauthenticated transfer of files
- Telnet and SSH—two commands used to remotely log into a UNIX computer
- Finger—a UNIX command providing information about users that can be utilized to retrieve the .plan and .project files from a user's home directory. These text files are used to store information about the user's location, near-future plans and the projects he or she is working on.
- NFS (network file system)—one method of sharing files across a local area network or through the Internet
- The e-mail subsystem
- UUCP (an acronym for *UNIX to UNIX copy*)—a protocol used for the store-and-forward exchange of e-mail

After gaining access to a system, a cracker can then install code (the portion of the computer program that can be read, written, and modified by humans) directly into the computer system or can add a transmitter device to allow for later installation.

For example, after gaining access to a targeted facility by posing as a member of the cleaning staff, a cracker could put a small computer, itself connected to the facility's main network, into the base of a lamp, with an infrared port (that enables users to transfer data from one device to another with infrared waves rather than cables) aimed outside through an office window or linked to a mobile phone. This setup could then provide the cracker with subsequent remote access to the device from anywhere in the line of sight (Ingles-le Nobel, 1999).

More advanced crackers can also use cellular modems to their advantage, but one major drawback to these is that they are potentially detectable by security radio frequency sweeps. For corporate espionage purposes, however, it is quite an easy matter for a cracker to pre-position several such cellular modems and then take advantage of security vulnerabilities to gain permanent entry into a desired system. For less than $1,000, crackers can order such devices from technology-oriented magazines and disguise them as lamps. Espionage on industrial computers can also be accomplished by using electromagnetic (EM) signals, but this means is quite expensive—in the range of $35,000 (Ingles-le Nobel, 1999).

Organizational Cracking Countermeasures: Patches

Responsible software vendors monitor incident reports closely and try to close the security gaps in their products. Also, new exploits are continuously being discovered, documented, and shared in the White Hacker and system security community. The vulnerabilities are addressed and solutions for repair are recommended. To prevent future intrusions, system administrators need to install updates for their systems' software called fixes or patches.

However, far too many systems officers fail to completely update the system programs, so that many gaps remain open for a while. There are a variety of reasons for the delay: the job may be too time-consuming, it may be too complex, or it may be given too low a priority rating by the organization. Also, some systems officers neglect parts of their security systems because some of the security measures create inconveniences for authorized users. For example, many system administrators remove a function that requires users to change their passwords frequently or that prevents the use of common passwords that can be easily stolen or mimicked.

Societal Cracking Countermeasures: Legislation

If caught for their exploits in the United States, crackers are often charged with "intentionally causing damage without authorization to a protected computer." A first offender typically faces up to 5 years in prison and pays fines of up to $250,000 per count, or twice the loss suffered by the victim (with the courts deciding in part by the range provided in the legislation and in part by the evidence provided in court). The victim can also seek civil penalties (Evans and McKenna, 2000).

If caught for cracking exploits in Canada, perpetrators often face a number of charges under that country's Criminal Code. In combating crack attacks, the following provisions of the Canadian Criminal Code are generally applied: theft, fraud, computer abuse, data abuse, and the interception of communications. The main prohibition in the Criminal Code is set out in section 342.1, entitled "unauthorized use of a computer" and often referred to by the legal community as the "computer abuse" offense. Section 342.1 of the Code is aimed at several potential harms: theft of computer services, invasion of privacy, and trading in computer passwords or cracking encryption systems. Section 430(1.1) describes the crime of "mischief" as it relates to data (Walton, 2000). Although the Canadian Criminal Code contains a number of provisions that can be utilized against persons perpetrating computer crimes, each offense falls into one of two categories, depending on its severity: an indictable offense or a summary conviction offense. Indictable offenses are more serious and can carry lengthy sentences.

In Europe, similar laws apply. In the United Kingdom, for example, there are a number of laws relating to computer crime, including the U.K. Data Protection Act of 1984, the Copyright Design and Patents Act of 1988, the Criminal Damage Act of 1971, the Theft Act of 1968, the Telecommunications Act of 1984, the Police and Criminal Evidence Act of 1984 (especially Section 69, relating to computer-generating evidence), and the Computer Misuse Act of 1990. Many crackers in the U.K. are under the impression that the only legislation pertaining to their activities is the Computer Misuse Act of 1990; they are often surprised when they are charged with offenses under the other relevant Acts (Mulhall, 1997).

Software to Stop Crackers

Hope lies on the horizon for individuals and organizations wanting to prevent crackers from intruding into their systems. Currently, there are some creative software products being designed to outsmart and stop crackers.

For example, startup company Amenaza Technologies is addressing intrusion risk reduction from a unique perspective—that of the attacker. Amenaza's SecurITree software creates an exploit route by linking various "approach" paths and vulnerabilities in the same way that a cracker might exploit a system. SecurITree lets security experts identify specific cybercrimes, such as theft of credit card information, and to work outward to model various ways that a cracker may pursue his or her objectives. The result is a decision tree showing all of the various combinations of paths leading to a successful outcome by the cracker. Once the path combinations are identified, and in order to calculate the relative value (representing the likelihood of an intrusion, typically defined as "I" for impossible or "P" for possible) of each path, SecurITree factors in a number of key variables such as the cost of the attack, the skill required to accomplish the act, and the probability of being caught. The program then allows the user to add in the profiles of potential crackers (thieves, terrorists, scriptkiddies, stalkers, and so on), allowing the decision tree to be "pruned" on the basis of cost, skills of intruders, and their aversion to being caught (Lindstrom, 2003).

Also, SecurITree provides users a way to identify "choke points" where security controls can be applied to protect multiple vulnerabilities along a path or a set of paths. An example of the latter would be a firewall protecting many systems from being attacked via the Internet (Lindstrom, 2003).

Flooding

When a cracker floods a site using a technique called distributed denial-of-service, or DDoS, he or she plants software programs (or scripts) on large computers with high-speed connections to the Internet (called servers). These planted machines are then known as zombies. Zombies lie in wait until the cracker sends them a signal to bombard a targeted site. On command, the zombies simultaneously send thousands or more fake requests for information to the targeted site. In an effort to try to handle so many requests, the computer soon runs out of memory and other resources. The computer either slows down dramatically, or it stops.

At the low end of flooding sophistication, denial-of-service (DoS) exploits use only a single computer on the Internet to originate the attack, and therefore can be more easily detected and guarded against than the more sophisticated DDoS, which use a large group of previously compromised systems to direct a coordinated, disturbed flood attack against a particular target.

Web sites such as Floodnet provide prefabricated software (i.e., Trin00, Tribal Flood Network, or Stacheldratht) that can be easily downloaded and used even by novice hackers to perform a simple DoS attack, causing a system to "overheat" so that it slows down or stops any attempts by registered users to log on. According to security experts, because the common gateway interface (CGI) scripts (a simple mechanism to pass information from a form on a Web site to the software on a Web server) for Web sites are poorly written, they can easily be compromised and broken into. Exploiting poorly written code is no great feat for crackers with plenty of time on their hands and a desire to infiltrate a system.

Industry experts, understandably, get upset about DoS exploits because such attacks are a costly form of vandalism. IBM, for example, estimates that online retailers can lose $10,000 or more in sales per minute if service is unavailable to customers (Evans, 2000).

Recent Flooding Cases: Mafiaboy and Aaron Caffrey

On the day that high-school student Mafiaboy (his real name is not available because he was tried as a juvenile offender) cracked into the Yahoo.com site in February 2000, the online search company was hard hit not only financially but also "psychologically." Simply put, the site was invaded and bombarded with enough confusing information that it caused the digital equivalent of a nervous breakdown. Yahoo.com's Internet service provider (ISP), Global Crossing, could normally absorb a few million bits of data each second, but on the day of the attack, it was clogged with as many as 1 billion bits per second. This kind of massive bombardment can be viewed as the equivalent of having millions of phantom users scream at once, "Yes, I heard you!" (Taylor, 2000).

Global Crossing took several hours to monitor their $500,000 routing machines to determine which one was being attacked. And when the engineers at this company saw the size of the barrage on the system—ten times as large as anything ever recorded—they were shocked. Within days of flooding Yahoo.com, Mafiaboy went on to flood other key online companies, including Amazon.com, eBay, CNN.com, ZdNet.com, E*trade.com, and Excite.com.

Apparently there were signs that such massive flooding or "shocking" could occur, but the warnings were largely ignored by the industry. In 1999, the FBI and a number of private security firms began detecting countless dormant "daemons" (a process running in the background that performs some service for other programs) appearing on servers across the United States. System security trackers warned companies to scan their servers with detection software, but far too few commercial sites paid heed to the warning. After the series of Mafiaboy shock attacks, however, the warnings were finally acted upon. Downloads of the FBI's scanning tool rose from 170 on Monday, February 7, 2000, to more than 4,000 on Thursday, February 10, 2000—the period associated with Mafiaboy's flooding exploits (Taylor, 2000).

Mafiaboy's computer cracking and mischief trial had the potential to redefine the concept of reasonable doubt in a relatively unexplored area of law. But, as is typical with most young crackers facing the prospect of a long and expensive trial, Mafiaboy admitted his part in the DoS attacks. He went before the Youth Court of Quebec and pleaded guilty to five counts of mischief, fifty-one counts of illegal access to a computer, and one count of breach of bail conditions. Judge Ouellet ruled that the teenager had committed a criminal act under the Canadian Criminal Code, and the judge sentenced him to 8 months in a youth detention center, ordered him to face one year of probation after his detention ended, and fined him $250. In a statement to the media, his lawyer expressed a common theme of regret among convicted young hackers (Evans, 2001, p. 6):

> If today, if placed in the same position, he would have contacted the companies and told them there was a major flaw in their security. At the time, it was the last thing on his mind. It was more of a challenge. It was not to willfully cause damage. . . . He had difficulty believing that such companies as Yahoo had not put in place security measures to stop him. He got results.

Besides Mafiaboy's, other flooding exploits have made the news in recent years around the world. For example, in 2002, a United Kingdom teenager was charged with cracking into and crippling a U.S. seaport's computer navigation system. In September 2001, Aaron Caffrey, a 19-year-old from Dorset, southwest England, was charged under the 1990 Computer Misuse Act in Great Britain and accused of unleashing a flood of data capable of shutting down the Port of Houston, Texas. This seaport is the sixth biggest shipping port in the world.

Caffrey denied the charges, saying that although the attack was apparently triggered from his computer, he was not the person behind the flooding exploit. In fact, in defending himself before the Southwark Crown Court, Caffrey gave a technical description of how computer crackers could assume the identity of unsuspecting computer users through tricks like "fishing out" a security password to steal someone's online identity, or installing a Trojan program—so named because it takes over a machine remotely. In his own defense, Caffrey affirmed, that his computer was completely and utterly vulnerable to many exploits ("Hacker Suspect," 2003).

Though he faced a possible prison sentence of 5 years, on Friday, October 17, 2003, a jury found Caffrey not guilty of the cracking charges. Outside the courtroom, when asked by reporters what advice he had for people interested in computer hacking, Aaron said, "Learning it [computer hacking] is just fine. Just don't do anything illegal." Like other talented young hackers before him who were caught for computer-related crimes, Aaron now wants to get a job as a computer security consultant ("PC Whiz," 2003).

Viruses and Worms

Viruses and worms can erase information from computers. Worms and viruses are part of a general category of programs called malicious code. Both viruses and worms exploit weaknesses in computer software, replicating and/or attaching themselves to other programs. They spread quickly and easily from system to system.

Technically speaking, worms are programs that spread with no human interaction after they are started, whereas viruses are programs requiring some action on the part of the user, such as opening an e-mail attachment. Viruses can be spread via floppy disks or CDs, as e-mail attachments, or in material downloaded from the Web. The majority of viruses that are currently a threat are spread by e-mail. Users are often enticed to open such email attachments because they are given intriguing (e.g., "I Love You") or legitimate-sounding subject lines, or because the e-mail appears to be from someone the user knows (i.e., a trusted source)—as occurs when the user's address book has been compromised. Worms and viruses can bypass security measures such as firewalls, erase data, and clog systems (Pethia, 2003)

In addition to their replicating ability, another bad thing about viruses is that they can be very destructive if they carry a "logic bomb," hidden code causing the virus to perform some potentially destructive action when specific criteria are met. These actions, or payloads, can vary from merely annoying—like altering a home page—to deleting files and reformatting hard drives (thereby erasing all information stored on them). Viruses not carrying a logic bomb, often referred to by experts as bacteria or rabbits, are not so destructive. They merely replicate, thus consuming resources.

One of the most talked-about insider malicious code incidents occurring in recent years involved Timothy Lloyd, an employee who planted a logic bomb in Omega Engineering's network in 1996 when he found out that he was about to be fired from the company. His act of sabotage allegedly cost the company $12 million in damages to the systems and networks. It also reportedly forced the layoff of eighty employees, and it cost the electronics firm its leading position in a competitive marketplace (Shaw, 2001).

Computer viruses have been a media item since the 1980s, with the first of the modern viruses thought to have been made in Bulgaria. Bulgaria occupied a central position in the virus industry because during one phase of the Cold War, the Eastern Bloc decided to manufacture viruses for electronic warfare. Bulgaria, known for its high-class computer scientists, was a natural choice for constructing these weapons. Thus, many talented Bulgarian software students came into contact with government-financed virus programming and later continued to develop viruses as a hobby. The most prominent of these students was one known as Dark Avenger (real identity not known), who has attained cult status among today's virus hackers (Nirgendwo, 2000).

The Michelangelo virus, discovered in 1991 and activated on March 6 (Michelangelo Buonarroti's birthday), 1992, attracted lots of media attention because it was at first believed to cause great damage to data and computers around the world. These fears turned out to be greatly exaggerated, however, because it turned out that the virus did not do anything to the computers it invaded (Nirgendwo, 1999)

Another virus incident of interest occurred in April 2003. A Swedish citizen (a minor, who could not be named) faced fines and a 2-year prison sentence for violating Swedish laws prohibiting the distribution of viruses and worms that caused changes in people's software without their permission. Though not a terrorist, this Swedish citizen admitted that he created and spread a computer worm detected in at least forty countries, causing him to make the media headlines worldwide. The worm he created and distributed did three destructive and/or annoying things ("Spreader of Multinational Virus," 2003):

1. It sent itself to every e-mail address the virus located on the infected computer's hard drive, not just those located in address books of e-mail programs.
2. It disabled antivirus software on the infected computer—with particular targets being the antivirus software products of F-Secure Corporation, Sophos Plc, and Symantec Corporation.
3. It generated a statement complaining about what the virus author claims was "discriminatory behavior" that he experienced during 8 years in the Swedish school system.

In the complaint, the perpetrator claimed that as he had routinely experienced difficulty speaking in front of groups, he had asked his school's officials if he could communicate mostly in writing. His request, however, was unsuccessful. Because of another virus command, the virus e-mailed this statement—in both the Swedish and English languages—thousands of times to national school authorities, to selected Swedish journalists, and to media outlets. Experts believe that the virus spread so rapidly in Sweden because virtually no major viruses had at that point been written in the Swedish language; the Swedes were therefore less cautious about opening attachments received in their own language ("Spreader of Multinational Virus," 2003).

Protecting Computers from Viruses and Worms

Since the time of Robert Morris's exploits in 1988 (see chapter 1), virus and worm detection and repair have become a standard operating procedure on corporate and home computers.

John McAfee, the developer of the McAfee antivirus software, claims that there are currently more than 58,000 virus threats, and antivirus company Symantec estimates that ten to fifteen new viruses are discovered daily. Basically, antivirus software keeps a database of "fingerprints," a set of characteristic bytes from known viruses, on file. The software searches files and programs on a computer for those patterns, and when it finds a fingerprint it recognizes as belonging to a virus, the antivirus software notifies the user that the virus is present. Heuristic programs also look for viruslike behavior in other computer programs, allowing the software to detect new viruses. Either way, however, antivirus software needs to be installed and updated regularly so that it can search a computer for new viruses that are created and released (Karp, 2002b).

Erasures caused by viruses and worms can be guarded against through frequent (under the purview of each company to decide how frequent), multiple, remote backups, in both geography and network topology, thus safekeeping backups on a different site and thus not directly connected to a segment of the network (Ingles-le Nobel, 1999).

After the Morris worm media frenzy in 1988, the United States Defense Advanced Research Projects Agency (DARPA) set up the Computer Emergency Response Team (CERT) and the CERT Coordination Center (CERT/CC) at Carnegie Mellon

University's Software Engineering Institute in Pittsburgh, Pennsylvania. CERT/CC serves as a focal point to help resolve computer security incidents and vulnerabilities.

On September 15, 2003, the Department of Homeland Security, in conjunction with the University, announced the creation of the U.S. Computer Emergency Response Team (US-CERT), designed to become the country's premier CERT and to supersede the existing one. The newly formed US-CERT is projected to grow to include partnerships with private sector security vendors and with other domestic and international CERT organizations. These groups will work together to coordinate national and international efforts to prevent, protect, and respond to the effects of cyberattacks across the Internet.

US-CERT is intended to improve warning and response time for computer security incidents by fostering the development of detection tools and utilizing common commercial incident and vulnerability reporting protocols. Also, US-CERT will collaborate with the private sector to develop and implement new tools and methods for detecting, and quickly responding to, vulnerabilities (Department of Homeland Security, 2003).

Tom Ridge, secretary of Homeland Security, remarked, "This new center for cybersecurity is a key element to our national strategy to combat terrorism and protect our critical infrastructure. The recent cyberattacks such as the Blaster worm and the SoBig virus highlight the urgent need for an enhanced computer emergency response program that coordinates national efforts to cyber incidents and attacks" (Department of Homeland Security, 2003, p. 1).

Without question, today's worms and viruses are causing damage more quickly than those created in the past, and they are spreading to the most vulnerable of all computer systems: those of home users. The Code Red worm spread around the world faster in 2001 than the Morris one moved in 1988. The Code Red worm also spread around the world faster than the Melissa virus in 1999. Months later, NIMDA caused serious damage within an hour of the first report of infection.

Blaster was even faster than Code Red. After 24 hours, Blaster had infected 336,000 computers, but Code Red had only infected 265,000 computers in the same amount of time. In both of these cases, 100,000 computers were infected in the first 3–5 hours. This "fast exploitation" means that security experts have little time to analyze the problem and to warn the Internet community—companies, government agencies, institutions, and home users. Also, system administrators and users alike, even when warned, have little time to protect their systems under these circumstances.

System administrators need to work quickly after a virus is identified, as the amount of damage done by viruses and worms because of service delays and stoppages can be high. For example, as of September 10, 2003, the Blaster worm was known to still be active, and the damages from it were estimated to be at least $525 million. Also, the SoBigF damages were estimated to range from $500 million to more than $1 billion (including lost productivity, wasted hours, lost sales, and extra bandwidth costs) (Pethia, 2003).

Elsewhere around the world, groups such as the National High-Tech Crime Unit (NHTCU) in the United Kingdom have started working with antivirus companies. Their objective is to identify patterns in the source code of the most damaging Internet worms and virus programs to determine whether they are the work of organized subversive groups or crime syndicates. Their hope is that critical investigations will expose clues to each author's identity, motive, and possibly future acts of sabotage buried somewhere in the lines of code.

The good news is that of the multitudes of viruses and worms emerging on the Internet each week, none to date has been traced to organized crime or to subversive elements whose aim is to disrupt a country's infrastructure. As increasingly sophisticated programs surface that are capable of taking vast computer networks offline, however, enforcement agents are getting ready for this type of cyberwarfare. Len Hynds, the head of the NHTCU, says, "It's a tactic that could be utilized. We've seen legitimate programs used in a way that allows people to have remote access to compromised systems. And, similarly, viruses, Trojans, and worms can be used by organized crime to launch attacks" ("News: U.K. Combs," 2003c, pp. 1–3).

Spoofing

Spoofing often includes attempts by crackers to create fake records or messages in a system—such as false bank accounts or forgeries. The easiest way to defend against this type of spoofing is to use backups for data and to operate a double-entry bookkeeping system (i.e., one that traces every record to its creation and that requires consistency among numerous, topologically separate sources).

Spoofing also includes disguising one computer user as another. Here, a cracker uses an intermediary system, called a proxy server, to create an anonymous or masked IP address (the numerical identifier by which computers address and recognize each other) so that his or her location cannot be traced, and/or to make a firewall believe that data comes from within the protected perimeter—thus permitting access to internal systems. Alternatively, the perpetrator uses false "reply to" or "from" information in an e-mail, making it appear that some innocent third party was the sender of the message. The latter practice, often employed by "spammers" (those who send unsolicited e-mails for commercial purposes and sometimes with the criminal intent to defraud), can be likened to placing a false return address on an envelope to be mailed.

By using another person's e-mail address, the spammer can avoid having e-mail bounce back to himself or herself because of invalid recipient addresses, and the spammer can also avoid receiving complaints from angry recipients of the unsolicited e-mail. The spammer's target—the person whose e-mail address appears in the "reply to" line—is typically inundated with angry e-mails from recipients that can number in the tens of thousands. The target can also suffer from a damaged reputation and the suspension of his or her e-mail accounts.

Though spoofing, as just described, is typically accomplished by manipulating the Internet's mail protocols, it does not require a lot of technical skill. There are even several Web sites devoted to the practice of helping crackers send prank e-mails with fake return addresses (Morano, 2003).

Another more complex way that a cracker could get another machine to execute rogue instructions is to exploit "buffer overflows," thus overloading the temporary data buffer on computers and thereby injecting code or data that the attacker wants to run on the target system. Buffer overflows, the result of faulty programs that do not adequately manage buffers, occur when a program writes data beyond the bounds of allocated memory. In each problem case, data is written in an unexpected location, causing unexpected results. Though often the program will abort, there are cases when the overflow can cause data to be written to a memory mapped file, thus altering data in the file on disk, or can cause security problems through "stack-smashing" attacks, which target a certain programming fault. These attacks alter the code of a running program by replacing portions of it with harmful code. Thus, relatively creative crackers can take advantage of a buffer overflow vulnerability through stack-smashing, followed by the running of any arbitrary code (Pipkin, 2003).

Spoofers exploit buffer overflows to get an interactive "shell" (the program that reads and executes commands that the user or the hacker enters on a keyboard) on the machine. In the most common type of attack, the perpetrator attempts to overflow the buffer of a remote daemon (earlier described) or service, to inject code into the program's address space, and to overwrite the return address of some function. Each line of code has an address that, once changed, can alter the control flow of a program. When this function completes, the program will not continue at the location that the original return address pointed to but will use the altered one instead. At the altered address the perpetrator's code is found and executed. The end result is that the shell will have the privileges of the program that was exploited, and the cracker will have a "back door" into the system (Pipkin, 2003). One such case occurred in Phoenix, Arizona. A cracker invaded the computer system of one of the public energy utilities, attaining "root"-level (administrator) privileges on the system that controlled the water gates from the water canals to the Grand Canyon south (Ingles-le Nobel, 1999).

A not-too-sophisticated spoof attack occurred on March 20, 2003, at the William Bee Ririe Hospital in Ely, Nevada. Here, crackers gained access to an undetermined amount of data that may have included 190 employees' social security numbers and bank information. To date, there have been no reported incidents of fraudulent use of this data. Though the source has not yet been traced, the hospital's IT (information technology) manager confirmed that the crackers used a masked IP address to hide the origin of the attack and to trick the security systems into believing that the communication originated at an authorized system (defined as spoofing) ("Hospital Hacked," 2003).

The incident was discovered early in the morning when the IT manager found an active data connection coming from outside the facility, routed through the emergency room and into the payroll department's computer. He became suspicious because at that hour (6 A.M.), no personnel were in the payroll office. The IT manager removed the network cable from the computer to interrupt the connection. He theorized that a computer game that had been downloaded by hospital employees from the Internet had contained a Trojan horse that may have served as a cyberspace beacon, leading the crackers to the system and enabling them to gain entry. Apparently, the log records for the facility indicated 80 to 200 electronic attacks per day. The incident, considered a spoof because of the masked IP address that was used, has resulted in upgraded security measures for the hospital computer system ("Hospital Hacked," 2003).

Fighting Spoofing

The National Infrastructure Protection Center (NIPC), part of the FBI, serves as a government center for investigating threats and providing warnings regarding attacks against critical U.S. infrastructures, including telecommunications, energy, banking, water systems, government operations, and emergency services (Karp, 2002a). The establishment of the NIPC followed a report by the President's Commission on Critical Infrastructure Protection with the mission to address the growing potential vulnerabilities of U.S. critical public and private IT infrastructures.

Creative research also plays a role in countering spoofing; sometimes even the White Hat hackers get the media's and the FBI's attention. For example, in July 2003, Sean Gorman made the headlines—not because he invaded a computer through spoofing, but because he produced for his doctoral dissertation charts detailing the communication networks binding the United States together.

This 29-year-old George Mason University graduate student mapped every business and industrial sector in the United States and layered on top of his map the fiber optic network that connects them. (Every optic fiber, thin as a hair, carries impulses for Internet traffic, telephones, cell phones, military communications, bank transfers, air traffic control, and signals to the power grid and water systems.) These charts are, essentially, treasure maps for terrorists wanting to destroy the United States' economy. For example, using Gorman's map, one can click on a bank in Manhattan and see who has communication lines running into it, or one can drill into a cable trench between Kansas and Colorado and determine how to create the most havoc with a hedge clipper (Blumenfeld, 2003, p. A3).

Gorman's motivation to develop these charts was a speech given by Osama bin Laden in December 2001. Bin Laden urged the destruction of the United States economy by saying, "This economic hemorrhaging continues until today, but requires more blows. And the youth should try to find the joints of the American economy and hit the enemy in these joints, with God's permission" (CBS, 2001). So, using mathematical formulas, Gorman probed for critical links, trying to answer the question, "If I were Osama bin Laden, where would I want to attack?"

Now that his doctoral dissertation is completed, Gorman spends much of his time briefing government officials and private sector CEOs on the critical joints of the American economy, particularly those involved in national security (Blumenfeld, 2003, p. A3).

The Federal Trade Commission (FTC) in the United States has set up a national spam database and is encouraging fed-up e-mail users to forward all the e-mail spam they receive. Last year, the FTC received more than 17 million complaints about spam messages, and nearly 110,000 complaints are received daily (Morano, 2003).

In June 2003, the U.S. Senate Commerce Committee approved legislation that could cost spammers who use false headers or misleading subject lines up to a year in jail and a maximum fine of $1 million. Known as the Can Spam Act, Section 877 requires that commercial e-mailers use clear and conspicuous identification to show that the message is an advertisement or solicitation. It also requires that the e-mail contain an opt-out provision. Under the bill, unsolicited commercial e-mail must contain the valid physical address of the sender. The bill also increases the penalties for address harvesting (scavenging public forums on the Internet for e-mail addresses) and dictionary attacks (generating massive numbers of e-mail addresses on the basis of electronic name dictionaries) using scripts or other automated means to establish multiple e-mail accounts to avoid detection and to intentionally relay or retransmit an unsolicited commercial e-mail (Jupitermedia Corporation, 2003).

Prior to the Can Spam Act's passage, on April 17, 2003, in Illinois, the FTC asked a district court judge to block an allegedly illegal spam operation that used deceptively bland subject lines, false return addresses, and empty "reply to" links to expose unsuspecting consumers—including children—to sexually explicit pornographic material. Saying the deceptive practices violated the Federal Trade Commission Act (FTC Act), the agency alleged that Brian Westby used the spam in an attempt to drive business to an adult Web site, Married But Lonely.

When consumers opened their e-mail messages, they were immediately subjected to sexually explicit solicitations to visit the defendant's adult-oriented Web sites. Because of the deceptive subject lines, consumers had no reason to expect to see such material, the FTC alleged. And, in some cases, consumers may have opened the e-mails in their offices, thereby committing unintentional violations of company policies. In other cases, children may have been exposed to inappropriate adult-oriented pornographic material, the FTC complaint noted. Furthermore, when consumers used the hyperlink or e-mail address to have themselves taken off the mailing list, they received an error message. They could not unsubscribe (Farrell, 2003). The FTC asked the court to order a halt to the deceptive spam, pending trial (Farrell, 2003).

Phreaking

Phreakers use technology to gain unauthorized access to the telephone system. How-to-phreak magazines such as *Phrack* and *Phun* are favored by today's phreakers, who tend to use sophisticated methods to make free telephone calls. These methods include reprogramming telephone company switches; using stolen or artificial card numbers to bill a call to another person or to an international conglomerate such as Coca-Cola; and using a PBX (private branch exchange, or a corporation's internal switchboard) to make free calls.

Phreakers, who from an early age seem to be infatuated with telephone networks, usually become more knowledgeable by reading standard, college-level telecommunications literature. They then master the jargon of telecommunications.

In the 1960s and 1970s, a collection of electronics enthusiasts called the Phone Phreaks specialized in fooling telephone companies' switches to connect free telephone calls over the continent through a technique called blue boxing. These blue boxes contained electronic components producing tones that manipulated the telephone companies' switches. Two of the most famous phreakers of that era were Joe Engressia and John T. Draper (Draper used a special whistle to manipulate the phone company's switching equipment; his exploits were noted in chapter 1).

Joe Engressia was a blind man who could perfectly whistle any note he heard. Joe was arrested twice after using his gift to connect free calls for some friends by simply whistling into the telephone receiver. Unlike Draper, Engressia never became famous or rich. After he was released from prison, he was hired by a small Tennessee company as a telephone repairman (Nirgendwo, 1999).

Another more recent phreaker who made media headlines in 1988 was Kevin Poulsen (also known as Dark Dante). Poulsen took over all the telephone lines going into Los Angeles radio station KIIS-FM, trying to win a contest to be the 102nd caller and win a Porsche 944 S2. In June 1994, Kevin, who continued to phreak, pleaded guilty to a total of seven counts of mail, wire, and computer fraud, money laundering, and obstruction of justice. He was sentenced to 51 months in prison and ordered to pay $56,000 in restitution to the victims of his crimes in the seven counts. At that time, it was the longest sentence that had ever been given for phreaking. Later, Kevin also pleaded guilty to charges of breaking into computers and obtaining information on undercover businesses run by the FBI ("Summary: Kevin Poulsen," 2003).

Modern-day phreaker Edward E. Cummings (a.k.a. Bernie S.), a native of Pennsylvania, was sent to federal prison in 1995 for his phreaking exploits, the first person to be imprisoned without bail for phreaking. Bernie S. used a modified Radio Shack speed dialer to make free telephone calls using public telephones. Bernie S., who has his own cult following in the hacker community (resulting from notoriety gained through *2600: The Hacker Quarterly,* a favorite Web site and magazine of hackers), says that what he did was not criminal activity, as the tones and information in his possession at the time of arrest were very easy to obtain (Schell, Dodge, and Moutsatsos, 2002).

Piracy, Intellectual Property Rights, and Copyright

The protection of intellectual property rights from attack by cybercriminals is, for many New Economy businesses (businesses started during the Internet boom of the late 1990s), as critical and financially important as dealing with crack attacks on computer networks.

Enacted in October 1998, in the United States, the Digital Millennium Copyright Act (DMCA) was intended to implement certain worldwide copyright laws to cope with emerging digital technologies. By protecting against the bypassing of encryption—

the mathematical conversion of information into a form from which the original information cannot be restored without using a special "key"—the DMCA encourages owners of copyrighted works to make them available on the Internet in a digital format without as much concern about unauthorized copying of those works.The DMCA also maintains that anyone who attempts to disable an encrypted, or protected, device should be liable for the harm caused to the property (Friedman and Papathomas, 2000).

In simple terms, intellectual property and copyright infringement is theft—taking what does not belong to the perpetrator of the encryption bypass, thereby depriving the copyright owners of royalties for the sale of their products.

Copying someone else's work without permission is, technically speaking, piracy. The harm is to the copyright owners, who are deprived of their product royalties. The term *software piracy* covers a number of different activities, including illegal copying of programs, counterfeiting and distributing of software, installing of software on more company computers than the company has licenses for, and informal sharing of copyrighted programs (or songs, CDs, DVDs) with friends who do not pay for them. Usually, piracy involves the purchasing of one legitimate piece of software, which is then illegally copied a number of times (Microsoft, 2003).

Internet piracy, in particular, refers to the use of the Internet for illegally copying or distributing unauthorized software. The offenders may use the Internet for all or some of their operations, including advertising, offering, acquiring, or distributing pirated software. An estimated 2 million Web pages offer, link to, or otherwise reference pirated software, also known as warez software. Moreover, a recent investigation indicates that more than 60 percent of the software sold through Internet auction sites is counterfeit, and more than 90 percent is sold in violation of the publisher's license agreement (Microsoft, 2003).

The owners of the product royalties are often not the only losers with these cybercrimes. Consumers acquiring counterfeit software often receive untested software that may have been copied hundreds or thousands of times and may seriously infect their computer hard drives with destructive viruses. In addition, consumers receive no technical support and no warranty protection with pirated software (Microsoft, 2003).

2600: The Hacker Quarterly

The entire subject of intellectual and property rights infringement and piracy has been highly controversial, not only within the jurisdiction of the United States, but also elsewhere. The first civil court test of the DMCA within the United States arrived with the new millennium.

Known as the Internet free speech and copyright case involving *2600: The Hacker Quarterly* and Universal Studios, the November 1999 controversial event arose from the hacker magazine's publishing, and linking their Web site to, a computer software program called DeCSS. The magazine said they did this as part of their news coverage about DVD decryption (decryption is the process of converting encrypted information back into its original, readable text).

Universal Studios, along with other members of the Motion Picture Association of America, filed suit against the hacker magazine in January 2000, seeking an order that it no longer publish the computer software program. Universal and the other MPAA members claimed that the software could be used as part of a process to infringe copyright on DVD movies. In its defense, the magazine argued that decryption of DVD movies was necessary for a number of reasons, including to make "fair use" (or publicly accessible rather than copyright protected) of movies and to play DVD movies on computers running the Linux operating system. In the end, the hacker magazine lost the suit ("Landmark Internet," 2001).

Upon hearing the court's decision, the head of the Motion Picture Association of America declared that the decision "nailed down an indispensable constitutional and congressional truth. It's wrong to help others steal creative works" (Dixon, 2001).

Dmitry Sklyarov and Elcomsoft

The following year, the first criminal case to be tried under the Digital Millennium Copyright Act began with an event on July 17, 2001, at the DefCon 9 hacker convention in Las Vegas. On this date Dmitry Sklyarov, a 27-year-old Russian Ph.D. student, cryptographer, and father of two small children, came to the hacker convention to talk about electronic book security and how he helped create the Advanced eBook Processor (AEBPR) software for his Russian employer, Elcomsoft.

After his speech at the convention and at the behest of Adobe Systems, Dmitry was charged on July 17, 2001, with distributing a product designed to circumvent copyright protection measures. He was eventually released on $50,000 bail but was not allowed to leave California. Finally, in December 2001, he was allowed to return to Russia to be with his family ("Dmitry—Status," 2002).

According to the Elcomsoft's Web site, the AEBPR software permits owners of electronic books to translate from Adobe's secure and copy-protected eBook format into the more common and unprotected portable document format (PDF)—which only works on legitimately purchased eBooks. In Russia, this software has been used by blind people to read otherwise inaccessible PDF user's manuals with reader software that uses PDF as an input format, as well as by people who wish to move their eBooks from one computer to another—much like one can move a CD from a player in the home to a player in the car ("Dmitry—Status," 2002).

On May 24, 2002, California Superior Court Judge Ronald Whyte shifted the attention away from Dmitry and shifted it onto Elcomsoft, making Elcomsoft the defendant in the trial. Dmitry 's charges were set aside by the prosecutors in exchange for his testimony in the case against his employers. The prosecutors said that the crux of the federal government's attack was Elcomsoft's AEBPR program, which allows users to disable copyright protections on Adobe eBook software. On December 17, 2002, a "not guilty" verdict was delivered ("Dmitry—Status" 2002).

Though Elcomsoft faced four charges related to directly designing and marketing software that could be used to crack eBook copyright protections, plus an additional charge related to conspiring to do so, the jury acquitted the company of all charges—positing that they believed the company hadn't meant to violate the law. "We didn't understand why a million-dollar company would put on their Web page an illegal thing that would (ruin) their whole business if they were caught," said jury foreman Dennis Strader. Though the jurors agreed with the prosecutors that the product was illegal under U.S. law, the company was acquitted because they didn't mean to violate U.S. law. Lawyers not involved in the case said the Elcomsoft verdict boded ill for future criminal prosecutions under the controversial copyright law. Evan Cox, an attorney with the San Francisco firm of Covington and Burlington, said, "This was the kind of case that the DMCA was meant to prevent. If this enforcement led to a not guilty verdict, you have to wonder what would lead to a successful case" (Borland, 2002, pp. 1–3).

The RIAA Lawsuits

On September 8, 2003, concerned about piracy and the loss of major revenues from CD sales, the Recording Industry Association of America (RIAA)—representing music companies such as Universal Music Group, Sony Music Entertainment Inc., Warner Music Group, BMG Entertainment, and EMI Group PLC—filed 261 lawsuits in courts across the United States, targeting the tens of millions of computer users who shared songs online. The RIAA said that the suits were just the first wave in what could ultimately be thousands of civil lawsuits in the United States. In Canada, legal experts say that it could be much harder to file similar suits because of major differences in Canadian copyright law (McKenna and Waldie, 2003).

One of their 2003 targets was Brianna Lahara, a 12-year-old student in New York. Though the RIAA said it was targeting people who had downloaded more than 1,000 titles from the Internet and was seeking damages of up to $150,000 per song, Brianna and her mother paid only $2,000 in damages, which is consistent with the amount of damages paid by other students who were similarly charged. The little girl was quoted as saying, "I am sorry for what I have done. I love music and I don't want to hurt the artists I love" (McKenna and Waldie, 2003).

French Court vs. Google, Inc.

In an international case, a French court ruled in October 2003, against Internet search powerhouse Google, Inc., in an intellectual property rights case that could have far-reaching technological and financial implications for Web search firms. The civil court in Nanterre, France, fined Google for allowing advertisers to link text Internet advertisements to trademarked search terms and it gave the search powerhouse 30 days to cease the practice.

When Internet users type in words or phrases in online searches, all search engines bring up links to other Web sites that carry the same terms. But Google also posts links to companies and organizations that have paid to be associated with certain keywords—even if they are trademarks belonging to somebody else. For example, Google users typing "Bourse des Vols" or "Bourse des Voyages"—trademarks for two French travel firms—were offered links to rival companies including low-cost airline EasyJet. The French firms Viaticum and Luteciel sued Google's French subsidiary for trademark violation and together won 75,000 euros (US$89,000) in damages in a court ruling in the same month (October 2003) (Associated Press, 2003).

This ruling is believed to be the first in which the owner of a trademarked term has successfully sued an Internet search service over the practice of allowing advertisers to use "protected" terms in text ads ("Google Loses," 2003).

Two Controversial "Cases" of Cracking

This chapter and the previous one have described a number of attention-getting cybercrimes that have resulted in criminal convictions and the awarding of penalties. However, there are also some interesting cases that have resulted in acquittals because of a lack of credible evidence regarding system vulnerability.

Jennifer Hargrove

One such case began in Idaho on March 27, 2003. The defendant, Jennifer Hargrove, had been employed by an insurance agency affiliated with Farmer's Insurance Group from 1990 to 1999 as a secretary and as a licensed agent. In 1999, Hargrove left Farmer's Insurance Group and became an agent for Allstate Insurance Agency. When it was discovered that Hargrove used information from her former employer to attract and serve customers at Allstate, she was charged by the State of Idaho with unauthorized access of her employer's computers ("Insufficient Evidence," 2003).

In her defense, Hargrove said that she took a copy of a client list with her, being under the impression that she was permitted to do so. A magistrate judge in Idaho had earlier agreed with the allegations of Farmer's Insurance group and found that Hargrove went into the computer base and retrieved the client list information, but on appeal, Chief Judge Darrel Perry concluded that the evidence presented to the district court was insufficient to sustain a conviction under the unauthorized access law.

First, there was evidence that the allegedly stolen information was available in paper form, to which Hargrove had access when employed at Farmer's Insurance Group. Therefore, he said, the state had failed to prove that the information could only have been obtained from the ex-employer's computer. Second, the court said that even if the information had not been available otherwise, there was no evidence presented by the state to prove that the defendant had, in fact, actually accessed or attempted to access the Farmer's Insurance computer system after she left. Third, the ex-employer testified that it was unlikely that anyone could access his computer system from a remote location, and he further testified that as far as he knew, Hargrove had not visited the office since her separation from service. Without such critical evidence, the conviction could not stand ("Insufficient Evidence," 2003).

Stefan Puffer

In February 2003, a Texas jury acquitted a computer security analyst who in 2002 had been accused of wrongful access to a county computer network. In March 2002, Stefan Puffer discovered that the Harris County district clerk's wireless computer network was unprotected. He worried that anyone with a wireless network card (a $30–$50 add-on device used to connect a computer to a wireless network) would have the ability to gain access to sensitive computers and files. Puffer demonstrated the problem to county officials and was indicted on two counts of fraud. He faced 5 years in jail and a $250,000 fine.

However, after only 15 minutes of deliberation, a jury found that the accused did not intend to cause any damage to the county's systems. Puffer's lawyer, in his closing argument, said that the Harris County district clerk called the authorities on Puffer in order to cover up the office's perceived incompetence, as evidence provided in the hearing showed that the county clerk was, indeed, embarrassed by Puffer's demonstration.

The widespread insecurity of the most commonly used wireless network version, known as IEEE 802.11b, such as the one accessed by Puffer, has been repeatedly demonstrated by White Hat hackers. Most cities are still filled with such vulnerable networks, many of which allow passersby to anonymously access networks, both public and private ("Man Who Exposed," 2003).

Issues and Controversies Related to System Vulnerabilities

The National Strategy to Secure Cyberspace

In an executive summary entitled *The National Strategy to Secure Cyberspace,* there is an overt statement recognizing that cyberspace—composed of hundreds of thousands of interconnected computers, servers, routers, switches, and fiber optic cables allowing the critical infrastructures to work—is, indeed, the nervous system of the global economy and of societal health and wellness. However, this executive summary declares, the global economy and the national security of the United States are also fully dependent upon information technology and information infrastructure—at the core of which is the Internet. The Internet, originally designed to share unclassified research among scientists who were thought to have no interest in abusing the network, today connects millions of other computer networks and controls electrical transformers, trains, pipeline pumps, chemical vats, radars, and stock markets (*The National Strategy to Secure Cyberspace,* 2003).

The 2003 reality is that in the United States and elsewhere, a primary concern is the threat of organized cyberattacks by Black Hats or terrorists capable of causing debilitating disruption to various nations' critical infrastructures, economies, and/or national security. Although the technical sophistication required to carry out such an attack is high—and partially explains the lack of a debilitating attack to date—remaining in denial that such an attack could occur is unacceptable. The executive summary statement outlines the threat (*The National Strategy to Secure Cyberspace,* 2003, p. vii):

> What is known is that the attack tools and methodologies are becoming widely available, and the technical capability and sophistication of users bent on causing havoc or disruption is improving. In peacetime, America's enemies may conduct espionage on our Government, university research centers, and private companies. They may also seek to prepare for cyberstrikes during a confrontation by mapping U.S. information systems, identifying key targets, and lacing our infrastructure with back doors and other means of access.

> In wartime or crisis, adversaries may seek to intimidate the Nation's political leaders by attacking critical infrastructures and key economic functions or eroding public confidence in information systems.

The National Strategy to Secure Cyberspace identifies eight key actions and initiatives required to reduce threats and related vulnerabilities (2003, p. 12):

1. Enhance law enforcement's capabilities for preventing and prosecuting cyberspace attacks.
2. Create a process for national vulnerability assessments in order to better understand the potential consequences of threats and vulnerabilities.
3. Secure the mechanisms of the Internet by improving protocols and routing.
4. Foster the use of trusted digital control systems/supervisory control and data acquisition systems.
5. Reduce and remediate software vulnerabilities.
6. Understand infrastructure interdependencies and improve the physical security of cybersystems and telecommunications.
7. Prioritize federal cybersecurity research and development agendas.
8. Assess and secure emerging systems.

The U.S. Department of Homeland Security, in particular, has addressed the vulnerability problem in a multipart effort: to reduce threat and deter malicious actors, to pass legislation and enforce these laws, to identify and remediate existing vulnerabilities, and to develop systems with decreased vulnerabilities and assess emerging technologies for vulnerabilities.

Software

Many problems arise with vulnerabilities in the technical systems, which invite attackers to exploit them. Often, these vulnerabilities start with poorly designed software. As Bruce Schneier stated in *Building Secure Software: How to Avoid Security Problems the Right Way* (Viega and McGraw, 2002), businesses and individuals would not have to spend so much time, money, and effort on network security if they were not hampered with such bad software security.

Without question, software security vulnerabilities are many and include such problems as:

- A killer packet that allows a perpetrator to crash a server by sending it a particular packet, or a piece of data transferred through the Internet
- Buffer overflows allowing an invader to take control of a computer by sending it a malformed message that the software is not programmed to react to effectively
- An encryption vulnerability that allows an intruder to read an encrypted message or to trick an authentication system

Software—well designed or not—has become the lifeblood of modern businesses. Thus, it has become deeply entwined in most people's lives. Moreover, with every new release, the software systems become more complex—and more vulnerable. There is an increased risk that "malicious functionality" will be added to a system either during the software's creation or afterward, particularly when the software is used for purposes other than the one for which it was primarily designed (Viega and McGraw, 2002).

Computers are extensible systems that are exposed to this risk at many points during their use. Some rogue programmer in the initial design team might modify the operating system software even before it is installed on a machine. Risk-unaware software developers might then introduce a security flaw when adding functionality to a networked program. Finally, software users in business may install applications that pose a risk to system integrity or, even worse, that propagate a virus.

Moreover, the systems themselves have become increasingly complex, and large parts of the existing software base were not designed or intended for Internet use. Says one Microsoft specialist about the software base concern ("But They Told Us," 2003, p. 1):

> Believe me, it ain't fun to work at Microsoft when we continually have bugs found in our products. It's the discussion at every lunch and every meeting I've been in lately. Are we working on answers? Yes (with more to come).

> Fifty million lines of code, some of which was written more than a decade ago. I remember using 386's about a decade ago in Fawcette's first offices. They were never attached to the Internet. We didn't have email. No Web. I'm sure that guys who were writing code back then had no idea their code would be permanently connected to everyone else's computers and that criminals would try to break into their computers.

In short, the existing code base is one major source of trouble. It cannot be easily reviewed or replaced because of the sheer number of lines of existing code and the similarly impressive number of installations of, for example, Microsoft's products on almost every office and home desktop computer. Moreover, fixing these problems will be a process of gradual improvement rather than a major one-time effort. The bottom line is that society will continue to see security problems in the foreseeable future because of flaws in software.

Patching

One way to secure software products is to have them tested by an "attack" team of experts who try to break into the software for the purpose of exploiting possible vulnerabilities. When vulnerabilities are found, a patch is produced and distributed. Although this approach has some benefits, it does not solve all of the software vulnerability issues. Some of those remaining unaddressed include these (Viega and McGraw, 2002):

- Software developers can patch only problems that they know about. Attackers may find problems never reported to developers.
- Patches are often so rushed for distribution to the market that they may be released before they have been fully tested, and they may introduce new problems of their own to a system.
- Patches often fix only the symptoms of a problem but do little to address the underlying cause of concern.
- Patches, though distributed, often go "unapplied," because system administrators tend to be overworked and do not take the time to install them. Also, system administrators often do not wish to make changes to a system that works.

For example, "never touch a running/working system" is one of the most important rules that system administrators learn at the very early stages of their careers. These system administrators need to accept the fact that a system exposing vulnerability is not a running system, although it quite nicely does the job for which it was designed.

The picture, however, is not all bad. Well-studied approaches in the software industry exist for building secure software systems. Designing a system for security, then carefully implementing and testing it, would be a much better approach than our current one for reducing vulnerability risks. However, taking such security measures is, indeed, expensive—which is a major factor for industry today.

An estimated selling price for a version of an Internet browser (such as Microsoft's Internet Explorer) that is built according to these refined coding standards could be as much as $10,000 (Preatoni, 2003). Are businesses and home users alike willing to pay this much money for software that is, in some cases, currently being distributed for free?

Attacks Made at the Source

On November 5, 2003, an incident was reported in the media in which a cracker broke into one of the computers on which the sources (or the program code) of the Linux operating systems are stored and from which they are distributed worldwide (Andrews, 2003). The Linux operating system is a collaborative piece of work developed by many programmers worldwide. Linux is widely used on Internet servers and is embraced by big corporations as an alternative to the Microsoft operating system.

A small group of Linux gatekeepers monitor its development and release contributed code segments to the master copy. Competitors and critics of Linux say that the process used in its development and updating is error-prone, lacking in quality, and unsecure.

In the case reported on November 5, 2003, the cracker inserted two lines of code in one of the sources for the kernel—the very heart of any operating system—program. These two lines would have allowed anybody with basic access rights to a Linux system to gain root (i.e., "superuser" or administrative) privileges. Andreas Dilger, one of the contributing developers of Linux, remarked that, had the change gone undetected, it might have taken a good while to find (Andrews, 2003).

Fortunately, as White Hat Linus Torvald (the "father" and namesake of Linux) was quick to point out, a variety of safeguards are in place in the master system to protect the source from being altered; thus, the cracker did not manage to break into this master system. That is, no real harm was done. Nevertheless, this exploit raised the alert level of the Linux group and gives a glimpse of what could be achieved by a more sophisticated cracker who could manage to break into the master machines, alter the code there, and trick the safeguards into believing that nothing suspicious had happened.

The present-day reality is that several million servers on the Internet use the license-free Linux operating system. These servers' administrators would have sooner or later updated their current versions of Linux to the one attacked by the November 5, 2003, cracker. Had that cracker been successful in getting into the master system and altering the code, the results could have been devastating.

Attacks Made to Data in Transmission

It has already been noted that the installed software on the millions of computers connected to the Internet is vulnerable. There is, however, a further vulnerability headache for system administrators: the data sent through the Internet are also susceptible to attack.

Simply put, the Internet is a network of networks. When a piece of information—be it an e-mail message, a Web page, or a bank statement—is transferred through the Internet, the data travel through many different hands. They are routed through the network from node to node.

The "client machine"—the computer requesting to view a Web page, for example—might reside in a home office connected through the high-speed Internet service of the local telephone company. The server—the computer on which the Web page is located—might be attached to a school, a library, or a university network provided by a government agency. The Web page data have to travel through one or more additional networks connecting the sender's and the receiver's networks. On their path through the Internet, the data will sometimes have to travel through twenty or thirty nodes. These nodes are owned by several different Internet service providers (ISPs), and some of them might be more trustworthy than others. In fact, some of these ISPs might have been victims of previous crack attacks.

This interconnectedness of the wired world opens a wide variety of opportunities for motivated crackers to attack the data, thereby having the data perform one or more of the cybercrimes described previously. Such an attack on data in transmission is known as a "man-in-the-middle" attack. Following are some particular types of data in transmission attacks:

- Eavesdropping—The data are watched as they travel through the Internet. Even when the data are encrypted, they might still be vulnerable to a man-in-the-middle attack.
- Tampering—The attacker maliciously modifies the data.
- Spoofing—The attacker pretends to send valid data, but in reality, the data are false.
- Hijacking—An attacker cuts an authenticated, authorized, and subsequently established connection between a sender and a receiver. The attacker then takes over the connection, intercepting and deleting the packets sent by the original sender and sending attack data instead.
- Capture/replay—An attacker captures a whole stream of data to be able to replay them later and repeat the effects. Thus, a bank transaction or a stock sales transaction might be repeated in order to empty the bank account of a targeted person.
- Man-in-the-middle—The attacker pretends to host the service that the client was requesting, by intercepting the data and replying to the information as if it came from the original server. The attacked client might be lured to expose private data such as credit card or bank account information to this false service. These stolen data can later be used to defraud the client.

Challenges Faced by System Administrators

In October 2003, a survey released by Deloitte & Touche LLP indicated that chief operating officers (COOs) of companies around the world are more nervous about terrorist attacks affecting business than are their American peers. For example, the survey found that 35 percent of Canadian COOs who responded to the survey were worried about global terrorist attacks, compared with 27 percent of their American counterparts. Economist Carl Steidtmann has proposed that U.S. executives might be less concerned and more complacent about terrorist and cyberterrorist attacks because they feel that their country has taken more steps to combat terrorism, such as introducing the Homeland Security Act of 2002 (Won, 2003). Following are a few of the areas that the survey found to be of concern to these worldwide COOs.

The Human Factor

Besides the factors already discussed regarding known vulnerabilities, one item that might be contributing to this concern is the human factor: system managers are a hopelessly overworked group who are high in demand and few in number. Unfortunately, the postsecondary educational systems of the world do not meet the demands of industry to generate enough skilled system managers—making their services quite costly. Thus, in many small- and medium-sized companies, system management is a part-time job, often given to a junior staff member who happens to be somewhat computer-savvy. Despite the shortage of highly qualified technical personnel, however, there is some seemingly good news for firms eager to save money by avoiding hiring a full-time system manager: most modern versions of operating systems such as Windows XP and the newer versions of Linux seem to be quite easy to manage. They are up and running in significantly less time than they required only a few years ago.

Wizards (i.e., software tools that automate common system administration tasks) for each and every subtask can help these novice system administrators to set up internal services (e.g., print and file services to share company internal printers and data or mail servers, as well as Web servers that are going to be connected to the Internet). The danger is that these novices, who theoretically do not fully know what they are doing, have to rely on the software manufacturer to do a perfect job in providing the necessary security on the installed services. Unfortunately, as discussed above, these software manufacturers do not have a stellar track record in providing secure systems.

Moreover, maintaining system security is a tedious job. To keep up with the many detected vulnerabilities, system managers have to keep track of a variety of information sources published by the operating system vendor, the vendor of the application software, the security companies, and various official agencies.

System managers must install fixes and patches for each and every loophole in the systems they are responsible for—a daunting task even for the committed professional, and even more daunting for the part-time system administrator who has other responsibilities within the organization.

Internet Protocol and IP Addresses

An earlier section in this chapter briefly described the working principle of data transport over the Internet. More technically speaking, three key protocols (i.e., a set of rules that govern how communication between two programs have to take place to be considered valid) are responsible for the proper transportation of data from point A to point B on the Internet. The most basic one is the Internet protocol.

The whole Internet is based on version 4 (IPv4) of this protocol, which was designed in the mid-1970s, and took its current form between 1977–1979. Unfortunately, it was not built with security features. This problem has long been known and was addressed in the latest version of the protocol, version 6 (IPv6). This version has support for much more secure communication on the Internet. However, it is not used, even though it is designed to solve a good part of the existing problems.

One reason IPv6 is not used is that it would be a major undertaking to convert the millions of connected machines on the Internet to the new protocol. As there is no central body managing the Internet, this effort would need to be coordinated with the many operators and participants on the Internet. No single organization can do this alone. Each organization would have to implement the update in close cooperation with its peering partners (i.e., other organizations with which the organization has agreed to exchange Intenet data) and with the networking companies that its networks are connected to. If any one organization made the conversion without taking care of the data exchange with its neighbors, this would sever the organization's links to the rest of the Internet.

Some countries, such as Japan, have committed to converting to a fully IPv6-based infrastructure as early as 2005. The European Union is in the initial steps of converting, and China is considering going this route in the near future. The main motivating force for moving to IPv6, however, especially in the Asian countries, does not lie in enhanced security features. Rather, the motivation lies in the fact that Internet addresses in version 4 of the protocol are running out faster in Asia than in the rest of the world. One reason for the upcoming shortage can be attributed to a faster-growing economy in Europe and Asia. Exacerbating the problem is that these areas started out with a much smaller piece of the Internet address "pie" when the distribution of addresses to world regions was initially decided in the early days of the Internet. Then one individual, John Postel, was charged with the administration of the Internet numbering system by the Defense Advanced Research Projects Agency (DARPA), which had funded the early versions of the Internet (Karrenberg, 2001). This task became too large for one individual and over the duration of 10 years a system of regional authorities responsible for roughly one continent each was developed.

An Internet address is a 32-bit number (i.e., a binary number that consists of 32 digits that are either 0 or 1) that uniquely identifies each computer attached to the Internet. Theoretically, more than 4 billion (4,294,967,296, to be exact) computers could be provided with an IP (Internet protocol) address and could simultaneously be connected to the Internet. This is almost enough for one address for each person on the planet.

Through the design of the protocol, this address space is used only sparsely; therefore, the theoretical maximum cannot be reached. For example, there are huge blocks in the address range that cannot be used at all. Also, other blocks are assigned to organizations that are not using all of their blocks, reducing the number of potentially connected machines further.

Each IP address is divided into a part that identifies a network (such as a school, a university, a government agency, or a company network) and another part designed to identify each computer in this network. An IP address is very comparable to a street name and a house number in a physical address. One cannot assign the address 1555 Wall Street to a house on Hollywood Boulevard; if there is no such house on Wall Street, then this address simply remains unused. The same phenomenon applies to IP addresses. Companies might receive a block of 256 addresses but use only 150 of them from their Internet Service Provider or directly from one of the regional numbering authorities. The unused addresses cannot be used anywhere else, and so the address space becomes depleted more rapidly than a first look at the number of available addresses would lead one to think.

Groups of network numbers have been distributed to four regional authorities: ARIN (American Registry for Internet

Numbers) for North America, a portion of the Caribbean, and sub-equatorial Africa; RIPE (Réseaux IP Européens) for Europe; APNIC (Asia Pacific Network Information Centre) for the Asia/Pacific region; and LACNIC (Latin American and Caribbean Internet Addresses Registry) for South America and the Caribbean. The initial allotment of addresses was based on a projected amount of use of these addresses, and a significantly higher share was assigned to the North American continent. Therefore, the remaining three authorities are running out of addresses much faster than ARIN and are much more motivated to move to IPv6.

IPv6 has ample IP addresses for future use. An address in the new and enhanced version 6 is a 128-bit number (i.e., a number consisting of 128 zeroes or ones) with which more than 3×10^{38} computers and other Internet-aware devices can be addressed. Even with a sparse usage of the address space, the likelihood that the world will run out of addresses in this century is very low. This drives the hope that the new protocol version will be introduced sooner rather than later, and that the world will soon see a much more secure version of the IP protocol coming into use.

The Domain Name System

Another known vulnerability contributing to the fears of the COOs surveyed is the domain name system.

It is a fact of life that humans generally seem to prefer working with meaningful names much more than meaningful numbers. For example, http://www.whitehouse.gov is easier for most people to remember than are the numbers 194.78.133.230 or 194.78.133.222, the IP (v4) addresses of the servers that house the Web site of the White House. The addresses in IPv6 will look somewhat like 5.40.161.101.255.255.0.0.80.191.119.8.13.201.78.118, and they will be nearly impossible to memorize quickly.

Computers, on the other hand, do not work very well using names. In fact, to find their way to a destination on the Internet, computers need the numerical representation of an IP address. To translate back and forth between names and numbers, the Internet uses the domain name system (DNS). The DNS maps the name of an Internet-attached computer to its IP address. As administration of the complete address and name system on the Internet is a problem far too big for any one organization, this responsibility is delegated downward from the four regional authorities described earlier to administrators of so-called top-level domains. These administrators, in turn, delegate authority to the administrators of second-level domains. At the top, or the root (as it is called in Internet terminology, because a widely branched tree of data grows from it) of this downward delegation mechanism are only thirteen so-called name servers worldwide—the "root servers." These servers are operated by the four regional authorities and are responsible at the root level for the domain name system, and they store the information about where the top-level servers can be found.

Top-level domains that are located mostly in the United States are indicated by .com for commercial organizations, .gov for government agencies, .edu for educational institutions, and .mil for military organizations. For other countries, a country top-level domain is used; for example, .ca is used for Canada, .uk is used for the United Kingdom, and .cn is used for China. There are several hundred of these top-level servers, which "point" downward to a set of servers that know the addresses of computers in the second-level domain. For example, whitehouse.gov is the domain name of the White House, and microsoft.com is the domain name for Microsoft, Inc.

An example will help clarify the domain name concept. An individual's home computer needs to find the numerical IP address of http://www.whitehouse.gov. To do this, it first asks the closest name server (or a computer that performs the mapping between host names and IP addresses for an organization). (Typically, one is provided by each Internet service provider.) However, this particular name server does not know the required information; it only knows the addresses of the thirteen root servers. So, the original computer or the first name server, depending on the type of query, will next ask one of the root servers to give it the address of the server that houses the .gov top-level domain. In turn, it will access this .gov server to find out the address of the server responsible for *whitehouse* within the .gov domain. It will get that IP address and will then ask the .gov server for the address of *www* in the second-level domain *whitehouse.gov.* This server will know the IP address (194.78.133.230), and, with this information, the original home computer can request the home page from the White House Web server.

Unfortunately, this whole system of connected servers is susceptible to attack—as a severe incident on October 21, 2002, revealed. Any server can be flooded with so-called denial-of-service (DoS) attacks, rendering it too busy to answer regular requests.

Such an attack was made to nine of the thirteen root servers in the October 2002 incident, making these servers inaccessible for more than one hour. If this should happen to all of the thirteen root servers, the complete DNS translation mechanism of the Internet would break down, and the Internet would become virtually unusable.

Another key concern is the data themselves. Data are stored on name servers, and these servers can be corrupted, either by being hacked into or by being fed with the wrong data. So, if a cracker maliciously changed data in the domain name system, large parts of the Internet might not be reachable any longer. Alternatively, users could be directed to forged sites while being led to believe that they were connected to the real sites.

Without a doubt, more secure versions of DNS would benefit all users of the Internet and would prevent disruption of the Internet's most essential services by malicious individuals, terrorist groups, or other organizations. The Internet Engineering Task Force (IETF) is a private organization set up by users and service providers on the Internet; it has established working groups for securing the DNS and the BGP routing service discussed in the next section (Internet Engineering Task Force, 2003). This group is making progress, but it suffers from coordination problems and technical difficulties. The U.S. government has identified the need to support this organization so that it can help solve problems more quickly.

Protocols

This chapter has discussed the problematic aspects of passing data through many hands before they reach their final destination. An additional problem worrying COOs around the world arises from vulnerabilities in the protocols that make this data passing and forwarding work.

Connecting a complete network to the Internet to become part of it involves setting up an exchange of information between specialized computer devices called routers. Each of these router machines at the border of a connected network stores a specialized map of the Internet and informs its neighbors about what it knows about its part of the Internet and about its neighbors and neighboring networks. This connection enables all of the routers to calculate the shortest, fastest, least-used, or cheapest path to a destination in the Internet. This path and routing information is exchanged through the border gateway protocol (BGP). The BGP is used in all border routers in the several tens of thousands of networks that together comprise the Internet.

All of these networks have their own administrators and administrative policies. Unfortunately, through the map propagation mechanism described above, false routing information can be injected into the Internet maps. For example, crackers can break into the network of an Internet service provider, or a disgruntled employee or other insider can reconfigure the border routers in a certain part of the Internet to tell the neighboring routers that a specific part of the Internet is reachable through a router that does not exist or that actually knows nothing about this part of the Internet.

Moreover, given the design of the BGP, the false information would be passed along to the core routers of the Internet, which would then learn about this new path and start sending data to the above, incorrect router. The router would drop or return the data sent to it. Thus, a "black hole" would be created—a region in the Internet that was not reachable from anywhere else.

Because the security features built into the BGP routing protocol are not unbreakable, and because some Internet service providers are not even using the available security features of the protocol, it becomes a rather easy task for an attacker to break into the protocol and propagate false information. Propagating false information can have a catastrophic cascading effect, as Americans and Canadians saw in the electrical blackout of the summer of 2003, when major parts of the eastern United States and Ontario were, literally, in the dark for a day or more. The cause of this blackout was the propagation of information in and about the electric grid that originated from a single point and led to the observed results. This analogy can easily be transposed to the Internet and its routers in which the injection of false information at one point in the Net can cause severe outages throughout large sections.

Address Verification and Out-of-Band Management

Today, it is almost impossible to find out where a denial-of-service attack originates. Because source addresses are easily forged, a perpetrator cannot always be found. Obviously, then, a technical infrastructure is needed that would allow for the verification of these addresses. Once such an infrastructure was in place, Internet operators could filter out forged addresses to prevent these attacks from causing harm.

An additional source of problems is the lack of "side roads" that could be used to get to the routers if the main paths were blocked, as is the case in a denial-of-service (DoS) attack. So far, Internet operators rely on the same communication lines to manage and administer the infrastructure as the data use to travel through the Internet. With separate control networks, also called out-of-band links, DoS attacks could be countered much more efficiently.

Implementation Issues

All of the recommended improvements discussed here would fall short if they were not widely employed by all, or at least a majority, of the operators and service providers on the Internet. Therefore, the Department of Homeland Security, in cooperation with the Commerce Department, has been pushing for public-private partnerships that will help ISPs to move to more secure protocols. Moreover, the Department of Homeland Security has been establishing a code of conduct that includes cybersecurity practices and cooperation in security questions (*The National Strategy to Secure Cyberspace,* 2003).

Digital Control, Supervisory Control, and Data Acquisition

In many sectors of public and private life, digital control systems, supervisory control, and data acquisition systems are used to operate and monitor equipment to control sensitive processes and physical functions in the United States and elsewhere around the world: power grids need to be monitored and controlled, water dams opened and shut, emergency services notified and dispatched. For public safety, some areas and industries are more important than others. The Department of Homeland Security has specifically identified the areas of water, transportation, manufacturing, chemicals, energy, health, and emergency services, to name just a few, as being of particular importance.

The Internet is a convenient and inexpensive tool that is increasingly used to transmit data to these control systems rather than using the closed networks of the past (*The National Strategy to Secure Cyberspace,* 2003). The convenient and inexpensive advantages of the Internet, however, are countered by the dangers and vulnerabilities that Internet technology brings with it. Consequently, the Department of Homeland Security maintains that special efforts need to be made to secure these very critical infrastructures.

A Theoretical Study: A Possible Coordinated Terror Attack

So far, much of this chapter has focused on the technical vulnerabilities that exist in computer systems, as well as some proposed recommendations for dealing with these. The following discussion of a possible coordinated terror attack will further illustrate how these vulnerabilities could be exploited to cause severe damage to a country, its citizens, and its economy—especially if such an attack were combined with a more conventional attack on its critical infrastructures, its telecommunication lines, its data exchanges, and its Internet hosting centers.

Step One: Damaging the Internal Network

Temmingh, a speaker at the DefCon hacker convention in Las Vegas in July 2003, described a frightening but very real scenario for attacking the infrastructure of a whole country. Though today's networks are pretty well protected against physical attacks from the outside, the internal systems remain a possible path for intrusion and damage. Because, as previously noted, patching and updating all servers in a network is a very time-consuming task, system administrators very rarely secure all computers in their network. They concentrate, instead, on the computers that are exposed to the outside world, because those are used to relay e-mail or to provide Web services or other forms of external communication (Temmingh, 2003).

To these internal networks, new machines are added on a regular basis, bringing unpatched and, therefore, unsecured versions of operating systems and application software into the network. The security problems these newly added computers expose are theoretically solved (the computers only would have to be installed with the most recent software releases) or are purely administrative. The list of ignored vulnerabilities is long and includes the following (Temmingh, 2003):

- Patches for known vulnerabilities are published and are accessible but are not installed on internal machines.
- Administrative passwords for the systems and databases are not set or are left at the default.
- Network drives are made accessible by other computers on the network (exported) without protection, so that internal users can access them with minimal hassle.

- Internal routers either have no monitoring passwords, or they have easily guessable administrative or unchanged default passwords.

The first step is to write the worm. All these small "holes" together produce a window of opportunity for a piece of malicious software that has security experts worried: a destructive worm. Such a worm would find a rich field of exploitable vulnerabilities in almost any existing internal network. What would make it even easier for such a worm to cause destruction is that these internal networks have a flat or rather simple structure in which, from a single compromised computer in the network, most others can be easily found and attacked. With a few simple tools, an attacker could easily find out whether another machine besides the one originally attacked is local—and therefore worth attacking—or is out in the Internet.

Furthermore, internal data traffic travels at the speed of the local network, which is typically between ten and ten thousand times faster than data that travel through the Internet, so a denial-of-service attack that originates at an internal computer is much more devastating than attacks from outside the internal network that are slowed down in Internet traffic jams. A machine under the control of a worm can pretend to be any other machine in the local network, redirecting traffic to itself and thus disrupting service and enabling more reconnaissance. It can do this by accessing data that was meant to be read by another computer, using that computer's identity, and thus potentially finding more vulnerable victims.

From there, a whole variety of damages could be inflicted—corrupting files, deleting disks, even changing the computers' BIOSes (software that is built into the hardware of any PC to access the operating system on the hard drives and boot up the machine) so that they could not be restarted. In concert with these damages, users could be confused with popup messages on their screens that say, "Your computer has been infected with a virus. Contact your system administrator immediately and read the following 25 characters to him or her: X#4X*& . . ."

This would keep a significant part of a system administrator's team busy, so that they would not easily find the time to take care of the underlying problem.

Without question, a sophisticated worm could coordinate these attacks in a well-staged manner. Before it went for the kill, this type of worm would first do its reconnaissance and exploit vulnerabilities by hitting its victims with a denial-of-service attack. This affectionately named ÜberWorm could gain additional sophistication by communicating with its descendants, with whom it infected other machines, so that a maximum level of infection would be reached before the network was taken down by a concerted effort.

Step Two: Breaching Perimeter Defenses

This, suggests Temmingh (2003), is a rather threatening but technical description of what a truly malicious worm could do to an internal network. The question remains, though: "How can the damaging code be injected into the network?" After all, there are firewalls, intrusion detection systems, and gateway virus scanners to protect most internal networks.

Breaching a network's perimeter defenses can simply be a matter of social engineering and some deception. Only a single user in the internal network would need to be persuaded to fall for a trick. The bait could be an e-mail that pretends to come from the marketing department of the organization that employs the user (such as marketing@companyname.com) and has an intriguing subject line such as "Our New Screensaver for Company XY." For maximum effect, this message would naturally have to be written in the native language of the user, something that most of today's worms don't take into account, and it should appear convincing enough to persuade the user to open the mail and click on the included link, which would activate the worm.

An advertised new company screen saver that is supposedly downloadable through an embedded link would be likely to work. The link could be disguised so that it was not obvious to the inexperienced user that the link did not point to a local server. Furthermore, an encrypted channel to the server containing the worm can be used; this would be comparable to the connection that most bank customers use to connect securely to their bank's Web site. Using a secure channel prevents the content screening devices on the organization's Internet gateway from detecting the malicious code in the downloaded screen saver, because the screening tools cannot look into the encrypted stream of data.

Temmingh (2003) told the audience at DefCon that an experiment employing the above scheme was performed on thirteen employees in the security department of a South African bank. Eight of the security employees were persuaded to download a modified worm that merely sent their usernames to the attacker. Five of these employees actually installed the software—in spite of the security warnings from the browser that "untrusted" content might be executed.

Step Three: Finding the Right E-Mail Addresses

Another component of a nationwide attack, said Temmingh (2003), would be for a malicious cracker to find the right e-mail addresses to send the worm to. A widely used Internet search engine such as Google, when fed with the company's or organization's domain name (e.g., @companyxyz.com), will return some e-mail addresses for almost any organization. For example, a search on the Turkish newspaper *Hurriyet* (@hurriyet.com.tr) returned thirty-eight e-mail addresses. This is the same mechanism that spammers use to compile their lists of addressees.

If a malicious organization wanted to attack an entire country, however, a little more effort would be needed. Primary targets for a concerted attack would likely be from both the private and the public sectors: telecommunications, energy facilities, water facilities, oil lines, transport lines, banks and financial institutions, government agencies, emergency services, and the military. The media would be also on the target list, in hopes that the reporting of the incident would upset the citizenry. In some countries, prominent businesses might contribute 60 percent or more to the gross domestic product (GDP) and would therefore likely be on the target list as well.

For all these branches of public and business life, there are either listings or specialized directories readily available on the Internet. For example, lists of all airlines, telecommunication companies, and media companies already exist on the Internet and need only be mined.

Public sector e-mail addresses are frequently divided into a tall hierarchy of departments, but a recursive Google search will find a good subset of them. In carrying out his experiment in the South African bank, Temmingh (2003) went so far as to introduce a computerized tool for use by crackers, with an easy-to-use graphical user interface that automated the time-consuming task of finding e-mail addresses. The tool started with a world map, highlighting the parts of the world where there was daylight at the corresponding time. This daylight area would move across the map with time passing and the parts on the left side of the map—the most recently lighted region—represent daybreak in that part of the world. This would be an important element in finding a good subset of addresses, as a cyberattack would be most successful in the morning when many people routinely arrive at work and read their e-mail messages. The tool then allowed the perpetrator to select a continent and a country and to "mine" the public databases for e-mail addresses that could be used for the above described attack.

An attack using this cyberapproach, combined with a real-world physical attack, could potentially have a devastating effect. The most amazing part of this theoretical study is that it could be easy to realize and would not require any very special skill set. It simply relies on the weaknesses of internal networks, on the excessive workloads of system administrators, and on relatively undereducated users.

Employing Countermeasures

Only two main countermeasures could be employed against such a cyberattack, warned Temmingh (2003): (1) Educate the users, and (2) don't throw technology after the problem but invest in educated system administrators. As mentioned earlier, most of the vulnerabilities of the internal systems are known, and patches and fixes exist that only need to be used. Other problems stem from mere administrative oversights, which can be addressed easily given sufficient time. Temmingh urges that society needs to make system administrators more aware of the internal weaknesses of their networks and to give them the time and the resources to fix the problems.

Honeypots and Controversies Surrounding Them

A new form of technology to counter cyberattacks and to learn more about the methods and tools crackers use is called honeypots or honeynets.

A honeypot or honeynet is a computer or network of computers set up to pretend that it offers some real service on the Internet. It might openly expose some vulnerabilities in order to attract an attacker to break into it. This honeypot computer is then closely monitored by an expert, with or without the help of specialized software tools, to find out how a cracker breaks into the system and what he or she does to compromise the system. It is critical that a honeypot designed for the purposes of observing human intruders looks and behaves as any normal system would look and behave. The maker of a honeypot must ensure that the intruder cannot detect that he or she is being observed. Honeypot software, therefore, tries not to modify the computer's software system but instead tries to analyze the Internet traffic to the computer without notifying the intruder that he or she is being watched (The Honeynet Project, 2003).

The Black Hats' newest trick is to use encrypted channels to attack computers and make the data unreadable for the observer. This trick also causes a malfunction of the analysis of the data on the network and malicious activity cannot be detected. Consequently, new tools have been developed for honeynets and honeypots to overcome this trick. Deep in the operating systems of the lures, modifications are now being made that allow circumventing of the encryption on the network.

In addition to gaining information about an attacker, honeypots can also be used to distract an attacker from targeting a real system. By diverting all traffic that is destined to the real machine to the honeypot first, the real machine would be protected. Only the traffic carrying the payload data (for example, a request for a Web page) would be let through to the live machine. All traffic on other channels (i.e., the channels used for file transfer, command shells, or mail traffic) would go to the honeypot, where it could be isolated and studied—and prevented from causing any real harm.

This interesting case of the use of a honeypot was reported by Lance Spitzner (2003):

> For years, attackers have exchanged stolen credit cards over the Internet—it's become a form of underground currency. Recently, however, honeypot technology was used to discover a level of automated credit card fraud researchers had never seen before: attackers connecting hacked databases of credit cards to automated networks.
>
> In April [2003], an attacker broke into a Microsoft Windows 2000 system at the Honeynet Research Alliance. . . . The attacker set up an IRC Bouncer (a program that relays Internet Relay Chat traffic, which is used widely in the Internet for online chatrooms) and used it to connect to several IRC channels dedicated to credit card exchange, hiding its true origin. Re-

searchers discovered attackers were building databases of hacked stolen credit cards, then using those databases to query cards, validate numbers, even get personal information, credit limit and purchase history of credit card users. These attackers needed very little expertise to pull this off, as most of the tools were readily available and documented on the Internet. This leads one to wonder what more advanced and skilled crackers might be doing.

Honeypots and the U.S. Fourth Amendment

The use of honeypots is not without controversy. Ownership of a network and the responsibility for maintaining it do not necessarily grant one the right to watch what that network's users are doing. Some hackers maintain that the Fourth Amendment to the U.S. Constitution prohibits government searches and seizures without a warrant and that it therefore might restrict the deployment of a honeypot for government employees or agents if the monitored users have a "reasonable expectation of privacy." The reality, though, is that crackers typically will not fall in this category, because the expectation of privacy cannot be upheld, so they will not be protected by this provision (Salgado, 2003).

The Federal Wiretap Act, as of January 26, 1998, prohibits anyone from listening in on an electronic communication in real time unless one of the Act's listed exceptions applies. So, even if the Fourth Amendment did not apply, a cracker may have other statutory privacy rights. Violation of the Act exposes the perpetrator—in this case, the organization setting up the honeypot—to civil and criminal liability (Federal Wiretap Act, 1998).

For honeypot operators, three exceptions to the Federal Wiretap Act prohibition, in particular, are relevant (Salgado, 2003):

- Provider protection: Internet service providers are allowed to listen in on data communications to prevent harm such as fraud and theft of service. It is currently unclear how the courts will rule on this provision, however, with regard to honeypots. A cracker could claim that the entire point of setting up the honeypot was to track the cracker's activity and not to protect any infrastructure. Setting up a honeypot purely for the purpose of studying others' activities, without combining it with a real production of a service that is protected by the honeypot, could very well be penalized under the provisions of the Act.

- Consent of party: If a user consents to the interception of his or her communications, monitoring of communications is allowed. By putting up an announcement on a service that by accessing the system, users consent to monitoring, system administrators can get around this protective provision of the Act. A perpetrator who continues the cracking session after seeing the warning can be believed to have consented to monitoring.
- Computer trespasser: Government agents can be authorized by a victim of a computer crack to intercept cracker communications to the victim's system. The government representative must be conducting an investigation and must reasonably believe that intercepted communications are relevant to this investigation.

Besides the just-cited legal issues involved in setting up a honeypot, there is yet another danger. Honeypots are meant to attract break-ins. Therefore, they need to be controlled very closely. Otherwise, a honeypot machine can be turned into a launch site for a cyberattack or into a distribution site for child pornography or stolen trade secrets. The operator of a neglected honeypot could, in fact, be held responsible for criminal negligence in not securing his or her system.

Operating Systems—Are Some More Secure Than Others?

In addition to all of the vulnerabilities discussed in this chapter, there is the question of whether some types of operating system software are more vulnerable to cracking exploits than others.

Over the past few years, security experts have been attempting to answer this question and to provide some solutions where needed. In 2003, according to the mi2g (2004) Intelligence Unit (a British security company that has been collecting and verifying data on overt digital attacks since 1995), it is mostly Linux—not Microsoft Windows—operating systems that are attacked. During August 2003, for example, 67 percent of all successful and verifiable digital attacks against online servers targeted Linux, followed by Microsoft Windows at 23.2 percent. Less than 2 percent of the attacked servers operated under the BSD variant of UNIX. According to the mi2g Intelligence Unit (2004), Linux remained the most attacked operating system online during all of 2003, with 51 percent of all successful overt digital attacks being perpetrated against Linux systems.

In the same study, government-run machines were considered separately. In August 2003, Microsoft Windows servers belonging to governments were the most attacked (51.4 percent), followed by Linux (14.3 percent). "The proliferation of Linux within the online server community coupled with inadequate knowledge of how to keep that environment secure when running vulnerable third-party applications is contributing to a consistently higher proportion of compromised Linux servers," says mi2g chair D. K. Matai. He adds that Microsoft deserves credit for having reduced the proportion of successful online hacker attacks perpetrated against Windows servers (Kapica, 2003).

According to a Netcraft survey that looked at a total of 44,946,965 servers for active sites on the Internet (Netcraft, 2003), the predominant Web server application in use was Apache, being used on 68 percent of the Web sites, whereas only 23 percent of the Web sites were using Microsoft products. Taking into account that Apache is run not only on Linux computers but also on other vendors' machines (such as Sun or Hewlett Packard), these figures lead to a general belief that about 2.5 times more Linux servers are used on the Internet than Microsoft servers, and therefore the mi2g attack numbers have to be weighted with this distribution. This leads to a somewhat more balanced picture.

About one-half of these servers had active content, meaning that those sites were not just used for parking domain names. When accessing a Web site with a parked domain name, the visitor will see a Web site showing an offer to buy the domain name or will see an "under construction" message. Interestingly, one-half of the domains on the Internet—that is, more than 20,000,000 domains—contain this sort of content, or are not reachable at all, because not even that minimal content was set up.

The mi2g study looked only at the number of online servers that were attacked. If one looks at the vast majority of Internet-connected PCs in private homes or on office desks—where Microsoft has a market share in the high 90 percent range—the picture looks very different. These machines are attacked by viruses that come in through e-mail attachments or are hidden in Web pages, and in most cases the user himself activates the malicious code by opening an attachment or surfing to a Web site. Siemens Business Systems, a prominent IT company, expects at least one-fifth of all desktop systems to switch to Linux as the operating system of choice by the year 2008 (Gulker, 2003). The main reason, they say, for this move away from Microsoft will be that Linux can provide equal productivity at a much lower cost, without Microsoft's restrictive licensing policies. Overcoming the current monoculture on the desktop will have the beneficial side effect that viruses and worms won't be able to spread as widely as they do now. Currently, viruses and worms can rely on finding a single type of operating system on nine out of ten computers on the Internet.

Around the quoted statistics, the fans of each operating system wage fierce discussion wars about which system is better and which is more secure. The one definitive conclusion possible is that the security of an operating system is a function not only of the type of operating system, but also of the knowledge, the skills, and the hard work of its administrators.

Legislative Countermeasures and Controversies

Many of the cybercrimes described in this and the previous chapter could not be successfully prosecuted by existing laws. In other cases, applying these existing laws meant stretching them a great deal. The Council of Europe recently recognized this problem and drafted a Convention on Cybercrime. The draft was opened to signature on November 23, 2001, and was signed by thirty-three nations. It was the first global legislative attempt of its kind to set standards on the definition of cybercrime and to develop policies and procedures that govern international cooperation to combat cybercrime.

Following are more details on its purpose (Council of Europe Press Service, 2001):

> The Convention will be the first international treaty on crimes committed via the Internet and other computer networks, dealing particularly with infringements of copyright, computer-related fraud, child pornography

> and violations of network security. It also contains a series of powers and procedures such as the search of computer networks and interception.
>
> Its main objective, set out in the preamble, is to pursue a common criminal policy aimed at the protection of society against cybercrime, especially by adopting appropriate legislation and fostering international co-operation.
>
> The Convention is the product of four years of work by Council of Europe experts, but also by the United States, Canada, Japan and other countries which are not members of the organisation.
>
> It will be supplemented by an additional protocol making any publication of racist and xenophobic propaganda via computer networks a criminal offence.

Critics of this Convention and of other legislative attempts warn that the Convention will fall short of fulfilling these high expectations unless more countries sign it and ratify it into national law. Moreover, the signatory countries are not the "problem countries." Crackers frequently route attacks through portals in Yemen or North Korea, where no comparable legislation exists and where cybercriminals are relatively safe from prosecution (Archik, 2002). Worse, these countries have not indicated that they plan to join the convention.

On the other hand, civil liberty groups point out that the Convention undermines privacy rights and grants too much surveillance power to authorities. European critics are concerned about the right to transfer European citizens' personal data outside of Europe by authorities to non-European authorities, and American organizations point out that the Convention allows for conducting surveillance and searches that would not be permitted by current U.S. law.

U.S. supporters of the Convention, however, say that the Convention indeed reflects the spirit of several bills passed or pending in Congress. The USA PATRIOT Act, for example, authorizes electronic intelligence gathering for the collection of evidence related to computer fraud, computer terrorism, and computer abuse. A part of the Homeland Security Act of 2002 (which created the Department of Homeland Security) is the Cyber Security Enhancement Act of 2002. It calls for increased penalties for computer-related crimes, including life imprisonment for crimes resulting in bodily harm and death, and harder sentences for other types of cyber offenses. Finally, the Cyberterrorism Preparedness Act of 2002 awards a 5-year grant to a nongovernmental entity to prepare and protect the U.S. information infrastructures and develop best practices to counter terrorist threats (Archik, 2002).

Conclusion

Without question, cyberwars of varying complexities and levels of harm are being waged daily. Whenever there is a regional conflict or a war, there is also an increased incidence of cyberattacks. Because of the power of the United States, American servers seem to be a primary target of cracker attacks, as is any country that hosts the annual G8 summit (Preatoni, 2003).

With increased hack attacks comes increased paranoia regarding an imminent cyberapocalypse (Yang, 2001). One reason for the increasing alarm is the apparent lack of effective legislation against cybercrime. Although the United States has tightened its legislative framework in this regard since September 11, 2001, there are other countries that hardly have any cybercrime legislation. Even where such laws exist, enforcing them seems to be extremely difficult.

For example, police forces in different countries, or even police from different regions within the same country, are notoriously secretive and reluctant to cooperate with each other. Moreover, Internet service providers (ISPs) that are a good source for information about the activities of their subscribers will often keep these records and log files confidential. The European Privacy Act requires ISPs to protect the log files from disclosure, and similar legislation exists in many other parts of the world.

The controversies surrounding cybercrime are, indeed, many and complex. Different groups of people who probably would not have engaged in conventional criminal activity years ago are beginning to be attracted to cybercrime because of the many vulnerabilities of the wired world and the relative ease with which these can be exploited. And compared to much old-fashioned crime, cybercrime is more convenient. The perpetrator can, in fact, stay at home and drink beer while committing a crime (Preatoni, 2003). Previously, criminals had to go out into the community to steal, attack, or fight.

Chapter 2 has not only discussed some of the problems and controversies regarding cybercrime and the common methods by which it is conducted, but this chapter has also described the challenging task of producing secure software systems and of securing internal networks. Several known vulnerabilities in the technical realm were described, and some potential solutions were presented. The chapter closed with a look at some of the legislative attempts to counter cybercrime and the controversies that arise with such legislation.

References

Andrews, J., 2003. "Linux: Kernel 'Back Door' Attempt." http://www.kerneltrap.org/node/view/1584 (cited November 5, 2003).

Archik, K. 2002. "Cybercrime: The Council of Europe Convention." Congressional Research Service Report for Congress: The Library of Congress. http://www.fas.org/irp/crs/RS21208.pdf (cited April 26, 2002).

Associated Press. 2003. "Handbag Maker Vuitton Sues Google." http://www.cnn.com/2003/TECH/biztech/10/24/france.google.ap/

Blumenfeld, L. 2003. "Student's 'Tedious' Thesis Is Terrorist's Treasure Map." *Toronto Star,* July 9, p. A3.

Bonisteel, S. 2001. "Mafiaboy Takes Rap on 55 Counts." http://articles.findarticles.com/p/articles/mi_m0NEW/is_2001_Jan_18/ai_69296380 (January 18, 2001).

Borland, J. 2002. "Elcomsoft Verdict: Not Guilty." http://news.com.com/2100–1023–978176.html (cited December 17, 2002).

"But They Told Us XP Was All New." 2003. *The Scobleizer Weblog.* http://paulbeard.no-ip.org/movabletype/archives/001131.html (September 16, 2003).

Computer Emergency Response Team Coordination Center (CERT/CC). 2004. "CERT/CC Statistics 1988–2003." http://www.cert.org/stats/cert_stats.html (updated January 22, 2004).

———. 2004. "CERT Coordination Center Incident Reporting System." https://irf.cc.cert.org/ (Version 2.1.1 cited May 31, 2004).

"Bin Laden Targets U.S. Economy." CBS News. 2001: http://www.cbsnews.com/stories/2001/12/26/attack/main322433.shtml (December 28, 2001).

Council of Europe Press Service. 2001. "First International Treaty to Combat Crime in Cyberspace Approved by Ministers' Deputies." http://press.coe.int/cp/2001/646a(2001).htm (September 19, 2001).

Department of Homeland Security. 2003. "DHS Establishes Computer Emergency Response Center for Cyber Security with Carnegie Mellon University." http://www.dhs.gov/dhspublic/display?content=1576 (September 15, 2003).

Dixon, G. 2001. "Hackers under Attack over Copyrights." *The Globe and Mail,* August 2, p. B22.

"Dmitry—Status." 2002. http://www.freesklyarov.org/ (cited May 26, 2002).

Evans, J. 2001. "Mafiaboy's Story Points to Net Weaknesses." IDC News Service, http://www.pcworld.com/news/article/0,aid,39142,00.asp (cited January 24, 2001).

Evans, M. 2000. "HMV Asks RCMP to Probe Web Attack." *The Globe and Mail,* February 12, p. B9.

Evans, M., and B. McKenna. 2000. "Dragnet Targets Internet Vandals." *The Globe and Mail,* February 10, pp. A1, A10.

Farrell, C. 2003. "FTC Asks Court to Block Deceptive Spam Operation." http://www.ftc.gov/opa/2003/04/westby.htm (cited April 17, 2003).

Federal Wiretap Act, Sec. 1343: Fraud by Wire, Radio, or Television. 1998. http://www.angelaw.com/weblaw/f_weblaw10.htm (cited January 26, 1998).

Friedman, M. S., and F. Papathomas. 2000. "Cybercrimes." *Computer Law Association,* 15, pp. 142, 144.

Garside, W. 1998. "White Paper: Lies, Damned Spies, and Computer Crime Statistics." http://www.computerweekly.com/Article42001.htm (cited July 22, 1999).

"Google Loses French Lawsuit." 2003. *The Globe and Mail,* October 20, p. B7.

Gulker, C. 2003. "Global IT Firm Predicts Linux Will Have 20 Percent Market Share by 2008." http://www.newsforge.com/business/03/08/13/1424212.shtml?tid=3 (cited August 13, 2003).

"Hacker Suspect Says His PC Was Hijacked." 2003. http://www.asianlaws.org/infosec/archives/10_03_hacker.htm (cited October 10, 2003).

Honeynet Project. 2003. "Know Your Enemy: Sebek 2." http://www.honeynet.org/papers/sebek.pdf. (cited November 17, 2003).

"Hospital Hacked: Computer Data Stolen from Rural Nevada Facility." 2003. *Cybercrime Law Report,* 3, pp. 6–7.

Ingles-le Nobel, J. 1999. "Cyberterrorism Hype." http://seclists.org/lists/isn/1999/Dec/0029.html (cited October 21, 1999).

"Insufficient Evidence: No Proof of Unauthorized Access." 2003. *Cybercrime Law Report,* 3, pp. 8–9.

Internet Engineering Task Force. 2003. "Active IETF Working Groups." http://www.ietf.org/html.charters/wg-dir.html (cited November 13, 2003).

Jupitermedia Corporation. 2003. "Senate Panel Overwhelmingly Passes Anti-Spam Bill." http://dc.internet.com/news/print.php/2224681 (cited June 19, 2003).

Kapica, J. 2003. "Linux Is Favourite Hacker Target: Study." *The Globe and Mail.* http://www.theglobeandmail.com (cited September 11, 2003).

Karrenberg, D. 2001. "Development of the Regional Internet Registry System. " http://www.cisco.com/warp/public/759/ipj_4-4/ipj_4-4_regional.html (cited December 2001)

Karp, J. 2002a. "Get Help Fighting Fraud Online." http://www.aafcil.com/articles/fightonlinefraud.asp (cited May 7, 2002).

———. 2002b. "Techtv: Viruses Explained." http://www.crime-research.org/eng/news/2002/10/Mess1102.htm (cited May 31, 2004).

"Landmark Internet Free Speech and Copyright Case." 2001. http://www.2600.com/news/view/article/211 (April 2, 2001).

Lindstrom, P. 2003. "Think Like an Attacker." *Information Security,* 6 (July), p. 38.

"Man Who Exposed County's Wireless Insecurity Found Innocent." 2003. *2600: The Hacker Quarterly,* http://www.2600.com/news/view/article/1546 (February 21, 2003).

McKenna, B., and P. Waldie. 2003. "Lawsuits Hit Net Music Downloaders." *The Globe and Mail,* September 9, pp. B1, B10.

Mi2G 2004. "Digital Attacks Report." http://www.mi2g.net/cgi/mi2g/frameset.php?pageid=http%3A//www.mi2g.net/cgi/mi2g/home_page.php (p 39. cited May 31, 2004)

Microsoft. 2003. "Internet Piracy." http://www.microsoft.com/piracy/ (August 1, 2003).

Morano, M. 2003. "E-Mail Spamming, Spoofing Growing 'Like Weeds in Yard.'" http://www.cnsnews.com/ViewCulture.asp?Page=%5CCulture%5Carchive%5C200304%5CCUL20030422a.html (April 22, 2003).

Mulhall, T. 1997. "Where Have All the Hackers Gone? Part 3: Motivation and Deterrence." *Computers and Security,* 16, pp. 291–297.

The National Strategy to Secure Cyberspace. 2003. http://www.whitehouse.gov/pcipb/cyberspace_strategy.pdf (cited September 19, 2003).

Netcraft. 2003. "Webserver Survey." http://news.netcraft.com/archives/2003/11/03/november_2003_web_server_survey.html (November 3, 2003).

"News: U.K. Combs Source Code for Cyberwarfare Clues." 2003. http://zdnet.com.com/2102-1105_2-5088392.html?tag=printthis (October 8, 2003).

Nirgendwo, 1999. *An English Translation of Linus Walleij's Copyright Does Not Exist.* Chapter 4: Underground Hackers. http://home.c2i.net/nirgendwo/cdne/ch4web.htm (cited August 23, 2000).

"PC Whiz Cleared in Houston Hacking." 2003. http://hightechmagazine.com/managearticle.asp?C=290&A=171 (cited October 19, 2003).

Pethia, R. D. 2003. "Viruses and Worms: What Can We Do about Them?" http://www.cert.org/congressional_testimony/Pethia-Testimony-9-10-2003/ (September 10, 2003).

Pipkin, D. 2003. *Halting the Hacker: A Practical Guide to Computer Security.* Upper Saddle River, NJ: Pearson Education.

Preatoni, R. 2003. *The Future Frontiers of Hacking.* Speech given at DefCon 11, Las Vegas, Nevada, July.

Richardson, R. 2003. "CSI/FBI Computer Crime and Security Survey." http://i.cmpnet.com/gocsi/db_area/pdfs/fbi/FBI2003.pdf (cited January 27, 2004).

Salgado, R. 2003. "Avoiding Sticky Legal Traps." *Information Security Magazine,* www.infosecuritymag.com (July 3, 2003).

Schell, B. H., J. L. Dodge, and S. Moutsatsos. 2002. *The Hacking of America: Who's Doing It, Why, and How.* Westport, CT: Quorum.

Shaw, E. D. 2001. "The Insider Problem." http://www.infosecuritymag.com/articles/january01/features4.shtml (January 2001).

Spitzner, L. 2003. "Hitting the Sweet Spot." *Information Security Magazine.* http://infosecuritymag.techtarget.com/2003/jul/honeypots.shtml (July 2003).

"Spreader of Multinational Virus Faces Fines, Prison." 2003. *Cybercrime Law Report,* 3, (April 21), p. 10.

"Summary: Kevin Poulsen, the Multi-Talented Hacker." 2003. http://livinginternet.com/i/ia_hackers_poulsen.htm (cited December 15, 2003).

Taylor, C. 2000. "Behind the Hack Attack." *Time,* February 21, pp. 19–21.

Temmingh, R. (SensePost). 2003. "Putting the Tea Back into Cyberterrorism." Speech given at DefCon 11. Las Vegas, Nevada, July.

Viega, J., and G. McGraw. 2002. *Building Secure Software: How to Avoid Security Problems the Right Way.* Boston, MA: Addison-Wesley.

Walton, D. 2000. "Hackers Tough to Prosecute, FBI Says." *The Globe and Mail,* February 10, p. B5.

Won, S. 2003. "Canadian COOs Wary of Terrorism: Survey." *The Globe and Mail,* October 21, p. B10.

Yang, J. 2001. 2001. "Government Jabs at Cyber Crime." http://abcnews.com/sections/wnt/DailyNews/cybercrime010721.html

3

Chronology

Cybercrime Timeline

1815 Ada Byron, one of the most interesting women in computer history, along with Charles Babbage, an English mathematician, predicted that a machine could be developed not only to compose complex music and graphics but also to be used for a variety of scientific and practical uses. Ada Byron, also known as Lady Byron, suggested to Babbage that he should write a plan for how a machine (dubbed the Difference Engine) might compile mathematical tables. Upon its completion in 1832, he conceived the idea of a better machine that could perform any kind of calculation. He completed the device in 1856, and called it the Analytical Engine. The latter is now regarded as the first computer. Unfortunately little remains of Charles Babbage's prototype computing machine because the British government suspended funding. Critical manufacturing tolerances required by Babbage's machine exceeded the level of technology available at the time. In modern days, the popular programming language ADA was named in Byron's honor for her contribution to mathematical science (Schell, Dodge, Moutsatsos, 2002).

1921 Kay McNulty Mauchly Antonelli was born in Pennsylvania. She later graduated from Chestnut Hill College, one of only three mathematics majors in a university class of ninety-two women. During the summer of 1942, when the United States Army was recruiting women with mathematics degrees to hand-calculate the firing trajectories of artillery for the war effort, Kay was successfully recruited to be a "human computer." She later married John Mauchly, a physics professor at Ursinus College and the coinventor (with J. Presper Eckert) of the first electronic computer in 1945, called the Eniac, or Electronic Numerical Integrator and Computer. This team of three from 1946 to 1950 worked on developing a new, faster computer called Universal Automatic Computer. It used magnetic tape storage to replace the previously used awkward punched data cards (Schell, Dodge, Moutsatsos, 2002).

1960s The infamous MIT all-male computer hobbyists were enjoying their hacking exploits. At this time, computers were mainframes locked away in temperature-controlled, glassed-in rooms. These slow-moving, expensive machines were known as PDP–1s, or Programmed Data Processor-1s, a Digital Equipment Corporation (DEC) computer. Using the PDP–1s, the White Hats in the MIT Tech Model Railroad Club created what they called hacks, or programming shortcuts, to enable them to complete their computer tasks more quickly. Their shortcuts were often more elegant than the original programs. The Club's talented White Hats became the nucleus of MIT's Artificial Intelligence (AI) Lab (Schell, Dodge, Moutsatsos, 2002).

1968 The Theft Act of 1968 was passed in the United Kingdom. It is still used today in the conviction of crackers (Schell, Dodge, Moutsatsos, 2002).

1969 This was the first year of ARPANET, or Advanced Research Projects Agency Network. ARPANET was the first transcontinental, high-speed computer network and was built by the United States Defense Department as an experiment in digital communications. By linking hundreds of universities, defense contractors, and research laboratories, ARPANET allowed AI researchers everywhere to exchange information with unprecedented speed and flexibility. This capability of working collaboratively advanced the field of information technology. The ARPANET, a network of DEC (Digital Equipment Corporation) machines, was meant to be a military defense technology that could withstand a nuclear attack because no central management body was established.

The operating system UNIX was developed at Bell Laboratory by researchers Dennis Ritchie and Ken Thompson. UNIX was greatly valued because its standard user and programming interface helped users with general computing, word processing, and networking. Today, it is still considered a very important operating system.

The first-ever Computer Science Man of the Year Award from the Data Processing Management Association was given to a woman, Rear Admiral Dr. Grace Murray Hopper. Among other notable achievements, Dr. Hopper wrote the computer language Cobol and contributed to the transition from primitive programming techniques to the use of a sophisticated compiler (a program that converts another program from human readable source language to machine language) (Schell, Dodge, Moutsatsos, 2002).

1970s Counterculture Yippie (a member of the Youth International Party) guru Abbie Hoffman started *The Youth International Party Line* newsletter to let other interested parties know the trade secrets of phreaking. Hoffman's publishing partner, Al Bell, changed the name of the newsletter to *TAP*, or *Technical Assistance Program.* Besides phreaking, other topics covered in the newsletter included explosives, electronic sabotage blueprints, and credit card fraud. Peculiar forms

1970s *(cont.)* of computer underground writing were also introduced in this publication, such as substituting *z* for *s* and *zero* for capital *O*. These trends have remained in the hacker community to the present day.

Dennis Ritchie invented a new computer language called C, which, like UNIX in the operating system world, was designed to be pleasant, nonconstraining to use, and flexible. Dennis Ritchie and his colleague Ken Thompson were among the first to realize that hardware and compiler technology had advanced enough that an entire operating system could be written in C. By 1978, the portability of the UNIX system to several machines of different types was demonstrated. The first widely available description of the C programming language, called the "White Book," appeared in the same year. Because both C and UNIX were based on the KISS (Keep It Simple, Stupid) idea, a programmer could easily hold the entire logical structure of C in his or her head while working, rather than needing to refer to a cumbersome manual (Schell, Dodge, Moutsatsos, 2002).

1971 John Draper made free long distance telephone calls using the whistle from a Cap'n Crunch cereal box. He was later imprisoned for this offense. Journalist Ron Rosenbaum's article in *Esquire* magazine on Draper's whistle-blowing phreaking exploits was what led to Draper's eventual arrest (Schell, Dodge, Moutsatsos, 2002).

The Criminal Damage Act of 1971 was passed in the United Kingdom and is still used today to prosecute crackers (Schell, Dodge, Moutsatsos, 2002).

1977 The Apple I Personal Computer (PC) computer was founded by two creative members of California's Homebrew Computer Club: Steve Jobs and Steve Wozniak. The Apple I was a kit computer, meaning that customers bought the workings and built their own case. At the time, many leaders in mainframe computer companies did not believe that personal computers were powerful enough to have a market. But sales of the Apple I and other more advanced PCs proved them wrong (Schell, Dodge, Moutsatsos, 2002).

1978 Two men from Chicago—Randy Sousa and Ward Christiansen—saw the need for a cybernetworking or social club. The pair created the first PC bulletin board system (BBS) for communicating with others in the computer underground. Their BBS was still in operation as of 2003 (Schell, Dodge, Moutsatsos, 2002).

1980s In the early 1980s, communication vehicles spreading the word about different high-tech exploits continued to expand. Two popular hacker groups, the Legion of Doom in the United States and the Chaos Computer Club in Germany, evolved and drew much talent into their ranks. Also, *2600: The Hacker Quarterly* emerged on the East Coast of the United States as a particularly exciting medium for phreakers. As of 2003, it was still considered a major communication medium for hackers.

The Comprehensive Crime Control Act gave the United States Secret Service jurisdiction over credit card and computer fraud.

The first of the modern computer viruses was thought to be created in Bulgaria (Schell, Dodge, Moutsatsos, 2002).

1981 International Business Machines (IBM) announced a new model of stand-alone computer called the PC, or personal computer. For many techies—both White Hats and Black Hats—the novelty of what the PC held inside became more exciting than what was inside sportscars. In particular, the Commodore 64 (a.k.a. Commie 64) and the TRS-80 (a.k.a. "Trash-S") became two favorite techie toys.

In Britain, the Forgery and Counterfeiting Act of 1981 was passed to help authorities convict criminals involved in these two activities (Schell, Dodge, Moutsatsos, 2002).

1982 A group of talented UNIX hackers from Stanford University and the University of California at Berkeley founded Sun Microsystems, Inc., on the belief that the UNIX operating system running on relatively inexpensive hardware would prove to be a winning combination for a variety of applications. Although still priced beyond most individuals' budgets, the Sun Microsystems networks increasingly replaced older computer systems (such as the VAX and other time-sharing systems) in corporations and universities across North America.

Richard Stallman founded the Free Software Foundation (FSF), dedicating his creativity to producing high-quality free software. He began constructing an entire clone of UNIX, written in C and available to the wired world free of charge. In 1984, his project, known as the GNU (Gnu's Not UNIX) operating system, quickly became a major focus for creative hacker activity. The GNU project's purpose was to engage White Hats in the development of a complete UNIX-style operating system that would allow for the distribution of free software. Free software enables a user to run, copy, distribute, study, change, and improve the software. For more than a decade after its inception, the Free Software Foundation largely defined the public ideology of the hacker culture (Schell, Dodge, Moutsatsos, 2002).

1983 The movie *War Games* was produced to expose to the public the hidden faces of Black Hat crackers in general and the media-exposed faces of the 414 cracker gang in particular. Despite the movie's intended purpose, it caused young women to become infatuated with (rather than put off by) computer "geeks."

After the 414 cracker gang entered a New York cancer hospital's computer system without authorization, they accidentally erased the contents of a certain hospital file as they were removing traces of their intrusion into the system. As a result, this New York hospital, as well as other industry and government agencies, began to fear that confidential or top-secret files could be at risk of erasure or alteration.

After the 414 gang became famous, other hackers developed a penchant for putting numbers before or after their proper names or for using a completely new "handle," or nickname. The 414 gang had derived their moniker from the Milwaukee area code (Schell, Dodge, Moutsatsos, 2002).

1984 The United Kingdom Data Protection Act was passed as a more effective means of curbing cracking activities than the Forgery and Counterfeiting Act of 1981.

The Telecommunications Act of 1984 (passed for the prevention of fraud in connection with the use of a telecommunication system) and the Police and Criminal Evidence Act of 1984 (which included a number of measures to prevent police from coercing a suspect to self-incriminate and confess to a crime—including cracking) were passed in the United Kingdom.

Steven Levy's (1984) book *Hackers: Heroes of the Computer Revolution* was released. It detailed the White Hat Hacker Ethic, which has been the guiding source for positively motivated White Hats since the 1960s (Schell, Dodge, Moutsatsos, 2002).

1986 In Britain, the convictions of Robert Schifreen and Steven Gold alluded to the term *criminal hacker* and triggered the public's fears about cybercrime. Schifreen and Gold were highly profiled crackers of the BT Prestel service, a text information retrieval system operated by BT Prestel and accessible over the public switched telephone system by means of a modem. Schifreen and Gold, although convicted on a number of criminal charges under the Forgery and Counterfeiting Act of 1981, had their convictions set aside when, in April 1988, the judges hearing the appeal felt that the spirit of the Forgery and Counterfeiting Act was being stretched to an unacceptable limit and that the Act was inappropriate for use in

1986 *(cont.)* cracking-related circumstances (Schell, Dodge, Moutsatsos, 2002).

1988 Robert Morris's Internet worm stole media headlines when he crashed 6,000 Internet-linked computers. He has the distinction of being the first person to be convicted under the Comprehensive Crime Control Act. Morris's defense was that although he had intended unauthorized access to a set of computers that the act categorizes as federal interest computers (computers of a department or agency of the United States), he had never intended to cause damage with his worm. For the court to find a violation of subsection of statute 1030(a)(5), the prosecution had to prove that Morris had intended to cause damage. In the end, the Second Circuit Court of New York found that intent to access the federal interest computer in question was sufficient by itself to warrant conviction, holding that the "intent" standard applied only to unauthorized accessing and not to the causing of damage. Morris received a sentence of 3 years' probation, 400 hours of community service, and a fine of $10,500.

Well-known cracker Kevin Mitnick secretly monitored the e-mail of security officials at the companies MCI and DEC to access proprietary information. As a result, Mitnick was convicted of damaging computers and stealing software and was sentenced to 1 year in prison, a story that was later to repeat itself (Schell, Dodge, Moutsatsos, 2002).

1988 The Copyright Design and Patents Act was passed in the United Kingdom.

Late 1980s Various United States defense agencies jointly set up the Computer Emergency Response Team (CERT) at Carnegie Mellon University to investigate the growing volume of cracker attacks on computer networks.

Kevin Poulsen took over all the telephone lines going into Los Angeles radio station KIIS-FM in an effort to be the 102nd caller and thereby win a Porsche 944 S2. Poulsen was later imprisoned.

A group of four female crackers was active in Europe during this time. Known as TBB (The Beautiful Blondes), they specialized in C64 (one of the earliest affordable home computers) exploits.

Computer abuse offenses were established under Canadian law after the failed prosecution of a cracker for theft of telecommunications services in the case of *Regina v. McLaughlin.*

1990 The Computer Misuse Act of 1990 was passed in Britain to more specifically deal with cracking exploits. Michael Colvin, then a member of Parliament, worked with the Department of Trade and Industry to get this bill through the British Parliament.

Early 1990s A "Hacker War" took place between two hacker clubs in the United States: the Legion of Doom (founded by Lex Luthor [real name not known] in 1984) and the Masters of Deception (founded by Mark Abene, a.k.a. Phiber Optik, in 1989). Named after a Saturday morning cartoon, the Legion of Doom had the reputation of attracting the best hackers in existence until one of the club's brightest members, Phiber Optik (Mark Abene), feuded with fellow Legion of Doomer Erik Bloodaxe (a.k.a. Chris Goggans). Abene was removed from the club, at which point he and some devotees formed a rival club. Online warfare (including jamming telephone lines, monitoring telephone lines and telephone calls, and trespassing the rival computer systems) between the two groups ensued for almost 2 years until United States federal agents moved in. Mark Abene received a 1-year jail sentence for his role in the online war.

With the advent of the Intel 386 chip (a microprocessor chip that was widely used in PCs) and its descendants, hackers could finally afford to have home ma-

Early 1990s *(cont.)* chines comparable in power and storage capacity to the minicomputers of 10 years earlier. However, affordable software for these machines was still not available (Schell, Dodge, Moutsatsos, 2002).

1991–1993 In 1991, a talented Helsinki University student named Linus Torvald began developing a free UNIX kernel (or central program that runs an operating system) for 386 machines using the Free Software Foundation's toolkit. Torvald's rapid success attracted many Internet hackers, who gave him their feedback on improving the product. Eventually, Linux was developed—a full-featured UNIX with entirely free and redistributable sources. By late 1993, Linux could compete on stability and reliability with the many commercial versions of UNIX, and it hosted vastly more free software (Schell, Dodge, Moutsatsos, 2002).

1992 The Michelangelo virus attracted a lot of media attention because it was believed to cause great damage to data and computers around the world. These fears turned out to be greatly exaggerated, however, as the virus actually did not do anything to the computers it invaded (Schell, Dodge, Moutsatsos, 2002).

1994 In the summer of this year, media headlines were captured by the story of a gang of crackers that broke into Citibank's computers and made unauthorized transfers from customers' accounts totaling more than $10 million. Though in time Citibank recovered all but about $400,000 of the illegally transferred funds, this ending to the story was not featured in the media (Schell, Dodge, Moutsatsos, 2002).

1994–1995 Hacktivists moved to the forefront. During these years, White Hat hacktivists squashed the Clipper proposal, which would have put strong encryption (the process of scrambling data into something that is seemingly unintelligible) under the control of the United States government (Schell, Dodge, Moutsatsos, 2002).

Mid-1990s Linux had become stable and reliable enough to be considered an operating systems platform by many commercial application software vendors (Schell, Dodge, Moutsatsos, 2002).

1995 In February, a University of Michigan student by the name of Jake Baker posted to the Internet a fictional story of rape, torture, and murder, using the name of a classmate of his as the victim. A few days later, he was arrested by the Federal Bureau of Investigation for interstate transmission of a threat to kidnap and was held without bond for 29 days on the grounds that he was too dangerous to release. Charges against Baker were eventually dropped in June of this year (Schell, Dodge, Moutsatsos, 2002).

Randal Schwartz, author of the popular books *Programming Perl* and *Learning Perl,* was convicted on charges of industrial espionage. While working as a system administrator for Intel, Schwartz performed some security tests using a program called Crack to uncover weak passwords (or a password that is easy to guess). When the Intel managers discovered this, Schwartz was assumed to be engaging in industrial espionage. They brought felony charges against him under Oregon's computer theft law. Schwartz was convicted in September 1995 on a reduced charge. He was sentenced to 5 years' probation, 480 hours of community work, 90 days of deferred jail time, and $68,000 of restitution to Intel.

Kevin Mitnick, cyberspace's most wanted hacker, was arrested by the FBI for his cracking exploits. Computer security consultant Tsutomu Shimomura, in close association with *New York Times* reporter John Markoff, helped the FBI locate Mitnick. Shimomura and Markoff later wrote a book together about the episode, entitled *Takedown: The Pursuit and Capture of Kevin Mitnick, America's Most Wanted Computer Outlaw—By the Man Who Did It.* The book was released in 1996.

1995 *(cont.)* Edward E. Cummings (a.k.a. Bernie S.), a man of *2600: The Hacker Quarterly* notoriety and a native of Pennsylvania, was sent to prison without bail for his phreaking exploits in using a modified Radio Shack speed dialer to make free phone calls. Bernie S., a creative man with his own cult following, said that what he did was not criminal activity, as the tones and information in his possession at the time of arrest were very easy to obtain (Schell, Dodge, Moutsatsos, 2002).

1996 Kevin Mitnick was arrested again, this time for stealing 20,000 credit card numbers. He was arrested in April 1996 and pleaded guilty to illegal use of stolen cellular telephones. His status as a repeat cyberoffender earned him the nickname "the Lost Boy of Cyberspace."

White Hat hacktivists mobilized a broad coalition not only to defeat the U.S. government's Communications Decency Act but also to prevent censorship of the Internet.

The CyberAngels started to appear online in an effort to stop cyberstalkers and cyberpornographers.

The Computer Fraud and Abuse Act (CFAA), the primary U.S. federal statute criminalizing cracking, was modified by the National Information Infrastructure Protection Act and codified at 18 U.S.C. subsection 1030. At its inception in 1984, the CFAA had only applied to government computers, including any computer used in interstate commerce. Now, though, the CFAA's much broader application reflected the United States government's resolve to combat cybercrime on a more comprehensive basis. A conviction for violation of most of the provisions of the CFAA included up to 5 years in prison and up to a $250,000 fine for a first offense, and up to 10 years in prison and up to a $500,000 fine for a second offense. The CFAA also permitted any person who suffered damages or losses through a violation of the CFAA to bring a civil action against the violator for damages.

The National Information Infrastructure Protection Act of 1996 (NIIPA) expanded the CFAA to include unauthorized access to and acquisition of information from a protected computer without the computer owner's authorization. Prior to the NIIPA amendments, in order to find a violation of the CFAA, the courts had interpreted the law as requiring that the accused must have intended commercial gain. The NIIPA amendments to the CFAA were the direct result of the First Circuit Court of Massachusetts's decision in the *United States v. Czubinski* case (see under 1997).

Timothy Lloyd, an employee who planted a logic bomb in Omega Engineering's network, cost the company $12 million in damages to the systems and networks (Schell, Dodge, Moutsatsos, 2002).

1997 Previously, in 1995, in the *United States v. Czubinski* case, an Internal Revenue Service employee was charged with gaining unauthorized access to confidential income tax records. Although the IRS employee was convicted at trial, the First Circuit Court of Massachusetts reversed the conviction on the appeal in 1997, finding that although Richard Czubinski had exceeded his authorization in viewing confidential income tax records, no evidence suggested that he had printed out or used the information he observed. Therefore, nothing of value was taken—as was required by the CFAA at the time for a conviction. The CFAA was modified as a direct result of this trial, and today, Czubinski's acts would constitute a misdemeanor offense under S. 1030(2)(4) of the CFAA (Schell, Dodge, Moutsatsos, 2002).

1998 Enacted in October, the Digital Millennium Copyright Act (DMCA) was intended to implement under U.S. law certain worldwide copyright laws to cope with emerging digital technologies. The DMCA provided protection against the disabling or bypassing of technical measures designed to protect copyright. Its sanctions apply to anyone who attempts to impair or

1998 *(cont.)* disable an encryption device protecting a copyrighted work (Schell, Dodge, Moutsatsos, 2002).

Late 1990s In the White Hat hacker laboratories around the world, activities centered on Linux development and the mainstreaming of the Internet. Many gifted White Hats launched Internet service providers (ISPs), selling or giving online access to many—and creating some of the world's wealthiest corporate leaders and stock option owners (Schell, Dodge, Moutsatsos, 2002).

1999 Two professional soldiers in the Chinese People's Liberation Army proposed a new way of waging war: by using terrorist attacks and cyberattacks on critical infrastructure as a way to keep a superpower adversary reeling.

In March, the world started to become familiar with the destruction caused by worms and viruses. The Melissa virus appeared on the Internet, spreading rapidly throughout computer systems in the United States and Europe and causing an estimated $80 million in damages. On December 9, David Smith pleaded guilty to state and federal charges associated with its creation (Schell, Dodge, Moutsatsos, 2002).

2000 In January, Universal Studios and other members of the Motion Picture Association of America took on *2600: The Hacker Quarterly* regarding an issue surrounding DVD decryption software. Universal Studios believed that software (discussed by *The Hacker Quarterly*) should not be used to copy DVDs and thereby infringe on copyright. At the end of the battle, the civil courts favored the position of Universal Studios and their arguments regarding the Digital Millennium Copyright Act.

In February, the high-profile case of a Canadian nicknamed Mafiaboy (his identity was not disclosed because he was only 15 years old at the time) raised concerns in North America about Internet security following a series of denial-of-service attacks on several high-profile Web sites, including Amazon.com, eBay, and Yahoo! On January 18, 2001, Mafiaboy pleaded guilty to charges that he broke into Internet servers and used them as launching pads for DoS attacks. In September 2001, he was sentenced to 8 months in a youth detection center and was fined $250.

In February, John Serabian, the CIA's information issue manager, said in written testimony to the United States Joint Economic Committee that the CIA was detecting with increasing frequency the appearance of government-sponsored cyberwarfare programs in other countries.

On May 23, Dr. Dorothy Denning, a cybercrime expert who was at that time affiliated with Georgetown University, gave testimony before the Special Oversight Panel on Terror in the United States. She commented that cyberspace was constantly under assault, making it fertile ground for cyberattacks against targeted individuals, companies, and governments—a point repeated often by White Hat hackers over the past two decades. She warned that unless critical computer systems were secured, conducting a computer operation that physically harms individuals or societies may become as easy in the not-too-distant-future as penetrating a Web site is today.

Around the time of Dr. Denning's speech, cyberexperts began to question whether a cyberapocalypse could surface as early as 2005.

IBM estimated that online retailers could lose $10,000 or more in sales per minute if service were not available to customers because of DoS attacks (Schell, Dodge, Moutsatsos, 2002).

2001 On April 4, Massachusetts Institute of Technology (MIT) announced that over the next decade, materials for nearly all courses offered at the university would

2001 *(cont.)* be freely available on the Internet. This was inspired by the White Hat spirit that has been the driving force behind the free information sharing movement since the 1960s.

On May 28, in a piece published in *The New Yorker,* Peter G. Neumann, a principal scientist at the technological consulting firm SRI International and a consultant to the U.S. Navy, Harvard University, and the National Security Agency (NSA), underscored his concerns about the negative impact of cybercriminals. He noted that he was worried about the cyberapocalypse because malicious hackers could now get into important systems in minutes or seconds and could wipe out one-third of the computer drives in the United States in a single day, or could shut down the power grids and emergency response systems of twenty states. He warned that such an apocalypse might not be too far away.

On July 19, the Code Red worm infected hundreds of thousands of computers worldwide in less than 14 hours, overloading the Internet's capacity and costing about $2.6 billion worldwide. It struck again in August. Carolyn Meinel, author of a number of hacking books, labeled the worm a type of computer disease that had computer security researchers more worried than ever about the integrity of the Internet and of the likelihood of imminent cyberterrorist attacks. She likened the Code Red worm to electronic snakebites that infected Microsoft Internet Information Servers (IIS)—the lifeline to many of the most popular Web sites around the world. Josef Chamberlin, a 34-year-old self-taught hacker, would later be hard at work at EDS, an international electronic data management company in Rancho Cordova, California, trying to track down the worm ("Code Red," 2001).

In July, a Russian named Dmitry Sklyarov was arrested at the DefCon hacker convention in Las Vegas after he gave a speech about the software he had developed for his Russian employer, Elcomsoft Co. Ltd.

The software in question allowed users to download eBooks from secure Adobe software to more commonly used PDF computer files. U.S. federal agents labeled him a cybercriminal who breached the Digital Millennium Copyright Act because his software allowed users to foil copyright protections put in place by eBook publishers, but both Sklyarov and his employer were eventually cleared by the courts of any wrongdoing. The conclusion was that his behavior was legal in the country where he had developed the software—Russia (Glasner, 2002).

In September, NIMDA (*ADMIN* spelled backwards) arrived, a blend of computer worm and computer virus. It lasted for days and attacked an estimated 86,000 computers. NIMDA serves as a good example of the increasing sophistication showing up in cyberattacks. Also, it demonstrated that some of the weapons available to organized and technically savvy attackers now had the capability to learn and adapt to their local environment (Schell, Dodge, Moutsatsos, 2002).

Also in September, Aaron Caffrey, age 19, from Dorset, England, was charged under the 1990 Computer Misuse Act and accused of unleashing a flood of data that shut down a Houston, Texas, seaport (the sixth biggest shipping port in the world). In his own defense, Caffrey claimed that his computer was completely and utterly vulnerable to many exploits. He was found not guilty of the cracking charges ("Hacker Suspect," 2003).

On September 11 at around 9 A.M. EST and within a span of 18 minutes, two U.S. passenger jets were deliberately crashed into the twin towers of the World Trade Center (WTC) in New York City, bringing down one of the most powerful symbols of capitalism in the world and killing thousands of innocent civilians and rescue workers. By 9:45 A.M., a third U.S. passenger jet was deliberately crashed on a helicopter landing pad beside the Pentagon in Washington, D.C., causing one

2001 *(cont.)* side of the five-sided structure to collapse and killing everyone aboard the plane and hundreds within the Pentagon building. At 10:08 A.M. a fourth passenger jet crashed in rural Sunset County, about 120 kilometers southeast of Pittsburgh, Pennsylvania. All 45 people on board that plane were killed as well. Authorities believed that the intended target of the Pennsylvania crash was the White House (in hopes of killing the president of the United States). This tragic set of events was not the apocalyptic work of cyberterrorists, but rather the work of about nineteen hijackers who social-engineered their way into North American mainstream society and onto four U.S. jets.

On October 8, the U.S. military retaliated for the airborne attacks on the WTC. Using waves of cruise missiles, satellite-guided bombs, and dropping food packages for the civilians, the United States and Britain launched their first offensive in a war against Afghanistan whose target was the military installations of the ruling Taliban.

On October 26, the USA PATRIOT Act of 2001 was enacted into law. This Act included several laws relating to computer crime and electronic evidence, giving the U.S. government greatly expanded surveillance and search powers.

On November 23, the Council of Europe opened to signature its newly drafted Convention on Cybercrime. The Convention was signed by thirty-three states. It had been recognized that many cybercrimes could not be prosecuted by existing laws, or that applying these existing laws to cybercrimes meant stretching the laws a great deal. The Convention was the first global legislative attempt of its kind to set standards on the definition of cybercrime and to develop policies and procedures to govern international cooperation to combat cybercrime.

2002 On November 25, the United States passed the Homeland Security Act of 2002, including section 225, known as the Cyber Security Enhancement Act of 2002.

2003 On January 24, President George W. Bush swore in Tom Ridge as the secretary of the Department of Homeland Security.

In February, the Prosecutorial Remedies and Tools against the Exploitation of Children Today (PROTECT) Act was passed in the United States. It was aimed at child pornographers, in particular.

Also in February, a Texas jury acquitted Stefan Puffer, a computer security analyst who had been accused in 2002 of wrongful access to a county computer network. In March 2002, Puffer discovered that the Harris County district clerk's wireless computer network was unprotected. Worrying that anyone with a wireless network card could gain access to sensitive computers and files, Puffer demonstrated the problem to county officials and was indicted on two counts of fraud. After only 15 minutes of deliberation, a jury found that Puffer had not intended to cause any damage to the county's systems (*2600: The Hacker Quarterly*, 2003).

In March, President George W. Bush and Tony Blair, the prime minister of the United Kingdom, waged war "in principle" against Iraq's leader Saddam Hussein, alleged to possess an arsenal of chemical and biological weapons of mass destruction, and against any state or anyone who aided or abetted terrorists. On March 19, the "war against terror" began.

On March 20, at the William Bee Ririe Hospital in Ely, Nevada, crackers gained access to an undetermined amount of data that may have included 190 employees' social security numbers and bank information. As of 2004, there had been no reported incidents of fraudulent use of these data (*Cybercrime Law Report*, 2003a).

2003 *(cont.)* Also in March, Jennifer Hargrove, formerly employed by Farmers Insurance Group, was charged with unauthorized access to her former employer's computer. Hargrove argued in her defense that she took a copy of a client list with her when she left, being under the mistaken impression she was permitted to do so. The judge concluded that the evidence presented to the district court was insufficient to sustain a conviction under the "unauthorized access" law (*Cybercrime Law Report,* 2003b).

In April, a Swedish minor was charged after he admitted to creating and spreading a computer worm in at least forty countries. He faces fines and a 2-year prison sentence for violating Swedish laws prohibiting the distribution of viruses and worms that caused changes in people's software without their permission (*Cybercrime Law Report,* 2003c).

Amenaza presented SecurITree, a software that utilizes a method of creating a likely hack attack by linking various "approach" paths and vulnerabilities in the same way that a cracker might exploit a system.

In the early summer, a poll of more than 1,000 U.S. adults by the Pew Internet and American Life Project found that one in two adults expressed concern about the vulnerability of the national infrastructure to terrorist crackers. The poll found that 58 percent of the women and 47 percent of men feared an imminent attack. More than 70 percent of the respondents were fairly confident that the United States government would provide them with sufficient information in the event of another terrorist attack ("Americans Concerned About Cyberattacks," 2003).

In July, Sean Gorman of George Mason University made media headlines when he produced for his doctoral dissertation a set of charts detailing the communication networks binding the United States together. Using mathematical formulas, Gorman had probed for critical infrastructure links in an attempt to answer the question, "If I were Osama bin Laden, where would I want to attack?" (Blumenfeld, 2003).

In July at the DefCon hacker convention in Las Vegas, R. Temmingh (2003) described the frightening possibility of someone attacking the infrastructure of an entire country. Though today's networks are fairly well protected against physical attacks from the outside, he proposed, the security and integrity of the internal systems remain a possible path for intrusion and damage.

The U.S. Federal Trade Commission (FTC) set up a national spam database and encouraged people to forward to the FTC all the e-mail spam they received. In 2002, the FTC had reported more than 17 million complaints about spam messages, with nearly 110,000 complaints being received daily.

In August, three crippling worms and viruses caused considerable cyberdamage and increased the stress levels of business leaders and citizens alike. The Blaster worm surfaced on August 11, 2003, exploiting security holes found in Microsoft Windows XP. The Welchia worm also surfaced on August 11; it targeted active computers, went to Microsoft's Web site, downloaded a program that fixes the Windows holes, and deleted itself. The most damaging of the three, though, was the e-mail-borne SoBigF virus, the fifth variant of a bug that initially invaded computers in January 2003 and that resurfaced with a vengeance on August 18. The damages for lost production and economic losses caused by these worms and viruses was in excess of $2 billion for just an 8-day period.

John McAffee, the developer of the McAfee antivirus software, claimed that there were more than 58,000 virus threats, and antivirus company Symantec estimated that 10 to 15 new viruses were discovered daily.

On August 14, the East Coast of the United States and the province of Ontario, Canada, were hit by an electrical blackout. This blackout, said to be the biggest

2003 *(cont.)* ever affecting the United States, lasted from hours to days, depending on the geographical location. Citizens in Manhattan were especially nervous, thinking that they were once again being targeted by terrorists. Some utility control system experts said that the two events—the August computer worm invasions and the blackout—might have been linked.

On August 29, Jeffrey Lee Parson was arrested and charged with intentionally causing and attempting to cause damage to a protected computer. He had used what was believed to be a variant of the Blaster worm (but likely not the original version) ("Minneapolis, Minnesota 18 Year Old," 2003).

On September 8, concerned about piracy and the loss of major revenues from CD sales, the Recording Industry Association of America (RIAA) filed 261 lawsuits in courts across the United States, targeting tens of millions of computer users who shared songs online. The RIAA said that the suits were just the first wave in what could ultimately be thousands of lawsuits in the United States. One of the much-written-about targets was Lahara, a 12-year-old student who lived in subsidized housing in New York (McKenna,Waldie, 2003; Damsell, 2003).

On September 15, the Department of Homeland Security, in conjunction with Carnegie Mellon University, announced the creation of the U.S. Computer Emergency Response Team (US-CERT). The newly formed unit was expected to grow to include other partnerships with private sector security vendors and other domestic and international CERT organizations.

Around the world, groups such as the National High-Tech Crime Unit (NHTCU) in the United Kingdom began working with antivirus companies to identify patterns in the source code of the most damaging Internet worms and virus programs to determine whether they were the work of organized subversive groups or crime syndicates. Their hope was that, buried somewhere in the lines of code would be clues to the author's identity, motive, and, possibly, future acts of sabotage.

On October 1, Symantec Corporation, a California security threat monitoring company, reported that Internet surfers in the United States and around the world needed to brace themselves for a growing number of sophisticated and contagious cyberspace bugs.

In October, an international consortium released a list of the top twenty Internet security vulnerabilities. The consortium included the United States Department of Homeland Security, the United Kingdom National Infrastructure Security Coordination Centre (NISCC), and the Government of Canada's Office of Critical Infrastructure Protection and Emergency Preparedness (OCIPEP), along with the SANS (SysAdmin, Audit, Network, Security) Institute in the United States. The consortium's hope was to define an absolute minimum level of security protection for computers connected to networks.

The Computer Security Institute (CSI) and Federal Bureau of Investigation (FBI) conducted a survey on computer crime. Of the 530 respondents (computer security practitioners in U.S. corporations, government agencies, financial institutions, medical institutions, and universities), more than one-half said that their organizations had experienced some kind of unauthorized computer use or intrusion during the previous year. An overwhelming 99 percent of the companies, however, thought that they had adequate protection against cyberintruders because their systems had antivirus software, firewalls, access controls, and other security measures. As in previous years, theft of proprietary information was reported to have caused the greatest financial losses to the respondents (Richardson, 2003).

In October, a French court ruled against Internet search powerhouse Google, Inc., in an intellectual property

2003 *(cont.)* rights case that could have far-reaching technological and financial implications for Web search firms. The court fined Google 75,000 euros for allowing advertisers to link text Internet advertisements to trademarked search terms and gave the search powerhouse 30 days to cease the practice. The ruling was believed to be the first in which the owner of a trademarked term successfully sued an Internet search service over the practice of allowing advertisers to use "protected" terms in text ads ("Google Loses," 2003).

Also in October, a survey released by Deloitte & Touche LLP indicated that chief operating officers (COOs) of companies around the world were more nervous about terrorist attacks affecting business than were their American peers. Economist Carl Steidtmann suggested that U.S. executives might be less concerned and more complacent about terrorist and cyberterrorist attacks because they felt that their country had taken more steps to combat terrorism, such as introducing the Homeland Security Act of 2002 (Won, 2003).

On November 5, the media reported that a cracker had broken into one of the computers on which the sources of the Linux operating systems are stored and from which they are distributed worldwide (Andrews, 2003).

The Controlling the Assault of Non-Solicited Pornography and Marketing Act of 2003 (Can Spam) Act of 2003 was passed by the United States Senate on November 25, aimed at commercial e-mailers and spammers. The bill was signed by President Bush on December 16, 2003, and took effect on January 1, 2004.

On December 14, eight months after Baghdad fell in the war in Iraq, United States soldiers found Saddam Hussein, disheveled and in hiding, 6 feet underground in a location about 9 miles from his hometown of Tikrit. He had a pistol but was taken into custody without firing it. U.S. forces also found other weapons and about $750,000 in U.S. bills with the former dictator.

The mi2g Intelligence Unit, a British security company that has collected and verified data on overt digital attacks since 1995, announces that Linux—and not Microsoft Windows—operating systems are the ones most frequently attacked. According to mi2g, Linux remained the most attacked operating system online during the year 2003, with 51 percent of all successful overt digital attacks being perpetrated against Linux systems (Mi2G, 2004).

2004 On January 21, the Recording Industry Association of America (RIAA) said it had identified 532 song-swappers by the trails their computers leave when they download illegal music. According to the CNN Web site, the 532 cases, at that time only identified by their IP addresses, were targeted in four lawsuits, three filed in New York and one filed in Washington, D.C. The new lawsuits were filed using the so-called John Doe process, allowing the recording industry to sue defendants whose names were not yet known (Rogers, 2004).

On January 26, the worm W.32.Novarg.A@mm, also known as MyDoom, spread throughout the Internet and wreaked havoc. It arrived as an attachment with the file extension .bat, .cmd, .exe, .pif, .scr, or .zip and affected the Windows 2000, Windows 95, Windows 98, Windows Server 2003, and Windows XP systems but not DOS, Linux, Macintosh, OS/2, UNIX, or Windows 3.x systems. The damage done by MyDoom was estimated to be $2 billion worldwide (Akin, 2004a, 2004b; Bloom, 2004).

References

Akin, D. 2004a. "MyDoom Virus Targets Utah Firm." *The Globe and Mail*, January 28, p. B6.

———. 2004b. "MyDoom Virus Variant Has Dangerous Quirks." *The Globe and Mail*, January 29.

"Americans Concerned about Cyberattacks." 2003. *The East Carolinian*. http://www.crime-research.org/eng/news/2003/09/Mess0502.html (cited September 5, 2003).

Andrews, J., 2003. "Linux: Kernel 'Back Door' Attempt." http://www.kerneltrap.org/node/view/1584 (cited November 5, 2003).

Bloom, R. 2004. "MyDoom E-Mail Virus Spreads Fast." *The Globe and Mail,* January 27, pp. A1, A4.

Blumenfeld, L. 2003. "Student's 'Tedious' Thesis Is Terrorist's Treasure Map." *Toronto Star,* July 9, p. A3.

"Code Red Havoc Reported to Have Cost $2.6 Billion." 2001. *The Globe and Mail,* September 6, p. B26.

Cybercrime Law Report. 2003a. "Hospital Hacked: Computer Data Stolen from Rural Nevada Facility." *Cybercrime Law Report,* 3 (April 21), pp. 6–7.

———. 2003b. "Insufficient Evidence: No Proof of Unauthorized Access," *Cybercrime Law Report,* 3 (April 21), pp. 8–9.

———. 2003c. "Spreader of Multinational Virus Faces Fines, Prison." *Cybercrime Law Report,* 3 (April 21), p. 10.

Damsell, K. 2003. "Microsoft Has Price on Hackers' Heads." *The Globe and Mail,* November 6, pp. B1, B10.

Glasner, J. 2002. "Jury Finds Elcomsoft Not Guilty." *Wired News.* http://www.wired.com/news/business/0,1367,56894,00.html (cited December 17, 2002).

"Google Loses French Lawsuit." 2003. *The Globe and Mail,* October 20, p. B7.

"Hacker Suspect Says His PC Was Hijacked." 2003. Asian School of Cyberlaws. http://www.asianlaws.org/infosec/archives/10_03_hacker.htm (cited October 10, 2003).

Levy, Steven. 1984. *Hackers: Heroes of the Computer Revolution.* New York: Dell.

"Man Who Exposed County's Wireless Insecurity Found Innocent," *2600: The Hacker Quarterly.* http://www.2600.com/news/view/article/1546 (cited February 21, 2003).

McKenna, B., and P. Waldie. 2003. "Lawsuits Hit Net Music Downloaders." *The Globe and Mail,* September 9: pp. B1, B10.

mi2g. 2004. "Digital Attacks Report." http://www.mi2g.net/cgi/mi2g/frameset.php?pageid=http%3A//www.mi2g.net/cgi/mi2g/home_page.php. p 39. (cited May 31, 2004)

Richardson, R. 2003. "CSI/FBI Computer Crime and Security Survey." http://i.cmpnet.com/gocsi/db_area/pdfs/fbi/FBI2003.pdf (cited January 27, 2004).

Rogers, J. 2004. "U.S. Suing 532 Song Swappers." CNN Online. http://cnn.com/2004/TECH/internet/01/22/online.music/index.html (cited January 21, 2004).

Schell, B. H., J. L. Dodge, and S. Moutsatsos. 2002. *The Hacking of America: Who's Doing It, Why, and How.* Westport, CT: Quorom.

Schwartz, Randal. 1993. *Learning Perl.* Cambridge, MA: O'Reilley.

———. 1996. *Programming Perl.* Cambridge, MA: O'Reilley.

Shimomura, Tsutomu, and John Markoff. 1996. *Takedown: The Pursuit and Capture of Kevin Mitnick, America's Most Wanted Computer Outlaw—By the Man Who Did It.* New York: Hyperion Press.

Temmingh, R. (SensePost). 2003. "Putting the Tea Back into Cyberterrorism." Speech given at DefCon 11. Las Vegas, Nevada, July.

U.S. Department of Justice. "Minneapolis, Minnesota 18 Year Old Arrested for Developing and Releasing B Variant of Blaster Computer Worm." 2003. U.S. Department of Justice Cybercrime Web Site. http://www.usdoj.gov/criminal/cybercrime/parsonArrest.htm (cited August 29, 2003).

Waldie, P. 2003. "Music Industry Hails $2,000 Win over Child." *The Globe and Mail,* September 10, pp. A1–2.

Won, S. 2003. "Canadian COOs Wary of Terrorism: Survey. *The Globe and Mail,* October 21, p. B10, 2003.

4

Biographical Sketches

Abene, Mark (a.k.a. Phiber Optik) (1972–)

A notorious phreaker, Mark Abene preferred breaking into telephone systems using a normal telephone receiver. A member of the Legion of Doom hacker group, and later the founder of the hacking group Masters of Deception, Abene was blamed for the American Telephone and Telegraph system crash in 1990. However, it was later learned that the crash was caused by a computer bug, not by Abene. The following year, Abene was investigated by the Secret Service and indicted for his phone hacking exploits with Southwestern Bell, New York Telephone, Pacific Bell, U.S. West, and the Martin Marietta Electronics Information and Missile Group. He served 10 months in prison. Because he was visited by so many journalists while he served time, the other inmates called him CNN ("Mark Abene," 2003). Upon his release from prison, Abene worked on penetration tests (a technical service aimed at compromising, from outside, the security of a company's information system) for an accounting firm and formed the now-defunct security company Crossbar Security ("Mark Abene," 2003).

Byron, Ada (1815–1852)

Ada Byron was one of the most interesting women in computer history. Born on December 10, 1815, Ada was the daughter of the famous poet Lord Byron. By the time she was 17, Ada was very interested in the power of mathematics—much to the relief of her mother, who had feared that Ada would become a poet like her father. In 1834, Ada was introduced to a researcher by the name of Charles Babbage, who spoke of a new calculating machine, dubbed the Analytical Engine. Later, Ada showed Babbage her translation of a piece written about the Engine in French, and after communicating further with Babbage, Ada published her own article in 1843. Her article included predictions that a machine could be developed not only to compose complex music and produce graphics, but also to be used for a variety of scientific and practical uses. Ada also suggested to Babbage that he should write a plan for how the Analytical Engine might calculate Bernoulli numbers (numbers that arise in the series expansion of mathematical functions and are very important in number theory and analysis). This plan was completed and is now regarded as the first computer program. Ada Byron married the Earl of Lovelace and had three children. She died in 1852. A popular, modern-day programming language was named ADA in her honor (Schell, Dodge, and Moutsatsos, 2002).

Caffrey, Aaron (1982–)

Besides those of Mafiaboy (see entry in this chapter), other flooding exploits have made the news in the early years of the twenty-first century. In September 2001, for example, Englishman Aaron Caffrey, age 19, was charged under the Computer Misuse Act of 1990 in Britain and accused of unleashing a flood of data to shut down the Houston, Texas, seaport—the sixth biggest seaport in the world. Caffrey denied the charges, saying that although the attack was apparently triggered from his computer, he was not the person behind the exploit. In defending himself before the Southwark Crown Court, he gave a technical description of how crackers could assume the identities of unsuspecting computer users through tricks such as "fishing out" security passwords to steal online identities. Though he faced a possible prison sentence of 5 years, the jury hearing his case believed his argument, and Caffrey was found not guilty of the cracking charges ("Hacker Suspect Says," 2003).

Cummings, Edward E. (a.k.a. Bernie S.) (1963–)

Modern-day phreaker and writer Edward E. Cummings, a correspondent for *2600: The Hacker Quarterly,* whose notoriety stemmed from a case that was widely publicized on the *2600* Web site, was sent to federal prison in 1995 for his phreaking exploits, the first person to be imprisoned without bail. Charged under a little known attachment to the Digital Telephony bill, Cummings was imprisoned for using a modified Radio Shack speed dialer to make free telephone calls using public telephones. Cummings, who has his own cult following in the hacker community, says that what he did was not criminal activity, as the tones and information in his possession at the time of arrest were very easy to obtain. While imprisoned, Cummings was severely beaten by another inmate. A description of Cummings's misfortunes and his thoughts on the bad publicity given to hackers can be found in the 2002 book *The Hacking of America: Who's Doing It, Why, and How* (Schell, Dodge, and Moutsatsos, 2002).

Denning, Dorothy (1945–)

Dr. Dorothy Denning is a professor in the Department of Defense Analysis at the Naval Postgraduate School. She previously taught at Georgetown University, where she was the Callahan Family Professor of computer science and the director of the Georgetown Institute of Information Assurance. Dr. Denning has published more than 100 articles and four books on terrorism and crime, conflict and cyberspace, information warfare and security, and cryptography. Her most recent book is called *Information Warfare and Security.* Well known for her expert testimony before the Special Oversight Panel on Terrorism in 2000, Dr. Denning has recently written a piece entitled, "Is Cyber Terror Next?" in the 2002 book *Understanding September 11.* She is the recipient of several awards, including the Augusta Ada Lovelace Award and the National Computer Systems Security Award ("Dorothy Denning," 2003).

Draper, John (a.k.a. Cap'n Crunch) (1945–)

John Draper, a phone phreaker, figured out how to make free telephone calls using a whistle found in Cap'n Crunch cereal. The whistle could produce a tone with the same frequency as the note that AT&T and other long-distance phone companies used at that time to indicate that long-distance phone lines were available. If either phone that was party to a call emitted this tone, the switch controlling the call would be fooled into thinking that the call had ended, and all billing for the call would stop.

Eventually, the authorities tracked down Draper, and he was convicted under Title 18, Section 1343 of the Criminal Code: fraud by wire. While he was serving time in federal prison, he was allowed to continue his computer programming. After Draper's release from prison, Steve Wozniak asked him to apply his talents to writing a word processing program for Wozniak's Apple II computer. The program, "Easy Writer," was eventually sold by IBM with their PCs. Today, Draper has his own security firm and is a book author. He has also recently developed Crunchbox, a firewall system that stops the spread of computer viruses (Webcrunchers International, 2003; "John Draper," 2003).

Gorman, Sean (1974–)

In July 2003, Sean Gorman made media headlines because he produced for his doctoral dissertation in public policy a set of charts detailing the communication networks binding the United States together. Gorman, a George Mason University graduate student, mapped every business and industrial sector in the United States and layered on top the fiber optic network that connected them. These charts were, essentially, treasure maps for terrorists wanting to destroy the United States economy. Using mathematical formulas, Gorman probed for critical links in an attempt to answer the question, "If I were Osama bin Laden, where would I want to attack?" After graduation, Gorman went on to brief government officials and private sector CEOs on the vulnerabilities of the American economy, particularly those involved in national security (Blumenfeld, 2003).

Jobs, Steve (1955–)

After studying physics, literature, and poetry at Reed College in Portland, Oregon, Steve Jobs sold his Volkswagen minibus in 1976 for the money to help start a company. Jobs, along with Steve Wozniak, started Apple Computer, Inc. They took the company public in 1980 at $22 per share, and in 1984, they reinvented the personal computer with the Macintosh. From 1986 through 1997, Jobs founded and ran NeXT Software Inc., a company that created hardware to exploit the full potential of object-oriented technologies (that deal with modeling aspects of the real world through computer programming). He sold the company to Apple in 1997.

In 1986, Jobs discovered and bought an animation company called Pixar Animation Studios. This company became the creator and producer of many of the top-grossing animated films of all time. These films have included *Toy Story, A Bug's Life, Toy Story 2,* and *Monsters, Inc.* Jobs was still involved with Pixar as of 2003. Since 1997, he has helped Apple Computer, Inc., create such products as iMac, iBook, iMovie, and iPod. He was also part of the team that positioned Apple to venture onto the Internet (Jobs, 2003).

Levin, Vladimir (1971–)

A graduate of St. Petersburg Technology University in Russia, mathematician Vladimir Levin allegedly masterminded the Russian cracker gang that tricked Citibank's computers into relinquishing US$10 million. He used a laptop computer in London, England, to access the Citibank network, and then obtained a list of customer codes and passwords. Then he logged on 18 times over a period of several weeks and transferred the money through wire transfers to accounts his group controlled in the United States, Finland, the Netherlands, Germany, and Israel. He was arrested by Interpol at Heathrow Airport in 1995 and was sentenced to 3 years in prison in the United States. He was also ordered to pay back more than $240,000 to Citibank—his share of the stolen money. Since this incident, Citibank has begun using the dynamic encryption card, an extremely tight security system possessed by other financial institutions in the world ("Vladimir Levin," 2003).

Mafiaboy (1985–)

Mafiaboy was involved in the most famous cracking attack in Canada's history. In February 2000, the high-profile case of this cracker (his identity was not disclosed because he was only 15 years old) raised concerns about Internet security. Mafiaboy pleaded guilty on January 18, 2001, to charges that he broke into Internet servers and used them to launch costly denial-of-service attacks on several high-profile Web sites, including Amazon.com, eBay.com, and Yahoo.com. In September 2001, the judge hearing the case sentenced him to 8 months in a youth detention center, ordered him to face 1 year of probation afterward, and fined him $250 (Schell, Dodge, and Moutsatsos, 2002).

Mitnick, Kevin (a.k.a. Condor) (1963–)

Once one of the Federal Bureau of Investigation's most wanted criminals and a past colleague of female cracker Susan Thunder, Kevin David Mitnick was put on probation in 1989 for a cracking offense. In 1992, Mitnick violated the terms of his probation and then went into hiding for almost 3 years. During this time, Mitnick cracked into computers, stole corporate secrets, scrambled telephone networks, and broke into the national defense warning system. In February 1995, Tsutomu Shimomura helped the FBI track him down. He was imprisoned in February 1995 on a 25-count indictment that included charges of wire fraud and illegal possession of computer files stolen from such companies as Nokia, Motorola, and Sun Microsystems. Mitnick was released from prison in January 2000 and now runs a computer security firm. His book, *The Art of Deception: Controlling the Human Element of Security,* is a top seller (tangINAyan, 2003a).

Morris, Robert (a.k.a. rtm) (1966–)

Robert Morris became known to the world when, in 1988, as a graduate student at Cornell University, he accidentally unleashed an Internet worm that he had developed, which infected and subsequently crashed thousands of computers. The son of the chief scientist at the National Computer Security Center, Morris introduced the word "cracker" into the vernacular with this incident. When the United States Secret Service raided the home of Erik

Bloodaxe (a Legion of Doom hacker) in 1990, they found a copy of the source code for Morris's Internet worm (tangINAyan, 2003b).

Poulsen, Kevin (a.k.a. Dark Dante) (1966–)

Kevin Poulsen's notoriety was the result of his taking over all of the telephone lines going into Los Angeles radio station KIIS-FM, ensuring that he would be the 102nd caller and win a Porsche 944 S2. During the investigation of the crime by the FBI, Poulsen went into hiding. Following a feature about the crime on a television episode of *Unsolved Mysteries,* Poulsen was arrested and spent 3 years in jail. Like many crackers after their release from prison, he was not legally permitted to use a computer for 3 years. A self-proclaimed "reformed and penitent" journalist, he went on to serve as editorial director for the SecurityFocus Web site ("Kevin Poulsen," 2003).

On November 23, 2003, one of his articles on the SecurityFocus Web site dealt with exploit code (software that makes use of vulnerabilities in computer systems). Poulsen's piece began: "Security pros gathering at a Stanford University Law School conference on responsible vulnerability disclosure on Saturday harmonized on the principle that vendors should be privately notified of holes in their products, and given at least some time to produce a patch before any public disclosure is made. But there was pronounced disagreement on the question of whether or not researchers should publicly release proof-of-concept code to demonstrate a vulnerability." Network defenders sometimes use proof-of-concept code to evaluate techniques to prevent a compromise, to help detect exploitation of a new vulnerability, and to test that a patch actually works (Poulsen, 2003). This stance seems to be a significant change from Poulsen's opinions in his youth.

Raymond, Eric Steven (1957–)

Eric Steven Raymond, annoyed by the fact that media people and the general population mistakenly used the word *hacker* when they really should use the word *cracker,* wrote *The Hacker's Dictionary* and *How to Become a Hacker.* He says that hackers build things, and crackers break them. Raymond's home page at www.catb.org notes, "As a public service and act of civil disobedience, we are proud to offer the DeCSS code that will allow you to circumvent the encryption on the DVDs you own." This DeCSS code was the subject of a controversy involving *2600: The Hacker Quarterly* and the Digital Millennium Copyright Act (see chapter 2). In 1998, Raymond cofounded (and has since served as president of) the Open Source Initiative, an educational organization that promotes cooperation between the hacker community and businesses, with the aim of spreading the open source development method (Raymond, 2003).

Ritchie, Dennis (a.k.a. dmr) (1941–)

Dennis Ritchie and his colleague Ken Thompson were the driving force behind Bell Laboratory's computer science operating group. There, in 1969, this White Hat team created UNIX—an open operating system for minicomputers. Not only did UNIX help users with general computing, word processing, and networking, but it also soon became a standard computer language. Although Ritchie is the author of the popular C programming language, he cites his favorite language as being Alef. As of 2003, Ritchie was the head of Lucent Technology's System Software Research Department ("Dennis Ritchie and Ken Thompson," 2003).

Shimomura, Tsutomu (1966–)

The author of the book *Takedown,* Tsutomu Shimomura is best known for tracking down and outsmarting Kevin Mitnick, the most wanted cracker in the United States, in the early 1990s. In December 1994, after his colleagues at the San Diego Supercomputing Center told Shimomura that someone had stolen hundreds of software programs and files from his work station, Shimomura went about searching for the perpetrator. He eventually led the Federal Bureau of Investigation, in February 1995, to an apartment complex in Raleigh, North Carolina, where they found and apprehended Kevin Mitnick. Tsutomu Shimomura still works for San Diego Supercomputer as a research fellow, and he has served as a consultant to the FBI, the Air Force, and the United States National Security Agency (NSA) ("Tsutomu Shimomura," 2003; Schell, Dodge, and Moutsatsos, 2002).

Sklyarov, Dmitry (1947–)

The July 2001 copyright infringement case of Russian Dmitry Sklyarov made headlines. Sklyarov was arrested at the DefCon 9 hacker convention in Las Vegas after giving a speech on a software package that he had developed for his Russian employer, Elcomsoft. The software allowed users to convert the copy-protected Adobe eBook file format to the more commonly used—and freely copyable—PDF computer files. United States federal agents labeled Sklyarov a cybercriminal who violated the Digital Millennium Copyright Act because his software allowed users to foil copyright protections put in place by eBook publishers. Immediately, the San Francisco-based advocacy group Electronic Frontier Foundation (EFF) lobbied heavily against his conviction, saying that jurisdictional issues applied and that Skylarov's activities were perfectly legal in Russia. In December 2002, both Sklyarov and his employer, Elcomsoft Co. Ltd., were cleared of any wrongdoing by the courts (Glasner, 2002).

Stallman, Richard (1953–)

The recipient of a $240,000 MacArthur Foundation genius grant, Richard Stallman is a White Hat who, as an undergraduate student at Harvard University, walked in with no prior arrangements and got a job at the prestigious MIT Artificial Intelligence Laboratory in 1971. Stallman is the founder of the GNU Project (an acronym for Gnu's Not Unix), launched in 1984 to develop the free operating system GNU. Because GNU is free software, everyone is free to copy it, redistribute it, and make changes to it—either large or small. Today, Linux-based variants of the GNU system, based on the kernel (or heart of an operating system) Linux (developed by Linus Torvald), are widely used.

In 1991, Stallman received the Grace Hopper award from the Association for Computing Machinery for his development in 1975 of the first Emacs text editor while he was employed at the MIT AI Lab. He has just released his latest book, *Free Software, Free Society: Selected Essays* (Stallman, 2003).

Thompson, Ken (1943–)

Ken Thompson and his colleague Dennis Ritchie were the driving force behind Bell Laboratory's computer science operating group. In 1969, this White Hat team at Bell created UNIX—an open operating system for minicomputers. UNIX helped users with general computing, word processing, and networking, and it soon became a standard computer language as well. Plan 9, a new operating system, was created as a descendant of UNIX by Thompson and a White Hat Bell Laboratory colleague, Rob Pike ("Dennis Ritchie and Ken Thompson," 2003). Thompson has since retired.

In 1984 when he was presented with the Association for Computing Machinery award, Thompson said: "You can't trust code that you did not totally create yourself." He went on to remark, "I have watched kids testifying before Congress. It is clear that they are completely unaware of the seriousness of their acts. There is obviously a cultural gap. The act of breaking into a computer system has to have the same social stigma as breaking into a neighbor's house. It should not matter that the neighbor's door is unlocked. The press must learn that misguided use of a computer is no more amazing than drunk driving of an automobile" (Thompson, 1995).

Wozniak, Steve (a.k.a. Oak Toebark, a.k.a. Woz) (1950–)

Born in 1950, Steve Wozniak got his ham radio license in grade 6 and later went on to receive a number of mathematics, science, and electronics awards. He graduated from the University of California at Berkeley in 1972. Wozniak and his friend Steve Jobs helped shape the computing industry; Wozniak's design of Apple's first line of products, the Apple I and II, influenced the later development of the popular Macintosh computer. For his achievements at Apple Computer, Wozniak was awarded the National Medal of Technology by the president of the United States in 1985. Wozniak convinced convicted phreaker John Draper to write the Easy Writer word processor program.

In 2000, Wozniak was inducted into the Inventors Hall of Fame and received the Heinz Award for Technology, the Economy, and Employment. Wozniak is co-founder of Apple Computer and founder of the Electronic Frontier Foundation and the

Children's Discovery Museum of San Jose. He serves on the board of directors for Jacent, a developer of telephony solutions, and for Danger, Inc., a developer of a wireless Internet platform; he also continues to do work for Apple (Wozniak, 2003).

References

Blumenfeld, L. 2003. "Student's 'Tedious' Thesis Is Terrorist's Treasure Map." *Toronto Star*, July 9, p. A3.

Denning, Dorothy. 1998. *Information Warfare and Security*. Reading, MA: Addison-Wesley.

———. 2002. "Is Cyber Terror Next?" In Craig Calhoun, Paul Price, and Ashley Timmer, eds. *Understanding September 11*. New York: New Press.

"Dennis Ritchie and Ken Thompson." 2003. http://tlc.discovery.com/convergence/hackers/bio/bio_02.html (cited November 19, 2003).

"Dorothy Denning." 2003. http://www.nps.navy.mil/ctiw/staff/denning.html (cited December 1, 2003).

Glasner, J. 2002. "Jury Finds Elcomsoft Not Guilty." *Wired News*. http://www.wired.com/news/business/0,1367,56894,00.html (cited December 17, 2002).

"Hacker Suspect Says His PC Was Hijacked." 2003. Asian School of Cyber Laws. http://www.asianlaws.org/infosec/archives/10_03_hacker.htm (cited October 10, 2003).

Jobs, S. 2003. "Resume." http://homepage.mac.com/steve/Resume.html (cited December 1, 2003).

"John Draper." 2003. http://tlc.discovery.com/convergence/hackers/bio/bio_03.html (cited November 19, 2003).

"Kevin Poulsen." 2003. http://tlc.discovery.com/convergence/hackers/bio/bio_07.html (cited November 19, 2003).

"Mark Abene." 2003. http://tlc.discovery.com/convergence/hackers/bio/bio_04.html (cited November 19, 2003).

"Mark Abene." 2003. http://www.Livinginternet.com/i/ia_hackers_abene.htm (cited November 21, 2003).

Poulsen, K. 2003. "SecurityFocus News: Exploit Code on Trial." http://www.securityfocus.com/news/7511 (cited December 1, 2003).

Raymond, Eric Steven. 1996. *The Hacker's Dictionary*. Cambridge, MA: MIT Press.

———. 2001. *How to Become a Hacker*. http://www.catb.org/~esr/faqs/hacker-howto.html.

———. 2003. "Resume of Eric Steven Raymond." http://www.catb.org/~esr/ (cited December 1, 2003).

Schell, B. H., J. L. Dodge, and S. Moutsatsos. 2002. *The Hacking of America: Who's Doing It, Why, and How.* Westport, CT: Quorum.

Shimomura, Tsutomu, and John Markoff. 1996. *Takedown: The Pursuit and Capture of Kevin Mitnick, America's Most Wanted Computer Outlaw—By the Man Who Did It.* New York: Hyperion.

Stallman, Richard. 2002. *Free Software, Free Society: Selected Essays by Richard Stallman.* Boston: Free Software Foundation

———. 2003. "Personal Home Page." http://www.stallman.org/ (cited November 20, 2003).

TangINAyan (real name unknown). 2003a. "Greatest Hackers in the Whole World: Legendary Computer Hacker Released from Prison." http://www.geocities.com/Vienna/4345/Hacking_News.htm (cited January 21, 2003).

———. 2003b. "Greatest Hackers in the Whole World: Robert Morris." http://www.geocities.com/vienna/4345/robert.htm (cited December 1, 2003).

Thompson, K. 1995. "September 1995 Classic of the Month: Reflections on Trusting Trust." http://www.acm.org/classics/sep95/ (cited September 5, 1995).

"Tsutomu Shimomura." 2003. http://tlc.discovery.com/convergence/hackers/bio/bio_11.html (cited November 19, 2003).

"Vladimir Levin." 2003. http://tlc.discovery.com/convergence/hackers/bio/bio_09.html (cited November 19, 2003).

Webcrunchers International. 2003. "The Story So Far." http://www.webcrunchers.com/crunch/story.html (cited November, 2003).

Wozniak, S. 2003 "Short Bio for Steve Wozniak." http://www.woz.org./wozscape/wozbio.html (cited December 1, 2003).

5

Cybercrime Legal Cases

This chapter discusses newsworthy cybercrime cases prosecuted in the United States under the computer crime statute 18 U.S.C. section 1030. In the United States, the primary federal statute criminalizing cracking was originally the Computer Fraud and Abuse Act (CFAA). It was modified in 1996 by the National Information Infrastructure Protection Act and codified at 18 U.S.C. subsection 1030, Fraud and Related Activity in Connection with Computers.

As previously noted in this book, after the World Trade Center terrorist attacks on September 11, 2001, the U.S. government passed a series of laws aimed to halt computer criminals as well as terrorists. The first part of this chapter summarizes the U.S. legislation aimed at fighting terrorism and cybercrime since September 11, 2001, and cites the particulars. The second part of this chapter describes trends in cybercrime in recent years. The third and largest part of the chapter describes cases prosecuted in the United States under the computer crime statute 18 U.S.C. section 1030.

Summary of Legislation

As of this writing (2004), the following statutes pertain to cybercrime in the United States under 18 U.S.C.:

- Section 1029: Fraud and Related Activity in Connection with Access Devices

- Section 1030: Fraud and Related Activity in Connection with Computers
- Section 1362: Communication Lines, Stations, or Systems
- Section 2510: Wire and Electronic Communications Interception and Interception of Oral Communications
- Section 2512: Manufacture, Distribution, Possession, and Advertising of Wire, Oral, or Electronic Communication Intercepting Devices Prohibited
- Section 2517: Authorization for Disclosure and Use of Intercepted Wire, Oral, or Electronic Communications
- Section 2520: Recovery of Civil Damages Authorized
- Section 2701: Unlawful Access to Store Communications
- Section 2702: Voluntary Disclosure of Customer Communications or Records
- Section 2703: Required Disclosure of Customer Communications or Records
- Section 3121: Recording of Dialing, Routing, Addressing, and Signaling Information
- Section 3125: Emergency Pen Register and Trap and Trace Device Installation

On October 26, 2001, the USA PATRIOT (Uniting and Strengthening America by Providing Appropriate Tools Required to Intercept and Obstruct Terrorism) Act was enacted into law. Within the PATRIOT Act of 2001, several laws relating to computer crime and electronic evidence were amended, and the U.S. government is considering more changes under proposals known as PATRIOT Act II.

In 2002, the Homeland Security Act was passed containing section 225, known as the Cyber Security Enhancement Act of 2002. The following titles, part of the act as a whole, were included (*Homeland Security Act of 2002,* 2002):

- Title I deals with the Department of Homeland Security (DHS) and its mission and functions.
- Title II deals with information analysis and infrastructure protection.
- Title III deals with chemical, biological, radiological, and nuclear countermeasures.
- Title IV deals with border and transportation security.

- Title V deals with emergency preparedness and response.
- Title VI deals with the internal management of the DHS.
- Title VII deals with general provisions and coordinating with nonfederal entities, the Inspector General, and the U.S. Secret Service.
- Title VIII deals with transitional items.
- Title IX deals with conforming and other technical amendments.

U.S. legislation in 2003 included the Prosecutorial Remedies and Tools against the Exploitation of Children Today Act (PROTECT Act)—legislation aimed at child pornographers. In February 2003, this piece of legislation was passed by the U.S. Senate by a vote of 84–0. Its intent was to assist law enforcement agents in their efforts to track and identify pedophiles using the Internet. It was also intended to permit the use of relevant images and graphics in prosecuting such cases. It is seen as a response to the April 16, 2002, Supreme Court decision that overturned most of the Child Pornography Prevention Act of 1966 (known as the CPPA). That case was *Ashcroft v. Free Speech Coalition* (00–795), 198F.3d 1083.

Also in 2003, the Can Spam Act was passed by the United States Senate on November 25 and was aimed at commercial e-mailers and spammers. The bill was signed by President Bush on December 16, 2003, and took effect on January 1, 2004. Its longer title was the Controlling the Assault of Non-Solicited Pornography and Marketing Act of 2003, a title that accurately reflects its purpose.

As of 2003, the Congress found that unsolicited commercial e-mail was estimated to account for more than one-half of all electronic mail traffic, up from an estimated 7 percent in 2001. Worse, Congress has noted that the volume of spam continues to rise—and that most of these messages are fraudulent or deceptive in one or more ways. It was for these important reasons that the Can Spam Act of 2003 was passed. Under the Act, chapter 47 of title 18, United States Code, was amended at the end of new section 1037, Fraud and Related Activity in Connection with Electronic Mail.

Offenders under the Can Spam Act are those being in or affecting interstate or foreign commerce who knowingly:

- Access a protected computer without authorization and intentionally initiate the transmission of multiple commercial e-mail messages from or through that computer

- Use a protected computer to relay or retransmit multiple commercial e-mail messages to deceive or mislead recipients or any Internet access service as to the origin of such e-mail messages
- Falsify header information in multiple commercial e-mail messages and intentionally initiate the transmission of such messages
- Register using information that falsifies the identity of the actual registrant for five or more e-mail accounts or online user accounts or two or more domain names, and intentionally initiate the transmission of multiple commercial e-mails from any combination of such accounts or domain names
- Falsely represent oneself to be the registrant or the legitimate successor in interest to the registrant of five or more Internet protocol (IP) addresses, and intentionally initiate the transmission of multiple commercial e-mail messages from such addresses

The punishment for an offense under the Can Spam Act is a fine, imprisonment for not more than 5 years, or both. The Can Spam Act is enforced by the Federal Trade Commission (FTC). Unique to this Act, within 6 months of the date of its enactment, the FTC transmitted to the Senate Committee on Commerce, Science, and Transportation and to the House of Representatives Committee on Energy and Commerce a report that set forth a plan and a timetable for establishing a nationwide marketing Do-Not-E-Mail registry ("The Can-Spam Act," 2004).

Other countries have enacted similar anti-intrusion legislation. For example, section 342.1 of the Canadian Criminal Code is aimed at several potential harms, including theft of computer services, invasion of privacy, and persons who trade in computer passwords or who crack encryption systems. Charges for violations are typically made pertaining to the sections of the Criminal Code dealing with theft, fraud, computer abuse, data abuse, and the interception of communications.

Trends and Observations in Cybercrime

Cybercriminals Tend to Be Male

The number of women is small, compared to the number of men, among those employed in the computer work world, involved in the computer underground, and caught and convicted for cybercrime.

For example, in a September 2003 study reported on the CNNmoney Web site, almost two-thirds of Americans with Internet access have at least one digital music file on their computers, but most downloaded music is held by a relatively small group of users. According to a study conducted by the NPD Group, a consumer research firm that tracks computer use online by about 40,000 computer users, only 8 percent of downloaders have more than 1,000 music files on their computers. But those large users apparently account for about 56 percent of an estimated 11.1 billion downloaded files, say the researchers. Moreover, the average number of music files held by heavy users is 2,300 songs. Apparently this typical active music downloader is young and male. NPD found that nearly 28 percent of active music downloaders are males age 18 to 25, and another 15 percent are teenaged boys age 13 to 17. Girls and women from the ages of 13 to 25 apparently make up only 18 percent of active music downloaders, but only about one in five downloaders is older than 36, and less than 5 percent are older than 50 (CNNmoney, 2003)

Another gender trend of note is that, of the women currently employed in the wired world, most say that they would leave if they had other career options. A 2001 survey of women in information technology fields conducted by the accounting firm Deloitte & Touche found that three of every five women in IT would choose another profession if they could. The reason given for this is a perceived glass ceiling. The women surveyed said that they were perceived to be less knowledgeable and qualified than the men that they worked with (Lancaster, 2001). This is in spite of the fact that, as shown in chapter 3, some of the innovators of the cyberworld have been female.

Cybercrime Could Move from Cyberspace to Outer Space

Some academics feel that cybercrime may, literally, move from cyberspace to outer space. For example, Leonard David, a space journalist, says, "Could a signal from the stars broadcast by an alien intelligence also carry harmful information, in the spirit of a computer virus? Could star folk launch a 'disinformation campaign'—one that covers up aspects of their culture?" (Kesterton, 2003, p. A24). These concerns deserve attention, says Richard Carrigan, Jr., physicist at the Fermi National Accelerator Laboratory in Batavia, Illinois. Those engaged in the Search for Extraterrestrial Intelligence (SETI), he maintains, should exercise caution when handling SETI downloads. He contends that we should think about decontaminating potential SETI signals for risk of computer-like viruses (David, 2003).

Computer Crime Cases

According to the United States Department of Justice, the following is a timeline of representative cybercrime headlines associated with individuals charged and convicted under the United States Computer Crime Statute, U.S.C. section 1030. To the right of each sample press release caption is the legal case citation from the U.S. Department of Justice website (http://www.usdoj.gov/criminal/cybercrime/cccases.html, 2004). These particular cases are presented chronologically. They are intended to provide an understanding of the kinds of cybercrime cases that have been successfully tried since 1998.

Note that this is a representative rather than a comprehensive list of legal cases for the past 6 years on the U.S. Department of Justice website. The site is updated on a regular basis and is in the public domain. The citing of these cases illustrates the types of cybercrime that are detected, tried, and prosecuted in the United States. Some of the more interesting cases described below were earlier discussed in this book.

1998

Eugene E. Kashpureff Pleaded Guilty to Unleashing Software on the Internet that Interrupted Service for Tens of Thousands of Internet Users

Worldwide (March 19, 1998) [*United States v. Kashpureff*] Eugene E. Kashpureff, the owner of AlterNIC, a Washington State–based commercial registration service for Internet domain names, was charged with computer fraud. Kashpureff admitted that on two occasions in July 1997, he released software on the Internet that interrupted service for tens of thousands of Internet users worldwide. Kashpureff, a self-described "webslinger," diverted Internet users attempting to reach the Web site for InterNIC, his chief commercial competitor, to his AlterNIC Web site, impeding those users' ability to register Web site domain names or to review InterNIC's popular electronic directory for existing domain names. Kashpureff worked to perfect this DNS corruption over a 1-year period, under the name Operation DNS Storm.

After launching his Internet attacks, Kashpureff boasted to the media about the effects of his scheme, claiming that he could divert all communications destined for China, the 100 most visited Web sites in the world, and the White House Web site. His crimes carry a maximum sentence of 5 years in prison and a maximum fine of $250,000.

Israeli Citizen Arrested in Israel for Hacking United States and Israeli Government Computers (March 18, 1998) [*United States v. Tenebaum*] The Israeli National Police arrested Ehud Tenebaum, an Israeli citizen, for illegally accessing computers belonging to the Israeli and United States governments, as well as for accessing computers at hundreds of other commercial and educational systems in the United States and elsewhere. The arrest of Tenebaum culminated several weeks of investigation into a series of computer intrusions into United States military systems that occurred in February 1998. As part of this investigation, the Department of Justice worked in cooperation with the Israeli Ministry of Justice, and the prompt arrest of Tenebaum demonstrated the effectiveness of international cooperation in cases involving transnational criminal conduct. Although the intrusions into United States military computers were treated as serious incidents, no classified information was ever compromised, and there has been no indication that the attacks were part of an organized military or state-sponsored campaign against the United States.

Juvenile Computer Hacker Cuts off FAA Tower at Regional Airport—First Federal Charges Brought against a Juvenile for Computer Crime (March 18, 1998) [*United States v. Unnamed Juvenile*] As a result of a series of commands sent from a cracker's personal computer, vital services to an FAA control tower were disabled for 6 hours in March 1997. The defendant also broke into a pharmacy computer and copied patient records. There was no evidence that he altered prescriptions or disseminated the information. These charges were the first ever to be brought against a juvenile by the federal government for commission of a computer crime. In accordance with federal law, the juvenile was not publicly named. It was alleged that the defendant temporarily disabled Next Generation digital loop carrier systems operated by Nynex at the Worcester Airport and in the community of Rutland, Massachusetts.

Loop carrier systems are programmable remote computers used to integrate voice and data communications for efficient transmission over a single, sophisticated fiber optic cable; in many respects, they serve the same function as a circuit breaker box in a home or an apartment.

The juvenile computer cracker identified the telephone numbers for the modems connected to the loop carrier systems providing service to the airport and the community, and on March 10, 1997, he accessed and disabled both in sequence. Public health and safety were threatened by the outage, which resulted in the loss of telephone service from 9:00 A.M. until approximately 3:30 P.M. to the FAA tower at the Worcester Airport, to the Worcester Airport Fire Department, and to other related services such as airport security, weather service, various private air freight companies, the main radio transmitter connected to the tower, and a circuit enabling aircraft to send an electric signal to activate airport runway lights on approach. The motive of the juvenile for his crimes are unknown.

1999

"Darkside Hacker" Pleads Guilty in Federal Court after Stealing National Internet Company Passwords (December 20, 1999) [*United States v. Miffleton*] Andrew Miffleton pleaded guilty in federal court to a charge of possession of unauthorized access devices. Miffleton, age 24, of Arlington, Texas, faced a maximum punishment of 10 years' imprisonment and a $250,000 fine. Miffleton had been associated with a group known as the Darkside Hackers, consisting of people with a very high level of computer knowledge and skill. The goal of the group members was accessing computer systems without authorization; they were also interested in using unauthorized access devices to fraudulently ob-

tain cellular telephone service through cloned cellular telephones or to obtain long-distance telephone service through stolen calling card numbers.

From May 1998 to February 1999, Miffleton, using the computer moniker Daphtpunk, hosted a Web page for the Darkside Hackers on his computer at his residence. In February 1999, Miffleton obtained, with the intent to defraud, a list of computer passwords from a national Internet company. This list contained root-level passwords that afforded the user complete control over a computer system. He gave these passwords to other members of the Darkside Hackers; he and others then used these passwords to access computer systems throughout the country without authorization. Miffleton's conduct resulted in a $90,000 loss to the Internet company. Miffleton also obtained the following unauthorized access devices with the intent to defraud their providers: approximately forty individual user-level passwords for an Internet service provider; approximately twenty electronic serial numbers/mobile identification number pairs for cellular telephone service; one AT&T calling card number; and approximately five credit card numbers.

Internet Service Provider Charged with Intercepting Customer Communications and Possessing Unauthorized Password Files (November 22, 1999) [*United States v. Alibris*] An Internet bookseller that also operated an Internet communications service was charged in federal court with intercepting electronic communications and with unauthorized possession of password files. Alibris, headquartered in Emeryville, California, was charged with ten counts of unlawful interception of e-mail and one count of unauthorized possession of passwords with intent to defraud. Alibris's corporate predecessor, Interloc, Inc., was an online bookseller that provided e-mail service to its book dealers and also operated a business called Valinet, which provided Internet service in the Greenfield, Massachusetts, area.

For periods of time between January and June 1998, Alibris allegedly intercepted e-mail messages directed by online bookseller Amazon.com to Alibris bookseller clients who had Interloc e-mail addresses. This interception was done, in part, to gain competitive advantage for Alibris by compiling a database of dealers' purchases and analyzing the bookselling market. In January 1998, Alibris altered its e-mail service so that it automatically intercepted and stored e-mail sent from Amazon.com to Alibris's customers. In a matter of weeks, Alibris allegedly intercepted and copied thousands of e-mail communications to which it was not a party and was not entitled. It was also alleged that Alibris obtained and retained unauthorized copies of the confidential and proprietary password files and customer lists of its competitor Internet service providers.

"Web Bandit" Sentenced to 15 Months' Imprisonment, 3 Years of Supervised Release, for Hacking USIA, NATO, Web Sites (November 19, 1999) [*United States v. Burns*] Eric Burns, age 19, a resident of Shoreline, Washington, who used the hacker handle (or screen name) ZYKLON, was sentenced to 15 months' imprisonment and 3 years of supervised release and was ordered to pay $36,240 in restitution. Burns pleaded guilty on September 7, 1999, to intentionally cracking into and damaging computers in Virginia, Washington state, Washington, D.C., and London, including computers hosting Web pages for the United States Information Agency and NATO, as well as the U.S. vice president's Web page. Burns also admitted that he had advised others on how to crack into computers at the White House in May 1999.

Burns designed a program he called Web Bandit to identify computers on the Internet that were vulnerable to attack. Using that program, he found that the computer server at Electric Press in Reston, Virginia (which hosted the Web pages for USIA, NATO, and the vice president) was vulnerable. Between August 1998 and January 1999, Burns hacked into the Electric Press server four times; these attacks affected the U.S. Embassy and Consulate Web sites, as well as others dependent on USIA for information. On one occasion, Burns made thousands of pages of information unavailable and caused the closing down of the USIA Web site for 8 days.

Burns also attacked the Web pages of approximately 80 businesses whose pages were hosted by Laser.Net in Fairfax, Virginia; the Web pages of two corporate clients of Issue Dynamics in Virginia and Washington, D.C.; the Web page of the University of Washington; the Web servers of the Virginia Higher Education Council in Richmond, Virginia; and an Internet service provider in London, England. The defendant usually replaced the attacked Web pages with his own, which often contained references to himself as ZYKLON and to his love for a woman named CRYSTAL. In May 1999, the White House Web server was attacked, and there was an attempt to replace the White House's Web site with a page that had references to ZYKLON and CRYSTAL. The White House was alerted to the attempt and had to shut down its Web server, disconnect both the public and private computer networks from the Internet for 2 days, and reconfigure the computer system. Although Burns took credit during Internet chat sessions for the attack, both before and after it was discovered, he told the court that he had simply provided advice to others about how to do it. Burns admitted, however, that his intrusions had caused damages exceeding $40,000.

"Phone Masters" Ringleaders Sentenced to Prison; 41-Month and Two-Year Terms to be Served by Telecommunications Hackers (September 16, 1999) [*United States v. Lindsly*] Corey Lindsly and Calvin Cantrell were sentenced for cracking into computer systems belonging to Sprint Corporation, Southwestern Bell, and GTE and for illegally obtaining long-distance calling card numbers and selling them. Lindsly, age 32, of Portland, Oregon, was sentenced to 41 months' imprisonment and ordered to pay $10,000 to the victim corporations. Calvin Cantrell, age 30, of Grand Prairie, Texas, was sentenced to 2 years' imprisonment and also ordered to pay $10,000 to the victim corporations. Both defendants pleaded guilty to charges of criminal fraud and related activity.

Lindsly and Cantrell were the ringleaders in a computer organization known as the Phone Masters, whose ultimate goal was to own the telecommunications infrastructure from coast to coast. In addition to the numerous telecommunications systems that they penetrated, the group also penetrated computer systems owned by credit reporting agencies, utility providers, and state and federal government agencies, including the National Crime Information Center (NCIC). These perpetrators organized their assaults on the computers through teleconferencing and utilized the encryption program PGP (Pretty Good Privacy) to hide data they traded with each other.

Kevin Mitnick Sentenced to Nearly Four Years in Prison; Computer Hacker Ordered to Pay Restitution to Victim Companies Whose Systems Were Compromised (August 9, 1999) [*United States v. Mitnick*] Kevin Mitnick, who pleaded guilty to a series of federal offenses related to a 2.5 year computer cracking spree, was sentenced in March 1999 to 46 months in federal prison. Mitnick, age 37, pleaded guilty to wire fraud, computer fraud, and illegally intercepting a wire communication. His active and damaging cracking career, which made him the most wanted computer criminal in United States history, ended when he was arrested in North Carolina in February 1995. Mitnick admitted breaking into a number of computer systems and stealing proprietary software belonging to Motorola, Novell, Fujitsu, Sun Microsystems, and other companies by using social engineering, cloned cellular telephones, sniffer programs, and cracker software programs. Mitnick acknowledged altering University of Southern California computer systems and using them to store programs that he had misappropriated; he also admitted stealing e-mails, monitoring computer systems, and impersonating employees of companies including Nokia Mobile Phones, Ltd., in an attempt to secure software that was being developed by those companies.

Mitnick had been previously sentenced to an additional 22 months in prison for possessing cloned cellular phones and for violating the terms of his supervised release after being convicted of an unrelated computer fraud charge in 1989. He violated the terms of his supervised release by cracking into Pacific Bell's voice mail and other systems and by associating with known computer crackers, including codefendant Lewis De Payne. Although Mitnick's victims allegedly suffered millions of dollars in damages, Mitnick was only ordered to pay just over $4,125. This nominal restitution amount was based on the court's determination that Mitnick would have limited earnings in the future. Additionally, Mitnick agreed that any profits he made on films or books based on his criminal activity would be assigned to the victims of his crimes for a period of 7 years following his release from prison.

Lewis De Payne, 39, who was charged along with Mitnick in the scheme to obtain proprietary software, had previously pleaded guilty to a federal wire fraud charge for attempting to obtain software from a cellular phone company.

2000

Juvenile Computer Hacker Sentenced to Six Months in Detention Facility (September 21, 2000) [*United States v. "Comrade"*] A 16-year-old from Miami pleaded guilty in this case and was sentenced to 6 months in a detention facility for intercepting electronic communications on military computer networks and for illegally obtaining information from NASA computer networks. Under statutes that apply to adults, these acts would have been violations of the Federal Wiretap Act and computer abuse laws. The juvenile, who was known on the Internet as "c0mrade," admitted that he was responsible for computer intrusions from August 23 to October 27, 1999, into a military computer network used by the Defense Threat Reduction Agency (DTRA), an agency of the Department of Defense charged with reducing the threat to the United States and its allies from nuclear, biological, chemical, and conventional weapons. He also admitted gaining unauthorized access to a computer server known as a router and installing a concealed means of access, or back door, on the server. This program intercepted more than 3,300 electronic messages to and from DTRA staff. It also intercepted at least nineteen user names and passwords for computer accounts of DTRA employees, including at least ten user names and passwords on military computers. The motive of this juvenile is unknown.

Chad Davis, "Global Hell" Hacker, Sentenced to Six Months in Prison, Three Years' Probation, for Army Network Hacks (March 1, 2000) [*United States v. Davis*] Chad Davis, age 19, of De Pere, Wisconsin, was sentenced to 6 months' imprisonment and 3 years of supervised release and was ordered to pay $8,054 in restitution. Davis pleaded guilty on January 4, 2000, to intentionally cracking into the United States Army's Web page in Washington, D.C., in June 1999. When he cracked into the Army Web site, Davis left the Global Hell signature page behind, temporarily halting public access to the Army's system. Public access was restored within 2 hours. Two months earlier, Davis's apartment in De Pere, Wisconsin, had been subject to a court-authorized search by federal agents investigating Global Hell, a hacker group. After the search, Davis admitted to being a member of Global Hell and cracking into a number of other Web sites, using the hacker handle (or screen name) "minphasr."

Boston Computer Hacker Charged with Illegal Access and Use of United Stated Government and Private Systems (February 23, 2000) [*United States v. Iffih*] A Boston man was charged with using his home computer to illegally gain access to a number of computers, including those controlled by NASA and an agency of the U.S. Department of Defense. Ikenna Iffih, age 28, was charged with intentionally intercepting and attempting to intercept login names and passwords transmitted to and through a NASA computer. He was also charged with intentionally and without authorization accessing and causing significant damage to a Web site owned by Zebra Marketing Online Services (ZMOS), which was used for interstate and foreign commerce. Iffih was also charged with willful and malicious interference with a U.S. government communication system (that of the Defense Logistics Agency), and obstructing, hindering, and delaying the transmission of communications over the system.

It was alleged that Iffih also accessed various computers operated by Northeastern University, from which he illegally copied a file containing the names, dates of birth, addresses, and social security numbers of numerous men and women affiliated with the university as students, faculty, administration, or alumni. Investigators were not aware of any use or dissemination of this information. Iffih's offenses carry a maximum penalty of 10 years' incarceration and a fine of $250,000.

2001

Former Financial Institution Employee Sentenced for Unauthorized Computer Access to Customer Account Information (December 14, 2001) [*United States v. Lukawinsky*] Markus P. Lukawinsky, age 32, of La Quinta, California, was sentenced to 12 months plus 1 day in prison, to be followed by 3 years of supervised release, and was required to pay restitution in the amount of $198,458.31 to the Greenwich consulting firm of Mars & Co. He admitted that from May 1999 through January 2000, he had transported computer equipment stolen from Mars & Co. worth more than $21,500 from Greenwich, Connecticut to La Quinta, California. Also, during approximately the same time period, he unlawfully accessed the computer systems of Mars & Co. without authorization to read and delete another person's e-mail. Lukawinsky's motive for these crimes is unknown.

Lukawinsky initially accessed the Mars & Co. computer network without authorization and downloaded several encrypted password files. He then used a decryption tool to decrypt numerous usernames and passwords. Thereafter, on at least five occasions, he reconnected to the Mars & Co. network and logged in as one of the employees whose usernames and passwords he had stolen. He did not compromise any confidential or proprietary information maintained by Mars & Co. on behalf of its clients; however, the judge in the case found that Lukawinsky's actions had resulted in a total loss of more than $198,000 to Mars & Co.: the stolen computer equipment, worth approximately $21,500, plus the expenditure by Mars & Co. of more than $176,000 to assess the damage and restore its computer network (including any corrupted data).

Chardon, Ohio Woman Sentenced for Computer Fraud via Unauthorized Access of Employer's Computer System (November 26, 2001) [*United States v. Brown*] Melissa S. Brown, age 30, of Chardon, Ohio, was sentenced for a computer crime to 3 years' probation, with a special condition that the first 7 months of her probation be served in home confinement with electronic monitoring. Brown was also ordered to pay $15,346.71 in restitution to Christian & Timbers, the victim of her offense.

Brown pleaded guilty to an indictment stating that in the early morning hours on April 14, 2001, she remotely logged on to the computer system of her employer, Christian & Timbers, an executive recruitment firm located in Beachwood, Ohio, from a company laptop computer located at her home. During the session, she logged on to the company's computer using the user ID and password of a coworker, without that coworker's knowledge or authorization, and transmitted computer codes, instructions, and/or commands to change the password of the company's chief information officer, who was on vacation at the time, thus preventing the CIO from gaining access to the company computer. The victim corporation was forced to conduct a thorough analysis of their entire computer network to see if any additional damage had been done or if any data had been improperly obtained by Brown. Brown admitted that her actions therefore caused Christian & Timbers to incur losses in the amount of $15,346.71.

Former Cisco Systems, Inc., Accountants Sentenced for Unauthorized Access to Computer Systems to Illegally Issue Almost $8 Million in Cisco Stock to Themselves (November 26, 2001) [*United States v. Osowski*] Accountants Geoffrey Osowski and Wilson Tang were each sentenced to 34 months in prison for exceeding their authorized access to the computer at Cisco Systems in order to illegally issue almost $8 million in Cisco stock to themselves. Osowski, 30, and Tang, 35, were charged with computer and wire fraud. They each pleaded guilty to one count of computer fraud, each agreed to the forfeiture of assets that the government had seized from them (including stock already liquidated for $5,049,057 worth of jewelry and an automobile), and each agreed to pay restitution in the amount of the difference between $7,868,637 and the amount that the government would recover from the sale of the seized items.

Man Indicted for Hacking Computers Belonging to Public Affairs Group (October 22, 2001) [*United States v. Khan*] Misbah Khan of Karachi, Pakistan, was charged with hacking into AIPAC's

(American Israel Public Affairs Committee) computer server in Silver Spring, Maryland, on November 1, 2000. He replaced AIPAC's Web page with a page boasting that AIPAC had been "hacked by Doctor Nuker, Founder Pakistan Hackerz Club, doctornuker@puckoff.com." The unauthorized Web page contained statements attacking the country of Israel and links to other anti-Israel or pro-Palestinian Web sites. In addition, Khan took confidential computer credit card account information belonging to AIPAC members and posted the information on the unauthorized Web page and on other sites, resulting in unlawful use of the credit card accounts.

Khan was charged with transmission of a computer command to intentionally cause damage to AIPAC's computers; intentionally accessing AIPAC's computer without authorization and obtaining information from that computer; knowingly possessing fifteen or more unauthorized "access devices" (credit card account numbers) with intent to defraud; and using unauthorized access devices to obtain items of more than $1,000 in value. The two computer offenses are punishable by up to 5 years in jail, the credit card offenses are punishable by up to 10 years in jail, and all four offenses carry fines of up to $250,000 and terms of supervised release of up to 3 years. "Doctornuker" was identified as Misbah Khan by the FBI computer crime squad, with the assistance of the FBI legal office at the U.S. Embassy in Islamabad, Pakistan. Following the indictment, a warrant was issued for the arrest of the defendant; however, as of this writing, Khan was still at large.

Hacker Sentenced in New York City for Hacking into Two NASA Jet Propulsion Lab Computers Located in Pasadena, California (September 5, 2001) [*United States v. Torricelli*] Raymond Torricelli, a.k.a. "rolex," the head of a group known as #conflict, was sentenced to 4 months in prison and 4 months of home confinement for breaking into two computers owned and maintained by NASA's Jet Propulsion Laboratory (JPL) and using one of those computers to host an Internet chat room devoted to hacking. Torricelli was also ordered to pay a $4,400 in restitution to NASA. Torricelli admitted that, in 1998, he was a computer hacker and a member of a hacking organization known as #conflict, and that he used his personal computer to run programs designed to search the Internet for computers that were vulnerable to intrusion. Once he found a vulnerable computer, his computer obtained unauthorized access to it by uploading a program known as rootkit which allows a cracker to gain complete access to all of a computer's functions without being given these privileges by the computer's authorized users. After gaining this unauthorized access to computers and loading rootkit, Torricelli, under his alias rolex, used many of the computers to host chat-room discussions in which he invited other chat participants to visit a Web site that enabled them to view pornographic images. Torricelli received 18 cents for each visit a person made to that Web site; these visits earned him approximately $300–$400 per week.

Torricelli also pleaded guilty to intercepting usernames and passwords traversing the computer networks of San Jose State University; he also pleaded guilty to possession of stolen passwords and usernames that he used to gain free Internet access, or to gain unauthorized access to still more computers. According to Torricelli, he used a password cracking program known as John the Ripper to decrypt the encrypted passwords he obtained. He also stole credit card numbers and stored them on his computer, and he admitted that he used one such credit card number to purchase long-distance telephone service. In addition to thousands of stolen passwords and numerous credit card numbers stored on Torricelli's computer, investigators found transcripts of chat room discussions in which he and members of #conflict discussed, among other things, breaking into other computers; obtaining stolen credit card numbers and using them to make unauthorized purchases (a practice known as carding); and using their computers to electronically alter the results of the annual MTV Movie Awards.

New York City Computer Security Expert Sentenced to 27 Months' Imprisonment for Computer Hacking and Electronic Eavesdropping (June 13, 2001) [*United States v. Oquendo*] Jesus Oquendo was sentenced to 27 months in prison for computer cracking and electronic eavesdropping in the first federal computer hacking case to go to a trial in the southern district of New York. During the first half of 2000, Oquendo was a computer security specialist at a company called Collegeboardwalk.com, which shared office space and a computer network with one of its investors, Five Partners Asset Management LLC.

Oquendo altered the startup commands on the Five Partners computer network to automatically send the company's password file to his e-mail account each time the computer was rebooted. After Collegeboardwalk.com went out of business in 2000, Oquendo began accessing the Five Partners network remotely over the Internet through a secure shell account (a secure mechanism used to log in and control a remote computer) he had illegally installed on the victim's network. In August 2000, he secretly installed what is known as a sniffer program on Five Partners' network—a program that intercepted and recorded electronic traffic, including unencrypted passwords—and sent these intercepted communications to himself at a secret e-mail account that he had opened under a false name.

One of the legitimate users on the Five Partners' network also had a computer account at a third company, RCS Computer Experience. Oquendo's sniffer program on the Five Partners computer intercepted this legitimate user's RCS password, enabling Oquendo to break into the RCS network, access the RCS password file, install a sniffer program on the RCS system, and delete the entire RCS database. Finally, he left the victims a taunting message on the network: "Hello, I have just hacked into your system. Have a nice day." In imposing the prison term, the judge determined that Oquendo's punishment should be increased because he used a special skill, his computer expertise, to commit his crimes. She also ordered him to pay restitution in the amount of $96,385 to RCS.

Former Lance, Inc., Employee from North Carolina Sentenced to 24 Months and Ordered to Pay $194,609 Restitution in Computer Fraud Case (April 13, 2001) [*United States v. Sullivan*] John Michael Sullivan, a former employee of Lance, Inc., was sentenced to 24 months' imprisonment, followed by a term of 3 years' supervised release. Sullivan was also ordered to pay restitution to Lance in the amount of $154,879.

Sullivan was hired by Lance on September 23, 1996, to develop part of a computer program for use by Lance's national sales staff to collect sales, inventory, and delivery information and transmit it by modem to company headquarters in Charlotte, North Carolina. Sullivan was demoted by Lance on May 8, 1998, because of poor performance on the job. On May 12, 1998, Sullivan inserted part of a "code bomb" or logic bomb in Lance's system, including a date trigger in the software that he wrote for hand-held computers used by the company's 2,000 sales representatives in the field. On May 22, 1998, Sullivan resigned his position with Lance. His logic or code bomb was triggered at noon on September 23, 1998, and caused the field staff's computers to become inoperative. Lance's operations were disrupted for several days, and its direct loss as a result of Sullivan's conduct was more than $100,000.

Former Cisco Employee Pleads Guilty to Exceeding Authorized Access to Obtain Information from Cisco's Computer Systems (March 21, 2001) [*United States v. Morch*] Former Cisco Systems, Inc., employee Peter Morch pleaded guilty to exceeding his authorized access to Cisco's computer systems and obtaining information valued at more than $5,000. Morch, a resident of San Francisco and a citizen of Canada and Denmark, admitted that in September and October 2000, while employed at Cisco Systems–Petaluma and shortly before his resignation from the company, he intentionally logged into the computer system both as an administrator and under his own username, exceeding his authorized access in order to obtain information that he knew he was not authorized to have. He used another software engineer's computer for these violations because it had a writeable CD drive. Morch admitted that he burned a number of CDs on the other employee's computer, obtaining proprietary materials relating to both released Cisco products and projects still in development.

The day before Morch left Cisco, he copied Cisco project ideas, general descriptions, requirements, specifications, limitations of design, and procedures for overcoming the design difficulties for a voice-over and optical networking software product. Shortly thereafter, he began working at Calix Networks, a potential competitor of Cisco. Morch copied Cisco's proprietary information onto a Calix laptop and the Calix network, presumably to get a head start in his new job at the company. Calix cooperated fully with the criminal investigation against Morch.

Ex-GTE Employee Pleads Guilty to Intentionally Damaging Protected GTE Computers (March 20, 2001) [*United States v. Ventimiglia*] Michael Whitt Ventimiglia, 32, pleaded guilty to intentionally damaging protected computers at his place of employment, GTE. In the early morning hours of May 15, 2000, Ventimiglia entered the GTE Network Service Support Center (NSSC) and entered commands into three different multistate GTE network computers used in interstate commerce and communication. These commands caused the computers to delete information stored on their hard disk drives and prohibited anyone from interfering with this destruction of data once it was initiated. The damage cost GTE at least $209,000. The maximum statutory penalty for Ventimiglia's offense is 5 years' imprisonment and a fine of up to $250,000.

Former Federal Court Systems Administrator Sentenced for Hacking into Government Computer System (January 22, 2001) [*United States v. Dennis*] Anchorage resident Scott Dennis, former computer system administrator for the U.S. District Court in Alaska, was sentenced on January 19, 2001, for interfering with a government-owned communications system. Dennis was sentenced to 3 months in jail and 3 months' home confinement, followed by 1 year of supervised release. He was also required to perform 240 hours of community service and allow authorities to monitor his computer activity. Dennis was charged with launching three denial-of-service attacks against the U.S. District Court for the eastern district of New York. Dennis overwhelmed the eastern district's server with e-mail messages to prove that it was vulnerable to outside attacks. He repeated this attack twice because he thought his cracking had gone unnoticed. The prosecution in the case contended that Dennis was upset about the New York court's plans to allow more users into a restricted e-mail list server.

2002

Disgruntled UBS PaineWebber Employee Charged with Allegedly Unleashing "Logic Bomb" on Company Computers (December 17, 2002) [*United States v. Duronio*] A disgruntled computer systems administrator for UBS (Union Bank of Switzerland) PaineWebber was charged with using a logic bomb to cause more than $3 million in damage to the company's computer network and was charged with securities fraud for a failed plan to drive down the company's stock by the activation of the logic bomb. Roger Duronio, 60, of Bogota, New Jersey, was charged with planting the logic bomb in some 1,000 of PaineWebber's approximately 1,500 networked computers in branch offices around the country. Duronio, who had repeatedly expressed dissatisfaction with his salary and bonuses at PaineWebber, resigned from the company on February 22, 2002. The logic bomb he allegedly planted, to cause computer damage which could then be contained, was activated on March 4, 2002.

In anticipation that the stock price of UBS PaineWebber's parent company, UBS A.G. (Aktiengesellschaft, a publicly traded company by Swiss, German, and Austrian law), would decline in response to damage caused by the logic bomb, Duronio also purchased more than $21,000 of put option contracts (a type of security that increases in value when the stock price drops) for UBS

A.G.'s stock. Market conditions at the time suggest there was no adverse impact on the UBS A.G. stock price.

Hacker Pleaded Guilty to Attacks on San Diego Auto Site (November 15, 2002) [*United States v. Suplita, III*] Stephen Suplita III, charged with cracking into the computer system of Fallbrook, California-based Enjoya.com and causing damage in excess of $10,000, admitted to using his personal computer to crack into the computer system of the e-commerce retailer and intentionally causing damage to their computer system from August through October 2000, which resulted in the loss of business transactions.

British National Charged with Hacking Into N.J. Naval Weapons Station Computers, Disabling Network after Sept. 11; Indictment Also Filed in Virginia for Other Military Intrusions (November 12, 2002) [*United States v. McKinnon*] An unemployed United Kingdom computer system administrator who allegedly broke into the computer network at the Earle Naval Weapons Station, stole computer passwords, and shut down the network in the immediate aftermath of the September 11 terrorist attacks was charged by a grand jury in Newark with intentional damage to a protected computer. Gary McKinnon, 36, of the Hornsey section of London, was charged for intrusions into ninety-two computer systems belonging to the U.S. Army, the Navy, the Air Force, the Department of Defense, and NASA. McKinnon's intrusions rendered the network for the Military District of Washington inoperable for three days. He was also charged in a Virginia indictment with intrusions into two computers located at the Pentagon into six private companies' networks. McKinnon was charged in Virginia with causing approximately $900,000 in damages to computers located in fourteen states.

Russian Computer Hacker Sentenced to Three Years in Prison (October 4, 2002) [*United States v. Gorshkov*] Vasiliy Gorshkov, age 27, of Chelyabinsk, Russia, was sentenced to serve 36 months in prison for conspiracy, various computer crimes, and fraud committed against Speakeasy Network of Seattle, Washington; Nara Bank of Los Angeles, California; Central National Bank of Waco, Texas; and the online credit card payment company PayPal of Palo Alto, California. He was also ordered to pay restitution of nearly $700,000 for losses he caused to Speakeasy and PayPal.

Gorshkov was one of two men from Chelyabinsk, Russia (the other was Alexy Ivanov, age 23), who were persuaded to travel to the United States as part of an FBI undercover operation to entice the persons responsible for these crimes to come to U.S. territory.

The operation arose out of a nationwide FBI investigation into Russian computer intrusions that were directed at Internet service providers, e-commerce sites, and online banks in the United States. In these cases, the crackers gained unauthorized access to the victims' computers to steal credit card information and other personal financial information, and they often tried to extort money from the victims with threats to expose the sensitive data to the public or damage the victims' computers. The crackers also defrauded PayPal through a scheme in which stolen credit cards were used to generate cash and to pay for computer parts purchased from vendors in the United States.

San Gabriel Valley, California, Man Pleads to Illegally Accessing Former Employer's Computers (September 9, 2002) [*United States v. Dopps*] Richard Glenn Dopps, age 35, pleaded guilty to a charge of obtaining information from a protected computer. Until February 2001, Dopps had been employed by The Bergman Companies (TBC), a contracting firm based in Chino, California. After leaving TBC to work for a competitor, Dopps used his Internet connection to gain access to TBC's computer systems on more than twenty occasions. Once Dopps was inside the TBC systems, he read the e-mail messages of TBC executives to stay informed of TBC's ongoing business and to obtain a commercial advantage for his new employer. Dopps's unauthorized access into TBC's computer system purportedly caused approximately $21,636 in damages and other costs to TBC. Dopps's offense carries a maximum sentence of 5 years in prison and a $250,000 fine.

San Fernando Valley Residents Indicted in Scheme to Hack into Software Firm Computer and Delete $2.6 Million Project (August 2, 2002) [*United States v. Marinella*] Two former employees of the Santa Monica office of an international software development company were indicted on federal charges of conspiring to enter the company's computer systems and unlawfully delete a $2.6 million software package being developed for a foreign client. Glenn Cazenave, age 44, and Amaya Marinella, age 31, were accused of conspiracy and of cracking into a computer system and causing damage.

The target of the scheme was Commerce One. Cazenave was hired to run Commerce One's engineering department, and Marinella was an employee of the company supervised by Cazenave. Although Cazenave was initially assigned to lead the multimillion-dollar Memec project, he was soon taken off the project and later was terminated by the company for unknown reasons. After Cazenave was terminated, Marinella allegedly provided Cazenave with the administrative password for the Commerce One server where the Memec project was located, so that Cazenave could delete the project file. Cazenave deleted the entire Memec project file on February 21, 2001. However, Commerce One personnel were able to retrieve the deleted information, which limited the company's losses to the cost of investigating the intrusion and ensured that the system was rendered no longer vulnerable to such attacks. Each offense carries a maximum possible sentence of 10 years in federal prison.

Twenty-Seven-Month Sentence in Internet Fraud Scheme to Defraud Priceline.Com and Others; Unauthorized Computer Access Conspiracy (May 17, 2002) [*United States v. Luckey*] Curtis Lawrence Luckey, age 26, was sentenced to a term of 27 months in prison for attempting to defraud Priceline.com and others using credit card information unlawfully obtained from a credit union employee. Luckey was also ordered to pay restitution in the amount of $116,869.30 and to serve a 3-year term of supervised release following his incarceration. On March 1, 2002, he pleaded guilty to wire fraud, conspiracy to obtain unauthorized computer access to customer account information from a financial institution, and credit card fraud.

Luckey admitted to masterminding a scheme to defraud Priceline.com, Southwest Airlines, the Hotel Reservations Network, Inc., a credit union, and the credit union's credit card holders by making fraudulent Internet credit card charges for hotel and airline reservations totaling more than $116,000. Luckey obtained confidential customer account and credit card information from credit union employee Tifane Roberts, who was subsequently terminated and convicted. Luckey then used the credit card information to make hotel and airline reservations over the Internet and telephone. Most of the reservations were made with Priceline.com, Southwest Airlines, and the Hotel Reservations Network, Inc. After making the reservations, Luckey typically enlisted another person to check into each hotel room using reservation and credit card information he supplied; the accomplices would then return the hotel room keys to Luckey, who then retained full use of the hotel rooms. No credit union customers lost any funds as a result of the fraud scheme, as all customer funds were federally insured by the National Credit Union Association.

Former Chief of Technology Charged with Intrusions, Transmitting Threats via the Internet (May 16, 2002) [*United States v. Blum*]

Raymond Blum, the former chief technology officer of Askit.com, a Manhattan-based computer consulting company, was arrested on charges of transmitting threats via the Internet to his former employer. In February 2002, shortly after Blum's departure from the company, Askit began to experience computer and telephone voice mail problems: unusual network traffic on the computer system that caused the computer network to fail, e-mail servers being flooded with thousands of messages containing pornographic images, and the voice mail system being altered so that certain customers calling the company were directed to a pornographic telephone service. At the time of this activity, Blum and Askit were in a dispute concerning the severance terms of his employment contract with Askit.

Following the intrusions directed against their computer and voice mail systems, Askit's chief executive officer (CEO) and its president began receiving threatening communications. For example, the CEO allegedly received an e-greeting card expressing sympathy at his "recent loss and bereavement." The president received an e-greeting card containing an image of a voodoo doll with pins stuck through various parts of the doll's body; the doll was wearing a name tag with the president's name. Askit's president also received an e-mail message telling him to "say goodbye to anyone who pretends to care about you"; this message was traced to a computer at Home Box Office, Blum's new place of employment. In April 2002, messages were posted on the customer service portion of Askit's Web site containing statements such as "You are doomed!" and "die." The message "die" was posted by a person identifying himself as "raymond" at an e-mail address associated with Blum. Blum's offenses carry a maximum sentence of 5 years in prison and a $250,000 fine.

Green Bay, Wisconsin Man Charged with Computer Intrusion, Software Piracy, and Numerous Destructive Acts (May 7, 2002) [*United States v. Konopka*] A thirteen-count indictment charged Joseph D. Konopka of Green Bay, Wisconsin, with trafficking in counterfeit goods (namely, Electronic Arts software), an offense punishable by 10 years in prison and a $2 million fine. Konopka was also charged with causing damage in excess of $5,000 to a protected computer owned by an Internet service provider known as Ultimate Fun World 2. This crime was punishable by 5 years in prison and a $250,000 fine. It was also alleged that Konopka intercepted electronic communications between customers of two Internet service providers known as Ultimate Fun

World and Infinity Technology. This crime was punishable by 5 years in prison and a $250,000 fine.

In the same indictment, Konopka was also charged with conspiring to damage or destroy communication facilities, energy facilities, air navigation facilities, and buildings used in interstate commerce. The indictment also alleged fifty-three separate overt acts that Konopka conspired to commit with others to cause power outages and other service interruptions, affecting in excess of 30,000 power customers and causing damages in excess of $800,000. Konopka was also charged with other crimes throughout Wisconsin: damaging the property of energy facilities; disabling an air navigation facility; interfering with the working and use of telecommunication systems; and using fire to damage buildings used in interstate commerce. Each of these crimes carried a penalty of 5–10 years in prison and a $250,000 fine; however, Konopka's use of fire to commit some of the alleged offenses was punishable by an additional 10 years in prison and a $250,000 fine. U.S. Attorney Steven M. Biskupic wouldn't attribute Konopka's alleged acts to a particular motive, but the indictment suggests that they were largely for his own entertainment.

Konopka is believed to be the leader of a band of vandals known as "The Realm of Chaos." Some of the group's members have been convicted in state courts and have helped investigators build a case against Konopka. Officials believe that he used an online chat room called "Teens for Satan" to contact potential recruits.

Creator of Melissa Computer Virus Sentenced to 20 Months in Federal Prison (May 1, 2002) [*United States v. Smith*] David L. Smith, age 34, of Aberdeen Township in New Jersey, pleaded guilty on December 9, 1999, in state and federal courts to developing the Melissa virus. Smith acknowledged that the Melissa virus caused more than $80 million in damage by disrupting personal computers and computer networks in business and government. He was ordered to serve 3 years of supervised release after completion of a 20-month prison sentence and was fined $5,000. Upon release, Smith was not to be involved with computer networks, the Internet, or Internet bulletin boards unless authorized by the court. Finally, Smith was sentenced to serve 100 hours of community service upon release. The judge said that Smith's supervised community service would somehow put to use Smith's technology experience.

U.S. Charges Engineer with Computer Intrusion, Destruction of Database at Manhattan Apparel Company (April 26, 2002) [*United

States v. Eitelberg] Richard Eitelberg was arrested and charged in Manhattan federal court with the unauthorized intrusion into the computer network of his former employer, MP Limited LLC, an apparel manufacturer and designer based in Manhattan. He was employed as the controller at MP and, in connection with his work, was given the password to permit him to remotely access the MP computer system from his home. Eitelberg stopped working at MP on February 1, 2002. On April 11, 2002, the records of all of MP's customer orders were found to have disappeared from the MP database. The computer records allegedly indicated that an individual accessed the MP computer system using a password from about 9:21 until 9:46 P.M. on April 10, 2002, and that orders in the database were deleted during this computer session. Phone records indicated that the phone line registered to Eitelberg's wife and located at their home was used to call MP's modem connection approximately thirteen times between February 27, 2002, and April 10, 2002, including the call made on the evening of April 10, 2002. Eitelberg's crime carries a maximum possible sentence of 5 years in prison and a fine of $250,000, or twice the gross gain or loss resulting from the crime.

Man Pleads Guilty to Unauthorized Access of Las Vegas Medical Imaging Computer System (April 17, 2002) [*United States v. Sandusky*] Scott Sandusky pleaded guilty to unauthorized access to a protected computer and was indicted by a federal grand jury in Las Vegas in May 2001. Sandusky, age 35, admitted to unlawfully accessing the computer system of Steinberg Diagnostic Medical Imaging (SDMI) of Las Vegas, Nevada, on three dates in 2001. Sandusky admitted that during those unlawful accesses, he knowingly transmitted codes or information and impaired SDMI's system by changing the administrative passwords, locking company personnel out of their own system, and crippling the business of SDMI. He had been terminated from his employment with a computer consulting business that assisted in setting up SDMI's computer system. Sandusky's offense is punishable by up to 5 years' imprisonment and a fine of $250,000 on each count.

Computer Operator Sentenced for Breaking Into Ex-Employer's Database (March 27, 2002) [*United States v. Leung*] On October 31, 2001, Washington Leung, a former employee in the human resources department at Manhattan insurance company Marsh Inc., pleaded guilty to accessing a protected computer without authorization and deleting approximately 950 files relating to employee compensation. He was sentenced to 18 months in prison.

A female employee at Marsh had complained that Leung was harassing her because she rebuffed his romantic advances. Leung was later terminated from Marsh and found employment at Viacom, Inc. In January 2001, Leung used a password belonging to another Marsh employee to obtain unauthorized access to the company's computer database and to delete approximately 950 files relating to employee compensation at Marsh. Leung also altered the female employee's compensation record to reflect a $40,000 increase in her salary and a $100,000 bonus.

Senior managers at Marsh received an e-mail with an attached file containing information from the deleted salary files. The e-mail appeared to have been originally sent from a Hotmail.com account whose user ID contained the female employee's last name, but she denied having established that account. A forensic image of Leung's computer at Viacom revealed that the e-mails to the senior managers at Marsh were sent from that computer. Leung's intrusion into Marsh's database cost the company thousands of dollars to secure its system from future unauthorized access, to re-enter deleted data, and to make other repairs. Leung was ordered to pay $91,814.68 in restitution to Marsh Inc.

Parma, Ohio, Man Indicted for Unauthorized Access into Computer System of Alltel Communications, Inc., Sending Threatening E-Mails (March 26, 2002) [*United States v. Rayburn*] Jimmie Earl Rayburn, age 44, of Parma, Ohio, was arrested by the FBI in connection with ten criminal charges related to computers and extortion. An indictment alleged that between January 28 and March 20, 2002, Rayburn, with the intent to extort money or other things of value from Alltel Communications, Inc., knowingly transmitted threats to damage a protected computer system and a threat to injure the property or reputation of another person. It was also alleged that Rayburn knowingly caused the transmission of programs, codes, information, or commands that intentionally caused damage to a protected computer system owned and/or operated by Alltel Communications, Inc. The maximum statutory penalty for the violations in the indictment is 2–10 years' imprisonment, a fine of up to $250,000, or both.

Former Computer Network Administrator at New Jersey High-Tech Firm Sentenced for Unleashing $10 Million Computer "Time Bomb" (February 26, 2002) [*United States v. Lloyd*] A former computer network administrator was sentenced to 41 months in prison for unleashing a $10 million "time bomb" that deleted all the sophisticated production programs of a New Jersey-based high-tech manufacturer of measurement and control instruments. Timothy Allen Lloyd, age 39, of Wilmington, Delaware, was the former chief computer network program designer for Omega Engineering Corp. but had been terminated from Omega on July 10, 1996, after working for the company for approximately 11 years. His indictment stated that the sabotage resulted in a loss to Omega of at least $10 million in sales and future contracts. Lloyd was found not guilty on a charge of transporting approximately $50,000 worth of computer equipment stolen from Omega to his Delaware residence. At the time of conviction, the case was believed to be one of the most expensive computer sabotage cases in U.S. Secret Service history in terms of the amount awarded in damages to the victim.

Former Chase Financial Corp. Employees Sentenced for Scheme to Defraud Chase Manhattan Bank and Chase Financial Corporation (February 19, 2002) [*United States v. Turner*] Patrice Williams, age 26, of Cleveland, Ohio, was sentenced to 12 months and 1 day in prison for a computer fraud conviction. Her codefendant, Makeebrah Turner, age 32, also of Cleveland, was also sentenced to the same length of prison term in connection with the offense. Turner and Williams each admitted that between approximately November 1999 and December 2000, while employed by Chase Financial Corporation, they knowingly and with the intent to defraud gained unauthorized access to one or more Chase Manhattan Bank and Chase Financial Corporation computer systems and obtained credit card account numbers and other customer account information for approximately sixty-eight accounts that they were not authorized to access in connection with their duties at Chase Financial Corporation. Turner and Williams admitted that the aggregate credit limits for the targeted accounts totaled approximately $580,700.

Turner and Williams further admitted that after fraudulently obtaining these credit card account numbers and customer account information, they distributed the information to others who, in turn, used the credit card accounts and other financial information to purchase goods and services valued at approximately $99,636.08, without the knowledge or consent of the account holders, Chase Manhattan Bank, or Chase Financial Corporation.

Orange County Computer Hacker Sentenced to Prison for Breaking into University Computers, NASA Systems (February 4, 2002) [*United*

States v. Diekman] Jason Allen Diekman, 20, a California man who admitted cracking into "hundreds, maybe thousands" of computers, was sentenced to 21 months in federal prison in three separate computer cracking cases and was ordered to pay a total of $87,736.29 in restitution to the victims of his crimes. In addition, once released from prison, Diekman must serve 3 years of supervised release with severe restrictions on his use of computers.

In the first case, Diekman cracked into NASA computers and used stolen credit card numbers to purchase more than $6,000 in electronic equipment. Diekman, who used the monikers Shadow Knight and Dark Lord, admitted gaining unauthorized "root-level" access to at least three computer systems at NASA's Jet Propulsion Laboratory (JPL), giving him control over all aspects of the computers. Diekman admitted that he had also caused $17,000 in damage to the NASA computer systems at Stanford, which were used to develop sensitive satellite flight control software used to control NASA satellites. Federal agents also discovered evidence on Diekman's computers indicating that he intercepted usernames and passwords from universities, including Harvard University.

While free on bond after pleading guilty in the first case, Diekman used his home computer to crack into computers at Oregon State University at Corvallis 33 times from February through April of 2001. He used the account of an OSU student to gain access to the school's computer system, where he stored computer programs to control Internet relay chat channels (similar to chat rooms that act as forums for text-based interaction between participants) on the Internet. In relation to this case, Diekman also pleaded guilty to a wire fraud charge. An internal investigation by AT&T into the theft of its services turned up recordings of telephone conversations in which the callers discussed defrauding Western Union, and these tapes were turned over to the FBI. On the tapes, Diekman—who was using an alias he has used in the past and who was identified by an FBI agent familiar with his voice—was heard discussing with others the possibility of obtaining fraudulent wire transfers from Western Union. Diekman also admitted that he had fraudulently obtained more than 8,000 minutes of long-distance services from AT&T.

In the third case, Diekman pleaded guilty to federal charges of cracking into Bay Area Internet Solutions, Inc., an Internet service provider in San Jose, California. Diekman and others again gained unauthorized root-level access, which gave them complete control of the computer systems and allowed them to obtain account information and passwords. They also used the company's computer systems to store computer exploits (programs that enabled unauthorized intruders to later gain access to that system and other computers) and caused more than $50,000 in damages to the company, due to the cost of investigating the intrusion and resecuring the systems.

Manhattan Paralegal Sentenced for Theft of Litigation Trial Plan (January 30, 2002) [United States v. Farraj] Said Farraj, a paralegal, was sentenced in Manhattan federal court to 2 years and 6 months in prison in connection with a scheme to sell to opposing counsel a confidential trial plan prepared by Orrick, Harrington, & Sutcliffe LLP, the law firm where he worked. Farraj pleaded guilty to conspiracy to commit wire fraud, transport stolen property interstate, and access a computer without authorization, as well as to substantive charges of interstate transportation of stolen property and unauthorized computer access. Yeazid Farraj, Said's brother, also pleaded guilty to a conspiracy charge for his participation in the same scheme.

Between May 20 and June 18, 2000, Farraj was employed as a paralegal at Orrick, which was one of several law firms representing the plaintiffs in the case of *Falise, et al.* v. *American Tobacco Co., et al.,* a mass tort case scheduled to go to trial on July 17, 2000. Attorneys working for Orrick had spent hundreds of hours preparing a trial plan at a cost of several million dollars. The trial plan exceeded 400 pages and included, among other things, trial strategy, deposition excerpts and summaries, and references to anticipated trial exhibits. In his capacity as a paralegal working on the *Falise* litigation, Farraj had access to the trial plan and obtained an electronic copy by downloading it from the Orrick computer system.

Three days later, using the alias FlyGuyNYt, Farraj transmitted to the defendants' attorneys an e-mail in which he offered to sell the trial plan. He negotiated the sale with an undercover FBI agent who was posing as defense counsel. Between June and July 2000, Farraj transmitted to the undercover agent various e-mails in which he agreed to sell the trial plan for $2 million and arranged to make the exchange for the money.

San Francisco Man Pleads Guilty to Unauthorized Access of Catholic Healthcare West Computer Causing Damage (January 18, 2002) [*United States v. Logan*] Michael Logan, 34, was charged with unauthorized access into a computer and utilizing a telecommunications device in interstate communications with intent to harass. Under a plea agreement, Logan pleaded guilty to the charge involving the telecommunications device. Logan admitted that he intentionally accessed a computer at Catholic Healthcare West (CHW) without authorization in November 1999 and then sent e-mail to approximately 30,000 CHW employees and associates. The e-mail purported to be from a named employee of CHW and contained insulting statements about that named employee and other CHW employees. Logan further admitted that his conduct caused damage of at least $5,000 to CHW; however, according to public records in the case, the damage was actually more than $25,000.

2003

Local FBI Employee Indicted for Public Corruption (November 5, 2003) [*United States v. Fudge*] On this date, a federal grand jury in Texas returned a ten-count indictment against Jeffrey D. Fudge, an FBI investigative analyst, charging him with eight counts of exceeding his authorized access to a government computer and two counts of making false statements. Fudge, age 33, had been an FBI employee since 1988. Fudge's crimes carry a statutory maximum sentence of 50 years' imprisonment and a $2.5 million fine.

Fudge's duties as an investigative analyst included conducting database searches using the FBI computer system, serving subpoenas, analyzing telephone records, and generally assisting FBI agents in conducting criminal investigations. The indictment charged Fudge with accessing FBI files and computer programs and disclosing information from the files to Fudge's friends and family members. He was also charged with accessing the FBI's computer system to determine whether the FBI was investigating particular people, including several locally prominent citizens, and with accessing FBI files to satisfy his own curiosity.

Disgruntled Philadelphia Phillies Fan Charged with Hacking into Computers Triggering Spam E-Mail Attacks (October 7, 2003) [*United States v. Carlson*] U.S. Attorney Patrick L. Meehan announced the unsealing of an indictment returned on September 25, 2003, against Allan Eric Carlson. FBI agents arrested Carlson at his home. Agents charged him with cracking into computers around the country (which he used as launch sites for his attacks), hijacking or "spoofing" the return addresses of reporters at the *Philadelphia Inquirer*, the *Philadelphia Daily News*, and the Philadelphia Phillies' offices, and using these e-mail addresses to launch spam e-mail attacks. He was also charged with identity theft for illegally using the e-mail addresses of the reporters.

Former Employee of Viewsonic Pleads Guilty to Hacking into Company's Computer, Destroying Data (October 6, 2003) [*United States v. Garcia*] A former employee of the Viewsonic Corporation pleaded guilty in a Los Angeles courtroom to a federal charge of cracking into the company's computer system and wiping out critical data, shutting down a server that was central to the company's foreign operations. Andrew Garcia, 38, pleaded guilty to charges of accessing a protected computer and recklessly causing damage. The charge carries a maximum sentence of 5 years in federal prison and a fine of $250,000.

Garcia had been the network administrator at Viewsonic, where he was in charge of several computer servers and had access to system passwords for management employees. Approximately 2 weeks after Garcia was terminated, he accessed the company's computer system and deleted critical files. The loss of these files rendered the server inoperative, and Viewsonic's Taiwan office was unable to access important data for several days.

President of San Diego Computer Security Company Indicted in Conspiracy to Gain Unauthorized Access into Government Computers (September 29, 2003) [*United States v. O'Keefe*] Brett Edward O'Keefe was charged in a six-count indictment with conspiring to gain unauthorized access to military, government, and private sector computers to obtain information for financial gain. The indictment alleged that O'Keefe, president of San Diego computer security company Forensic Tec Solutions, along with his co-conspirators, tried to gain unauthorized access to government and military computers, copy computer files, and take the files to the media to generate public visibility for the company—thereby generating new clients and increased profits for Forensic Tec. O'Keefe and his co-conspirators also sought to gain unauthorized access to private sector computers to copy information and use this information to contact the victim companies to solicit their business. The government agencies targeted by O'Keefe included the National Aeronautics and Space Administration (NASA), the United States Army, the United States Navy, the Department of Energy, and the National Institutes of Health.

Juvenile Arrested for Releasing Variant of Blaster Computer Worm that Attacked Microsoft (September 26, 2003) [*United States v. Unnamed Juvenile*] A juvenile was arrested in connection with the release of the RPCSDBOT variant of the Blaster computer worm, which directed infected computers to launch a distributed denial-of-service attack against the Microsoft Corporation. The arrest was for an act of juvenile delinquency, based on intentionally causing damage and attempting to cause damage to protected computers. Because of his age, the identity of the juvenile, the details of the investigation, and the charge could not be disclosed to the public. U.S. Attorney John McKay commended the Washington Cyber Task Force on its investigation and thanked Microsoft Corporation for its assistance to law enforcement. He said that computer crackers, whether adult or juvenile, need to understand that they will be pursued and held accountable for malicious activity.

Minneapolis, Minnesota, 18-Year-Old Arrested for Developing and Releasing B Variant of Blaster Computer Worm (August 29, 2003) [*United States v. Parson*] Jeffrey Lee Parson, age 18, of Minneapolis, Minnesota, was arrested on one count filed in Seattle, Washington, charging that he intentionally caused and attempted to cause damage to a protected computer. The crime carries a maximum prison sentence of 10 years and a $250,000 fine. The complaint alleged that Parson knowingly developed and released onto the Internet the B variant of the Blaster computer worm, infecting at least 7,000 computers and causing them to attack or attempt to attack Microsoft (especially its Web site www.windowsupdate.com). Parson intentionally caused significant damage to Microsoft and to other victim computers that significantly exceeded the $5,000 threshold set forth in 18 U.S.C. subsection 1030(a)(5)(B)(i).

Former Computer Technician in Douglasville, Georgia, Arrested for Hacking into Government Computer Systems in Southern California (August 25, 2003) [*United States v. Wiggs*] Walter Wiggs, a 44-year-old resident of Douglasville, Georgia, was arrested on federal charges of gaining unauthorized access to a protected computer. According to the criminal complaint filed, Wiggs was previously a computer technician for Technology for Business Corporation (TFBC), a Manhattan Beach–based company specializing in developing customized software for numerous government agencies and private companies, including an interactive voice response system for telephone call centers.

After being laid off from TFBC in June 2003, Wiggs used a computer at his home to gain unauthorized access to approximately thirteen computers that used TFBC's interactive voice response software, including systems used by the Los Angeles County Department of Children and Family Services, the City of

San Diego, the City of Modesto, and the Orange County District Attorney's Office. By deleting critical configuration files from the system, Wiggs caused significant disruption between July 1 and 4, 2003, to the Los Angeles County Child Protection Hotline, a hotline used by citizens, police officers, hospitals, and mental health workers to report cases of child abuse or neglect that required an immediate response.

Russian Man Sentenced for Hacking into Computers in the United States (July 25, 2003) [*United States v. Ivanov*] Alexey V. Ivanov, age 23, formerly of Chelyabinsk, Russia, was sentenced to 48 months in prison, to be followed by 3 years of supervised release, for charges of conspiracy, computer intrusion, computer fraud, credit card fraud, wire fraud, and extortion. Ivanov and others, operating from Russia, had cracked into dozens of computers throughout the United States, stealing usernames, passwords, credit card information, and other financial data and then extorting those victims with the threat of deleting their data and destroying their computer systems. Ivanov was found to be responsible for an aggregate loss of approximately $25 million.

FBI Employee Arrested and Charged in Three Federal Indictments (July 17, 2003) [*United States v. Castillo*] Mario Castillo, a 36-year-old FBI language specialist, was arrested in El Paso, Texas, in connection with three separate federal grand jury indictments.

The first charged Castillo with six counts of unauthorized access of a FBI computer to obtain information for private financial gain and four counts of making false statements to federal officials when questioned about other paid employment, financial indebtedness, providing confidential information to unauthorized persons, and ties and associations with a convicted felon. The second indictment charged Castillo with collecting more than $1,000 in money and property from trafficking in and using stolen cellular telephones. The third indictment charged Castillo with possession of child pornography, receiving child pornography via the Internet, and receipt of obscene material. On May 9, 2003, FBI agents seized from Castillo's home a computer containing several video files and more than a dozen images depicting minors engaged in sexually explicit conduct.

Queens, New York, Man Pleads Guilty to Federal Charges of Computer Damage, Access Device Fraud, and Software Piracy (July 11, 2003) [*United States v. Jiang*] Juju Jiang, 24, of Flushing, New York, pleaded guilty to a five-count indictment relating to computer fraud and software piracy. Between February 14, 2001, and December 20, 2002, Jiang, without permission, installed special keylogging software (to track and store the key strokes that a user enters) on computer terminals at Kinko's stores to record activity on those computers and to collect computer usernames and passwords of Kinko's customers. He then used the confidential information he obtained to access, or attempt to access, bank accounts belonging to others and to fraudulently open online bank accounts. During this time, he possessed more than fifteen computer usernames and passwords belonging to others, which he used to access these individuals' bank and financial services accounts, open online bank accounts in their names, and transfer funds into the new, unauthorized accounts. Jiang also pleaded guilty to continuing these fraudulent activities while free on bail after his arrest on December 20, 2002. His crimes each carry a maximum sentence of 5 years in prison and a $250,000 fine.

Jiang admitted that the keylogging software he installed could damage the Kinko's computers. He also pleaded guilty to two counts of software piracy for his online sale in 2000 of copies of Microsoft Office 2000 Professional Edition in violation of Microsoft's copyright on its software. These charges each carry a maximum term of 1 year in prison and a $100,000 fine.

Kazakhstan Hacker Sentenced to Four Years Prison for Breaking into Bloomberg Systems and Attempting Extortion (July 1, 2003) [*United States v. Zezev*] Oleg Zezev, a.k.a. "Alex," a citizen of Kazakhstan, was convicted on extortion and computer cracking charges and sentenced to 51 months in prison. This sentence is among the longest ever imposed for a computer intrusion charge. Zezev was accused of cracking into Bloomberg L.P.'s (a market data distributor) computer system, trying to steal confidential information belonging to Bloomberg and its customers, and trying to then use that information to threaten Bloomberg founder Michael Bloomberg. Zezev demanded $200,000 or threatened that he would disclose the stolen information to Bloomberg's customers and the media in an attempt to harm Bloomberg's reputation.

Zezev was the chief information technology officer at Kazkommerts Securities in Almaty, Kazakhstan. In 1999, Bloomberg had provided database services to Kazkommerts, in the process providing Kazkommerts with software needed to gain access to Bloomberg's services over the Internet. Those services were canceled by Bloomberg in 1999 because Kazkommerts did not pay its bill. In March 2000, Zezev manipulated the software to bypass Bloomberg's security system and gain unauthorized access to Bloomberg's computer system, posing as different legitimate Bloomberg customers and employees. On eleven separate occasions during March 2000, Zezev illegally entered Bloomberg's computer system and accessed various accounts. He then copied various information from these accounts, including e-mail screens, credit card numbers, screens relating to internal functions of Bloomberg, and various internal information that was accessible by Bloomberg employees.

Southern California Man Who Hijacked Al Jazeera Website Agrees to Plead Guilty to Federal Charges (June 12, 2003) [*United States v. Racine*] John William Racine II, a Web site designer from Norco, California, admitted to federal authorities that he was responsible for a hijacking of Arabic-language news station Al Jazeera's Web site. Racine was charged with wire fraud and unlawful interception of an electronic communication.

Al Jazeera Space Channel, based in Doha, Qatar, is an Arabic-language media organization that provides, in addition to its satellite television news service, English- and Arabic-language news through its Aljazeera.net Web site. After learning in March 2003 that the Web site contained images of captured American prisoners of war and soldiers killed in action during Operation Iraqi Freedom, Racine gained control of the Aljazeera.net domain name by defrauding Network Solutions, Inc., where Al Jazeera maintained an account for its domain name and e-mail services. Racine then diverted the Web site traffic to another Web site he had designed featuring an American flag in the shape of the continental United States and the words "Let Freedom Ring. . . ." Racine also intercepted approximately 300 e-mail messages destined for Aljazeera.net and diverted the messages to an e-mail account under his control.

Racine further admitted to FBI agents that he created a false photo identification card to impersonate an Al Jazeera systems administrator and forged the systems administrator's signature on a Network Solutions "Statement of Authorization" form. Racine then sent the fraudulent documents to Network Solutions by facsimile, tricking the company into giving him control of the Al Jazeera account. While Racine maintained control of Al Jazeera's domain name, Internet users were unable to access the Al Jazeera news Web sites, and Al Jazeera was unable to receive e-mail sent to the domain.

Computer Hacker Sentenced to One Year and One Day and Ordered to Pay More than $88,000 Restitution for Series of Computer Intrusions and Credit Card Fraud (June 12, 2003) [*United States v. Shakour*] Adil Yahya Zakaria Shakour, age 19, of Los Angeles, California, pleaded guilty on March 13, 2003, to committing computer fraud and credit card fraud. Shakour committed a series of intrusions into four separate computer systems: a server at Eglin Air Force Base, a federal military base in Florida, during which he compromised the integrity of the system and defaced the Web site; computers at Accenture, a management consulting and technology services company based in Chicago, Illinois; an unclassified network computer at the Sandia National Laboratories in Livermore, California; and a computer at Cheaptaxforms.com, a North Carolina subsidiary of Pro Systems, Inc. When cracking into the North Carolina site, he obtained customers' credit card information and other personal information from the Web site, which he then used to purchase more than $7,000 worth of items for his personal use.

Shakour was sentenced to 1 year and 1 day in federal prison, a 3-year term of supervised release, and a $200 special assessment. He was also ordered to pay $88,253.47 for damages, investigation, and repairs in restitution. As part of his sentence, the court restricted his computer use during the supervised release period following his federal prison term.

Three Californians Indicted in Conspiracy to Commit Bank Fraud and Identity Theft (May 12, 2003) [*United States v. Thomas et al.*] Dorian Patrick Thomas, age 27, Daryen Craig Simmons, age 38, and David Raphel King, aged 24, all of Sacramento, California, were indicted on twenty-two counts of conspiracy, bank fraud, and identity theft charges. Thomas, a former financial institution employee, was charged with conspiring to obtain unauthorized computer access to his financial institution's information, commit computer fraud, unlawfully use another person's means of identification, and commit bank fraud. He allegedly obtained confidential member profile information of account holders (including account holder name, address, date of birth, driver's license number, social security number, credit card account information, account balance information, and other personal information) through his financial institution's computers and provided it to others, including King.

Thomas was purportedly compensated by King and others for providing this information. The indictment charged Simmons with conspiring with Thomas and King in bank fraud, attempted bank fraud, and unlawful use of another person's means of identification. King was charged with the same conspiracy as well as with ten counts of bank fraud. Both Simmons and King allegedly made and obtained false identification documents in the names of, along with fictitious financial instruments bearing the names and/or account information of, the original account holders.

The offenses are punishable by a maximum sentence of up to 30 years, a 5-year term of supervised release, and a $1 million fine on each bank fraud count; up to 15 years imprisonment, a 3-year term of supervised release, and a $250,000 fine on each identity theft count; and up to 5 years' imprisonment, a 3-year term of supervised release, and a $250,000 fine on the conspiracy charge. Fortunately, all customer funds were federally insured, so no customers of the financial institution lost any funds as a result of these identity theft and bank fraud schemes..

Ex-Employee of Airport Transportation Company Guilty of Hacking into Company's Computer (April 18, 2003) [*United States v. Tran*] Alan Giang Tran, age 28, previously employed by the Airline Coach Service and Sky Limousine Company, pleaded guilty to a federal charge of cracking into the company's shared computer system and wiping out the company's customer database and other records and shutting down the company's computer server, Internet-based credit card processing system, and Web site. Tran was charged with intentionally causing damage to a protected computer by knowingly causing the transmission of a program, information, code, or command, a felony offense.

Tran, the network administrator at the company's facility in Inglewood, California, had recently been terminated by the company. On January 5, 2003, the company's computer system was attacked, passwords on the system were changed, and specialized software applications were deleted. Because employees could not use the computer system, the company was unable to dispatch drivers to pick up clients, and the company suffered thousands of dollars in losses. Federal investigators executed a search warrant at Tran's home, where they found several computers, a file folder marked "retaliation," and information regarding the company's computer systems. The charge to which Tran pleaded guilty to carries a maximum possible sentence of 10 years in federal prison.

Student Charged with Unauthorized Access to University of Texas

Computer System (March 14, 2003) [United States v. Phillips] Christopher Andrew Phillips, a 20-year-old student at the University of Texas at Austin, was charged with unauthorized access to a protected computer and using another person's means of identification with intent to commit a federal offense. Phillips allegedly wrote and executed a computer program that permitted him to gain unauthorized access to a database at the University of Texas at Austin and to download tens of thousands of names and social security numbers. On March 5, 2003, Secret Service agents carried out search warrants at Phillips's homes in Austin and Houston and seized several computers; on a computer found in his Austin home, agents recovered downloaded names and social security numbers and the computer program used to access the UT database. Phillips turned himself in to the United States Secret Service office in Austin. There was no indication that the stolen data was further disseminated or used to anyone's detriment.

St. Joseph Man Pleads Guilty in District's First Computer Hacking Conviction (March 13, 2003) [*United States v. Gerhardt*] This was the first conviction for computer cracking prosecuted by a new Computer Crimes and Child Exploitation Unit. Richard W. Gerhardt, age 43, admitted that he had gained unauthorized access to the network computer system of Nestle USA while employed as an information systems consultant, working primarily at the Friskies Petcare plant in St. Joseph, Missouri, a subsidiary of Nestle USA. Gerhardt's cracking activity allegedly resulted in a loss to Nestle USA of about $10,000. Under the terms of the plea agreement, Gerhardt was to pay that amount in restitution to the company. He also agreed to perform 250 hours of community service, either during a term of supervised release following a prison sentence or as a condition of probation. This community service was to take the form of speaking to groups to advise them of the dangers of computer cracking and to warn them that cracking can result in a federal felony conviction.

California Woman Convicted for Unauthorized Computer Access to Customer Account Information in Credit Union Fraud Prosecution (March 10, 2003) [*United States v. Northern*] Charmaine Northern, age 23, employed as a member service representative of Schools Federal Credit Union in Sacramento, California, admitted that between January 22, 2001, and October 26, 2002, she used the credit union computer to obtain customer account information, including names, social security and driver's license numbers, and addresses, to open accounts in the names of others and incur unauthorized charges. Some of the credit card accounts were opened on the Internet. After the credit cards were established in the names of other customers, Northern used the credit cards to make numerous purchases. The estimated amount of the fraudulent transactions was more than $53,000. Northern's offense carries a maximum prison sentence of 5 years, a fine of $250,000, and a 3-year term of supervised release. No financial institution customers lost any funds as a result of the offense, as all customer funds were federally insured.

Los Angeles, California, Man Sentenced to Prison for Role in International Computer Hacking and Internet Fraud Scheme (February 28, 2003) [*United States v. Pae*] Thomas Pae, age 20, was sentenced on charges of wire fraud, conspiracy, and credit card fraud for his involvement in an international computer cracking and Internet fraud scheme targeting Santa Ana, California–based Ingram Micro, the world's largest wholesale distributor of technology products. Pae pleaded guilty to the charges and admitted that in 2001 he had participated in a scheme with computer crackers in Romania who had gained unauthorized access to Ingram Micro's online ordering system and placed hundreds of thousands of dollars in orders for computer equipment. The stolen equipment was sent to locations controlled by Pae and his co-conspirators in the Los Angeles area and was then repackaged and sent to eastern Europe, where it was likely re-sold.

Pae also admitted purchasing credit card numbers from crackers on the Internet and using the cards to purchase computer chips, hard drives, personal digital assistants, and other items from Handspring.com, Amazon.com, and Egghead.com. He also admitted that he and his co-conspirators attempted to purchase more than $500,000 in computer equipment and other items from Ingram Micro and the other online retailers. Pae was ordered to pay $324,061 in restitution to the victims of his crimes. In addition, he received a 33-month prison term, followed by 3 years of supervised release. Six other defendants involved in the scheme also pleaded guilty.

Former Employee of American Eagle Outfitters Indicted on Charges of Password Trafficking and Computer Damage (February 26, 2003) [*United States v. Patterson*] Kenneth Patterson, a 38-year-old employee of American Eagle Outfitters in Greensburg, Pennsylvania, was charged with trafficking in passwords and similar information that would allow others to gain unauthorized access to the company's computer network. Patterson posted and maintained at a Yahoo! group discussion board the username and password combinations of certain legitimate American Eagle Outfitters users, together with detailed instructions on how to crack into the wide area network (WAN) of American Eagle Outfitters using those passwords. He was also charged with a series of computer intrusions into the American Eagle Outfitters computer network from November 27 to December 1, 2002, intending to deny computer services to American Eagle Outfitters stores in the United States and Canada during the beginning of the Christmas shopping season. These denial-of-service (DoS) attacks were quickly identified by company personnel, however, and corrective actions were implemented that limited their intended economic impact. Patterson's crimes carry a maximum total sentence of 11 years in prison, a fine of $350,000, or both.

Ohio Man Attacked NASA Computer System, Shutting Down E-mail Server (February 13, 2003) [*United States v. Amato*] Dino A. Amato, age 37, of Medina, Ohio, was charged with knowingly violating the regulations and orders of NASA for the protection and security of property and equipment in the custody of, and under contract with, NASA. According to court documents, between November 5 and 14, 2001, Amato, a contract employee with Affiliated Computer Services at the NASA Glenn Research Center in Cleveland, Ohio, knowingly and willfully violated NASA regulations by downloading a compressed or "zipped" computer file from the Internet. He transmitted this file to an e-mail account on the NASA e-mail server on at least seven different occasions, knowing that the file would slow the computer system drastically or would cause it to completely stop processing e-mail messages at the Glenn Research Center. Apparently, Amato's actions caused such a disruption in the flow of electronic communications on the Glenn Research Center e-mail server that NASA's computer security department incurred losses of approximately $12,000 in inspecting, diagnosing, and repairing the e-mail server. Amato's crime is punishable by a maximum statutory penalty of up to 1 year's imprisonment, a fine of up to $100,000, or both.

Pittsburgh, Pennsylvania, Man Convicted of Hacking a Judge's Personal E-mail Account (January 23, 2003) [*United States v. Ferguson*] Brian T. Ferguson, age 43, was found guilty of breaking into the America Online (AOL) account of Common Pleas Court

Judge Kim D. Eaton, who handled his divorce case, on three occasions. He obtained personal e-mail messages belonging to Judge Eaton, computer files, and other information that was part of her AOL account. Eaton testified that Ferguson appeared before her in April 2002 and handed her several e-mail messages she had written to friends and relatives. The e-mails contained personal information about her children's activities, and Ferguson's remarks led Eaton to believe he was threatening her. Ferguson's offense is punishable by up to 3 years in prison, a fine of $300,000, or both.

2004

U.S. Charges Hacker with Illegally Accessing New York Times Computer Network (January 8, 2004) [*United States v. Lamo*] Adrian Lamo, age 22, was charged in Manhattan federal court with cracking into the internal computer network of the *New York Times.* Lamo reportedly cracked into the *New York Times's* internal computer network on February 26, 2002, and accessed a database containing personal information (including home telephone numbers and social security numbers) for more than 3,000 contributors to the *New York Times's* op-ed page. Lamo added an entry to that database for himself, listing personal information including his cellular telephone number, (415) 505-HACK, and a description of his areas of expertise as "computer hacking, national security, communications intelligence." While inside the newspaper's internal network, Lamo set up five fictitious user identification names and passwords for the *New York Times'* account with LexisNexis, an online subscription service that provides legal, news, and other information for a fee. Over a 3-month period, those five fictitious user IDs/passwords conducted more than 3,000 searches on LexisNexis, costing approximately $300,000. Lamo could face up to five years in prison and a $250,000 penalty.

In an interview with a reporter from the online publication *SecurityFocus* on the same day as the crack, Lamo admitted responsibility for the *New York Times* intrusion. In interviews with other members of the press, Lamo also accepted responsibility for other cracks. He further admitted responsibility for the computer intrusion to representatives of the *Times,* providing details of how he cracked their computer network.

References

"The Can-Spam Act." 2004. http://www.spamlaws.com/federal/108s877.html (cited January 29, 2004.)

CNN.com. 2004. "Terror Financing Case in Florida Puts the PATRIOT Act to the Test." http://www.cnn.com/2004/LAW/01/19/attacks.professor.ap/index.html (cited January 19, 2004).

CNNmoney. 2003. "Profiling the Music Pirates." http://money.cnn.com/2003/09/10/technology/pirates/index.htm?cnn=yes (cited September 10, 2003).

David, Leonard. 2003. "Keeping Watch for Interstellar Viruses." http://www.space.com/scienceastronomy/space_hackers_031111.html.

Homeland Security Act of 2002. 2002. http://www.whitehouse.gov/deptofhomeland/analysis (cited January 23, 2004).

Kesterton, M. 2003. "Social Studies: Hackers from Outer Space?" *The Globe and Mail*, November 18, p. A 24.

Lancaster, H. 2001. "Women Bump into Tech Glass Ceiling." *The Globe and Mail*, August 25, p. S7.

U.S. Department of Justice. 2004. "Computer Crime and Intellectual Property Section." http://www.usdoj.gov/criminal/cybercrime/cccases.html (cited December 29, 2003).

6

Agencies and Organizations

This chapter provides an overview of the agencies and organizations committed to fighting cybercrime. The chapter opens with government and government-affiliated agencies having this objective in the United States and elsewhere. Listed next are independent organizations having this commitment, followed by suppliers of products and services for halting cybercrime.

Government Agencies

Department of Homeland Security
Homeland Security Operations Center
Washington, DC 20528
Tel: 202-282-8101
E-mail: HSCenter@dhs.gov
Web: http://www.dhs.gov

The creation of the Department of Homeland Security (DHS) was the most significant transformation of the U.S. government since 1947, when Harry S. Truman merged the various branches of the U.S. Armed Forces with the Department of Defense to better coordinate the nation's defense against military threats. The DHS represents a similar consolidation, both in style and in substance.

In the aftermath of the terrorist attacks against the United States on September 11, 2001, President George W. Bush decided that twenty-two previously disparate domestic agencies needed to be coordinated into one department to better protect the nation against threats to the homeland. Accordingly, the new department's priority objective is to protect the nation against further terrorist attacks. Component agencies will assist in analyzing threats and intelligence, guarding borders and airports, protecting critical infrastructures, and coordinating the responses to future emergencies. Besides providing a better-coordinated defense of the U.S. homeland, the DHS is also dedicated to protecting the rights of American citizens and enhancing public services (such as natural disaster assistance and citizenship services) by dedicating offices to these important missions.

U.S. Department of Justice
10th & Constitution Ave. NW
Criminal Division (Computer Crime & Intellectual Property Section)
John C. Keeney Building, Suite 600
Washington, DC 20530
Tel: (202) 514-1026
Fax: (202) 514-6113
Web: http://www.cybercrime.gov

The U.S. Department of Justice set up the Computer Crime and Intellectual Property Section (CCIPS) of the Criminal Division to deal with cybercrime in particular. CCIPS's Web site informs the public about its wide field of activities.

Federal Bureau of Investigation (FBI)
J. Edgar Hoover Building
935 Pennsylvania Ave. NW
Washington, DC 20535-0001
Tel: (202) 324-2000

NIPC (National Infrastructure Protection Center)
Information Analysis Infrastructure Protection
Washington, DC 20528
Tel: (202) 323-3205
Fax: (202) 323-2079
E-mail: nipc.watch@fbi.gov

In cooperation with the Department of Homeland Security, the Federal Bureau of Investigation (FBI) operates the Center for National Infrastructure Protection. The FBI has also constructed a number of cybercrime fighting units across the United States.

NSA National Computer Security Center (NCSC)
NSA INFOSEC Service Center (NISC)
INFOSEC Awareness, Attn: Y13
Fort George G. Meade, MD 20755-6000
Tel: (800) 688-6115

The National Computer Security Center (NCSC) provides solutions, products, and services and conducts defensive information operations for information infrastructures critical to U.S. national security interests.

The NCSC, a part of the National Computer Security Agency (NSA), provides information systems security standards and solutions. Working in partnership with industry, academic institutions, and other U.S. government agencies, including the National Institute of Standards and Technology (NIST), the NCSC initiates needed research and develops and publishes standards and criteria for trusted information systems. The NCSC also promotes information systems security awareness, education, and technology transfer through cooperative efforts, public seminars, and an annual National Information Systems Security Conference.

Independent Organizations

CERT (Computer Emergency Response Team)
CERT Coordination Center Software Engineering Institute
Carnegie Mellon University
5000 Forbes Avenue
Pittsburgh, PA 15213-3890
E-mail: cert@cert.org
Tel: (412) 268-7090 (24-hour hotline)
Fax: (412) 268-6989
To report security incidents:
http://www.cert.org/reporting/incident_form.txt
To report system vulnerabilities:
http://www.cert.org/reporting/vulnerability_form.txt

The CERT Coordination Center (CERT/CC) is a center for Internet security founded in 1988 following the Morris worm incident—an exploit that reportedly brought 10 percent of the existing Internet systems to a halt in November 1988. At that time, the Defense Advanced Research Projects Agency (DARPA) charged the Software Engineering Institute (SEI) at Carnegie Mellon University with starting a center to coordinate communication among experts during security emergencies and to help prevent future incidents.

Due to the rapid development of the Internet and its use in many critical applications, the amount of damage and the difficulties in detecting intrusions have grown significantly. Thus, the CERT/CC role has been expanded in the past two years. CERT/CC has become part of the SEI Networked Systems Survivability Program, with its primary goal being to ensure that appropriate technology and systems management practices are used to resist attacks on networked systems and to limit damage and ensure continuity of critical services in spite of successful attacks, accidents, or failures.

United States Computer Emergency Response Team (US-CERT)

US-CERT is jointly run by the Department of Homeland Security and CERT at Carnegie-Mellon University, and can be contacted through any one of these organizations.
E-mail: info@us-cert.gov

With the recent development of the Department of Homeland Security, and in collaboration with the CERT/CC, the newly named US-CERT is intended to become the new focal point for identifying and responding to computer security incidents in the United States. Its main mission is to coordinate previously dispersed efforts to counter the threats from all forms of cybercrime. In doing so, the newly formed US-CERT takes on responsibilities for:

- Analyzing and reducing cyberthreats and vulnerabilities
- Disseminating cyberthreat warning information
- Coordinating incident responses

ICANN (Internet Corporation for Assigned Names and Numbers)
4676 Admiralty Way, Suite 330
Marina del Rey, CA 90292-6601
Tel: (310) 823-9358
Fax: (310) 823-8649
E-mail: icann@icann.org

In 1998, a broad coalition of the Internet's stakeholders—the business community, the academic community, the technical community, and the user community—founded the Internet Corporation for Assigned Names and Numbers (ICANN) to serve as a technical coordination body for the Internet. ICANN assumed responsibility for tasks previously performed by the United States Internet Assigned Numbers Authority as well as by other key groups. ICANN manages the assignment of identifiers that must be globally unique for the Internet to function properly. These identifiers include:

- Domain names
- IP addresses
- Protocol parameters and port numbers

ICANN has also assumed responsibility for the operation of the Internet's root server system. ICANN is a nonprofit, private sector corporation also charged with the promotion of competition and the achievement of a broad representation of the user community.

ISOC (Internet Society)
Internet Society International Secretariat
1775 Wiehle Ave., Suite 102
Reston, VA 20190
Tel: (703) 326-9880
Fax: (703) 326-9881
Web: http:/www.isoc.org

The Internet Society (ISOC) is a professional membership society with more than 150 organization and 16,000 individual members in over 180 countries. It provides leadership in addressing issues that confront the future of the Internet and is the organizational home for the groups responsible for Internet infrastructure standards, including the Internet Engineering Task Force (IETF).

IETF (Internet Engineering Task Force)
IETF Secretariat c/o Corporation for National Research Initiatives
1895 Preston White Dr., Suite 100
Reston, VA 20191-5434
Tel: (703) 620-8990
Fax: (703) 620-9071
E-mail: ietf-secretariat@ietf.org

The Internet Engineering Task Force (IETF) is a large, open, international community of network designers, operators, vendors, and researchers concerned with the evolution of the Internet's architecture and its smooth operation. IETF membership is open, and the actual technical work is performed in groups organized into several areas, including routing, transport, and security. Much of the work of the IETF is handled via mailing lists, as the IETF holds meetings only three times per year. The working groups are managed by area directors, who are members of the Internet Engineering Steering Group (IESG).

The Internet Architecture Board (IAB) provides architectural oversight and adjudicates appeals when someone complains that the IESG has failed in meeting its objectives. The IAB and IESG are chartered by the Internet Society (ISOC) for meeting these purposes. The general area director serves as the chair of the IESG and of the IETF and is an ex officio member of the IAB.

Free Software Foundation (FSF)
59 Temple Place, Suite 330
Boston MA 02111-1307
Tel: (617) 542-5942
Fax: (617) 542-2652
E-mail: gnu@gnu.org

The Free Software Foundation (FSF), founded in 1985, is dedicated to promoting computer users' rights to use, study, copy, modify, and redistribute computer programs. The FSF promotes the development and use of free software, particularly the GNU operating system (used widely today in its GNU/Linux variant), and free documentation. The FSF also helps to spread awareness of the ethical and political issues of freedom in the use of software.

Though other organizations distribute freely what software happens to be available, the Free Software Foundation concentrates on the development of new free software. The FSF also makes free software into a coherent system, thus eliminating the need to use proprietary software. The FSF distributes copies of GNU software and manuals for a distribution fee and accepts tax-deductible gifts to support GNU development. Most of the FSF's funds come from its distribution service.

W3C (The World Wide Web Consortium)
Massachusetts Institute of Technology (MIT)
Computer Science and Artificial Intelligence Laboratory (CSAIL)
200 Technology Square
Cambridge, MA 02139
Tel: (617) 253-2613
Fax: (617) 258-5999

In October 1994, Tim Berners-Lee founded the World Wide Web Consortium (W3C) at the MIT Laboratory for Computer Science in collaboration with CERN (Conseil Européen pour la Recherche Nucléaire, or the European Organization for Nuclear Research), the world's largest particle physics center, and an initiator of many advances in information technologies. The Consortium also received support from DARPA and the European Commission to advance its mission.

The Consortium's purpose is to promote "interoperability" and to encourage an open forum for Web development discussion. The Consortium concentrates its efforts on three principal tasks:

- The promotion and development of its vision for the future of the World Wide Web
- The design of Web technologies to realize this vision
- The standardization of Web technologies

Suppliers of Products and Services

Security Training, Education, and Certification

SANS (SysAdmin, Audit, Network, Security) Institute
8120 Woodmont Ave., Suite 205
Bethesda, MD 20814
Tel: (301) 654-SANS (7267)
Fax: (540) 548-0957
E-mail: info@sans.org
Web: http://www.sans.org

The SANS Institute offers conferences and training courses to provide a certification in security knowledge, the Global Information

Assurance Certification (GIAC), which has gained industry-wide acceptance.

ISC(2) (International Information Systems Security Certification Consortium, Inc.)
(ISC)2 Services
2494 Bayshore Blvd., Suite 201
Dunedin, FL 34698
Tel: (888) 333-4458
Fax: (727) 738-8522
E-mail: infoisc2@isc2.org
Web: http://www.isc2.org

The ISC(2) has developed the Common Body of Knowledge (CBK) in IT security. The CBK is a compilation and distillation of all security information collected internationally of relevance to information security (IS) professionals. ISC(2) has also defined the CISSP (Certified Information Systems Security Profession) certification, which sets standards for testing individuals who seek certification on their IT security knowledge.

Academic Degrees

A number of universities in the United States and around the world have identified information technology security as an independent area of specialization. To this end, there are a growing number of dedicated undergraduate and graduate degrees in information technology with a security specialization. Some of these educational institutions are listed here.

James Madison University
Commonwealth Information Security Center
800 S. Main St.
Harrisonburg, VA 22807
Tel: (540) 568-6211

Mary Washington College
James Monroe Center
1301 College Ave.
Fredericksburg, VA 22401
Tel: (540) 654-1000

Idaho State University
Computer Information Systems Department
921 S. 8th Ave.
Pocatello, ID 83209
Tel: (208) 282-3585

University of Advanced Technology
Admissions
2625 W. Baseline Rd.
Tempe, AZ 85283-1042
Tel: (800) 658-5744 or (602) 383-8228
E-mail: admissions@uat.edu

University of Ontario Institute of Technology
Admissions (graduate program under development)
2000 Simcoe St.
North Oshawa, ON L1H 7L7
Canada
Tel: (905) 721-3190 or (866) 844-8648
Fax: (905) 721-3178
E-mail: info@uoit.ca or admissions@uoit.ca

Antivirus Software

There are two main types of virus scanning software. One type is used on the individual machine that is going to be protected, and the other type scans the traffic to and from the Internet at a gateway, looking for potentially harmful code. Both versions not only try to remove any attached viruses from programs and documents, but also inform the user about actions taken.

The companies listed here offer a broad portfolio of antivirus products for gateway-based and local installation. The products differ mainly in licensing and packaging schemes. The products are regularly tested by the computer security organizations and publications. Depending on the set of criteria, the outcomes of these evaluations show different products at the top of the list. Most of the listed companies also provide information services for their customers and the general public to inform them about the latest worm and virus threats and vulnerabilities, and possible countermeasures.

Aladdin-Esafe
Aladdin Knowledge Systems, Ltd.
15 Beit Oved St.
Tel Aviv, Israel 61110
Tel: 972-(0)3-636-2222
Fax: 972-(0)3-537-5796

Aladdin Knowledge Systems, Inc.
2920 N. Arlington Heights Rd.
Arlington Heights, IL 60004
Tel: (800) 562-2543 or (847) 818-3800
Fax: (847) 818-3810
E-mail: sales@us.aks.com

F-Secure
Corporate Headquarters
Tammasaarenkatu 7 PL 24 00180
Helsinki, Finland
Tel: 358–9-2520-0700
Fax: 358–9-2520-5001

F-Secure Inc.
100 Century Center Ct., Suite 700
San Jose, CA 95112
Tel: (408) 938-6700
Fax: (408) 938-6701
E-mail: SanJose@F-Secure.com

Network Associates—McAfee
Corporate Headquarters (including McAfee Security, Sniffer Technologies, and Magic Solutions)
3965 Freedom Cir.
Santa Clara, CA 95054
Tel: (972) 963-8000
Web: http://www.mcafee.com/

Sophos
Global Headquarters
The Pentagon
Abingdon Science Park
Abingdon OX14 3YP

United Kingdom
Tel: 44-1235-559933
Fax: 44-1235-559935
E-mail: sales@sophos.com

Sophos Inc.
6 Kimball Ln.
4th Floor
Lynnfield, MA 01940
Tel: (781) 973-0110

Symantec Corporation
20330 Stevens Creek Blvd.
Cupertino, CA 95014
Tel: (408) 517-8000
Web: http://www.symantec.com

Trend Micro, Inc.
10101 N. De Anza Blvd.
Cupertino, CA 95014
Tel: (800) 228-5651
E-mail: info@trendmicro.com

Firewalls

Firewalls are devices used to control the data traffic flowing into and out of a corporate network to and from the Internet. With firewalls, unwanted data traffic can be blocked, and access to the network can be controlled. Many of the available firewall products allow users to build a secure tunnel or virtual private network through the Internet so that two or more sites of an organization can use the Internet as a medium to communicate. Data are encrypted by one firewall before being sent, and the receiving firewall decrypts the data. This minimizes the risks of a man-in-the-middle attack (see chapter 2). The suppliers listed below have all provided strong products for these tasks over the past several years.

Check Point Software Technologies, Inc.
800 Bridge Pkwy.
Redwood City, CA 94065
Tel: (650) 628-2000

Fax: (650) 654-4233
E-mail: info@checkpoint.com

Cisco Systems, Inc.
Main Corporate Headquarters
170 W. Tasman Dr.
San Jose, CA 95134
Tel: (408) 526-4000 or (800) 553-NETS or (800) 553-6387
E-mail: info@cisco.com

NetScreen Technologies, Inc.
805 11th Ave.
Building 3
Sunnyvale, CA 94089
Tel: (408) 543-2100
E-mail: info@netscreen.com

Nokia
Head Office
Keilalahdentie 2-4
P.O. Box 226
FIN-00045 Nokia Group
Finland
Tel: 358-7180-08000

Nokia, Inc.
Nokia 545
Whisman Rd.
Silicon Valley Campus
Mountain View, CA 94043
Tel: (650) 625-2000
Fax: (650) 691-2170

Nortel Networks
Corporate Headquarters
8200 Dixie Rd.
Brampton, ON L6T 5P6
Canada
Tel: (905) 863-0000

SonicWALL, Inc.
1143 Borregas Ave.
Sunnyvale, CA 94089-1306
Tel: (408) 745-9600
Fax: (408) 745-9300
E-mail: info@sonicwall.com

Symantec
For Symantec's listing, refer to the Antivirus Software section.

Watchguard
505 Fifth Ave. S
Suite 500
Seattle, WA 98104
Tel: (206) 521-8340
Fax: (206) 521-8342
E-mail: information@watchguard.com

Intrusion Detection Systems (IDS)

Intrusion detection systems complete the set of technical precautions that an organization can take. Intrusion detection systems, or IDS, assist in detecting whether a security breach actually has happened in a network. These systems examine the computer itself for unwanted changes or data transfers in the network, noting anomalies.

Cisco
For Cisco's listing, refer to the Firewall section.

Internet Security Systems
Global Headquarters
6303 Barfield Rd.
Atlanta, GA 30328
Tel: (888) 901-7477
Web: http://www.iss.net/contact.php

Symantec
For Symantec's listing, refer to the Antivirus Software section.

Tripwire, Inc.
Headquarters
326 SW Broadway, 3rd Floor
Portland, OR 97205
Tel: (503) 276-7500
Fax: (503) 223-0182
Web: http://www.tripwire.com

7

Print and Nonprint Resources

Resource materials in print about cybercrime and its various forms—such as cracking and the computer underground (CU)—are abundant. This chapter focuses on three types of materials: books, Web sites dealing with cybercrime and computer intrusion, and films portraying cybercrime.

The U.S. Department of Justice's Computer Crime and Intellectual Property Section (CCIPS) has an e-mail service giving updates on cybercrime. To receive these updates, send a blank message to cybercrime-subscribe@topica.com to be added to the e-mail list. The www.usdoj.gov/criminal/cybercrime/index.html site has links to the following topics:

- Computer crime
- Intellectual property crime
- Cybercrime documents
- Cyberethics information

This Department of Justice Web site also has general information such as how to report Internet-related crime; how private industry can help fight cybercrime; law enforcement coordination of high-tech crimes; legal issues dealing with electronic commerce, encryption, and computer crime; federal code related to cybercrime; intellectual property crime; international aspects of computer crime (such as the Council of Europe Convention on Cybercrime); privacy issues in the high-tech context; prosecuting crimes facilitated by computers and by the Internet; protecting critical infrastructures; searching and seizing computers and obtaining electronic evidence in criminal investigations; and speech issues in the high-tech context.

Books

Arguilla, J., and David F. Ronfeldt. ***Networks and Netwars: The Future of Terror, Crime, and Militancy.*** Santa Monica, CA: Rand, 2001.

This book describes a new, emerging spectrum of cyberconflict. The book discusses, among other topics, netwar (conflicts that terrorists, criminals, gangs, and ethnic extremists wage) and how to combat it.

Berkowitz, B. D. ***The New Face of War: How War Will Be Fought in the 21st Century.*** New York: Simon and Schuster, 2003.

This book discusses the information war, how it has revolutionized combat, and how the war against cyberterrorists can be fought and won.

Blane, J. V. ***Cybercrime and Cyberterrorism: Current Issues.*** Commack, NY: Nova Science, 2003.

This book discusses various topics on cybercrime and cyberterrorism, including how the two differ.

Bond, C. S. ***Cybercrime: Can a Small Business Protect Itself? Hearing before the Committee on Small Business, U.S. Senate.*** Collingdale, PA: DIANE, 2002.

This book gives ideas for how small business owners can protect their computer systems from cybercrime.

Brill, A. E., F. N. Baldwin, and Robert John Munro. ***Cybercrime and Security*** (3-Binder Set). New York: Oceana, 1998.

This rather advanced publication, prepared by leading experts in cybercrime and security, offers management strategies and solutions for system administrators. The book alerts readers to potential threats, discusses cybercrime legislation, and covers privacy issues, encryption, and computer security.

Casey, E. ***Digital Evidence and Computer Crime.*** San Diego, CA: Academic, 2000.

This book details the law as it applies to computer networks and cybercrime, and it describes how evidence stored on or transmitted by computers can play a role in a wide range of crimes, such as homicide, rape, abduction, child abuse, solicitation of pornography, stalking, harassment, fraud, theft, drug trafficking, computer intrusions, and terrorism.

Chirillo, J. ***Hack Attacks Encyclopedia: A Complete History of Hacks, Phreaks, and Spies over Time.*** New York: John Wiley and Sons, 2001.

Written by a security expert, this book covers historic texts, program files, code snippets, hacking and security tools, and more advanced topics such as password programs, Unix/Linux systems, scanners, sniffers, spoofers, and flooders.

Clifford, R. D. ***Cybercrime: The Investigation, Prosecution, and Defense of a Computer-Related Crime.*** Durham, NC: Carolina Academic, 2001.

Intended primarily for a legal audience, this book covers legal topics such as what conduct is considered a cybercrime, investigating improper cyberconduct, trying a cybercrime case as a prosecuting or defending attorney, and handling the international aspects of cybercrimes.

Cole, E., and Jeff Riley. ***Hackers Beware: The Ultimate Guide to Network Security.*** Upper Saddle River, NJ: Pearson Education, 2001.

This book is written by experts in computer security and is intended for network security professionals. It describes UNIX and Microsoft NT vulnerabilities; protection against intrusions; and trends and critical thoughts regarding system administration, networking, and security.

Feinstein, D. ***Improving Our Ability to Fight Cybercrime: Oversight of the National Infrastructure Protection Center: Congressional Hearing.*** Collingdale, PA: DIANE, 2003.

This current text speaks frankly in the wake of the World Trade Center attacks about protecting the United States' ability to fight cybercrime. Important issues are also discussed regarding the National Infrastructure Protection Center.

Furnell, S. ***Cybercrime: Vandalizing the Information Society.*** Reading, MA: Addison-Wesley, 2001.

Written by a British computer security expert, this book gives a thorough overview of cracking, viral code, and e-fraud and covers a wide range of crimes and abuses relating to information technology. Unlike many other books, this one does not require advanced technical knowledge to understand. Thus, it is a good basic text for understanding cybercrimes.

Garfinkel, W., G. Spafford, and Debby Russell. ***Web Security, Privacy, and Commerce.*** Sebastopol, CA: O'Reilly and Associates, 2001.

Intended primarily for a business audience, this book covers issues of Web security, privacy, and commerce, including such advanced topics as the public key infrastructure, digital signatures, digital certificates, hostile mobile code, and Web publishing.

Goodman, S. F., and Abraham D. Sofaer. ***The Transnational Dimension of Cybercrime and Terrorism.*** Prague: Hoover Institute, 2001.

Intended for a more advanced audience, this book covers the issues of transnational cybercrime and terrorism.

Gunkel, D. J. ***Hacking Cyberspace.*** Boulder, CO: Westview Press, 2000.

The author, writing for an advanced audience, examines the metaphors of new technology and how these metaphors impact the implementation of technology in today's world. This book combines philosophy, communication theory, and computer history.

Himanen, P., M. Castells, and Linus Torvald. ***The Hacker Ethic and the Spirit of the Information Age.*** New York: Random House, 2001.

This is one of the few books available that focuses on the White Hat Hacker Ethic, values, and beliefs—especially their belief that individuals can create great things by joining forces and using information in imaginative ways.

Howard, M., and David E. LeBlanc. ***Writing Secure Code,* 2d ed**. Redmond, WA: Microsoft Press, 2002.

Drawing on the lessons learned at Microsoft during the 2002 Windows security push, the authors offer a three-pronged strategy for securing design, defaults, and deployment. This is an advanced book written for security professionals.

Juergensmeyer, M. ***Terror in the Mind of God.*** Berkeley: University of California Press, 2000.

This book discusses what terrorist groups may be likely to commit crimes against states. The author focuses on the theological justifications for violence and the bases for the decision to use violence. The book also discusses common themes and patterns in the cultures of violence and offers ideas about the future of religious violence.

Klevinsky, T. J., A. K. Gupta, and Scott Laliberte. ***Hack I.T.: Security through Penetration Testing.*** Upper Saddle River, NJ: Pearson Education, 2002.

This book introduces the complex topic of penetration testing and its vital role in network security. Written for advanced professionals, the book discusses hacking myths, potential drawbacks of penetration testing, war dialing, social engineering methods, sniffers and password crackers, and firewalls and intrusion detection systems.

Komar, B., J. Wettern, and Ronald Beekelaar. ***Firewalls for Dummies.*** New York: John Wiley and Sons, 2003.

This book presents the latest facts about firewalls, to help businesses and individuals protect their computer systems. The authors are computer security experts.

Levy, S. ***Hackers: Heroes of the Computer Revolution.*** New York: Penguin, 2001.

This book, written for young students, talks about MIT's Tech Model Railroad Club and some of the great White Hat hackers of all time.

Lilley, P. ***Hacked, Attacked, and Abused: Digital Crime Exposed.*** London: Kogan Page Limited, 2003.

This book gives practical advice for a business audience on protecting a network against intrusions. The book discusses organized digital crime, cyberlaundering, fraudulent Internet sites, viruses, Web site defacement, aspects of electronic cash, identity theft, information warfare, denial of service attacks, and invasion of digital privacy.

Littman, J. ***The Fugitive Game: Online with Kevin Mitnick.*** Boston: Little, Brown, 1996.

The author explores the online pranks of convicted cracker Kevin Mitnick, offering insights into social engineering as well.

Loader, B., and Thomas Douglas. ***Cybercrime: Security and Surveillance in the Information Age.*** New York: Routledge, 2000.

These two writers for the journal *Information, Communication, and Society* focus on the growing concern over the use of electronic communications for criminal activities and the appropriateness of the countermeasures currently used to deal with cybercrime. The wide range of topics includes the legal, psychological, and sociological aspects of cybercrime. This advanced book is intended for practitioners, graduate students, and faculty.

Maiwald, E. ***Network Security: A Beginner's Guide.*** New York: McGraw-Hill, 2001.

Despite its title, this book is written for network administrators who run a network but need to secure it as well. Topics include antivirus software, firewalls, and intrusion detection.

McClure, S., J. Scambray, and George Kurtz. ***Hacking Exposed: Network Security Secrets and Solutions,*** **4th ed**. New York: McGraw-Hill, 2003.

This book discusses an offensive approach to security and presents an extensive catalog of the weaponry that Black Hat crackers use. The book gives detailed explanations of concepts such as war dialing and rootkits and discusses how to use the more powerful and popular hacker software. The language and concepts are advanced and are intended for system administrators.

McClure, S., S. Shah, and Shreeraj Shah. ***Web Hacking: Attacks and Defense.*** Upper Saddle River, NJ: Pearson, 2002.

This book talks about what can happen when vulnerabilities go unrepaired. It is an informative guide for Web security guidance.

McIntosh, N. ***Cybercrime.*** Chicago: Heinemann Library, 2002.

This book gives a sound but elementary introduction to the topic of cybercrime for students aged 9–12.

Meinel, C. P. ***The Happy Hacker,* 4th ed.** Tuscon, AZ: American Eagle, 2001.

This is part of a series of books by the same author on how to hack. The basic theme is that hacking is fun, but cracking is not. The book is especially useful for neophytes in the field.

Mitnick, K., and William L. Simon. ***The Art of Deception: Controlling the Human Element of Security.*** New York: John Wiley and Sons, 2002.

This book, cowritten by cybercriminal-turned-security expert Kevin Mitnick, offers advice about securing business computer systems and insights about social engineering.

Newman, J. Q. ***Identity Theft: The Cybercrime of the Millennium.*** Port Townsend, WA: Loompanics Unlimited, 1999.

This book gives a nontechnical overview of identity theft, particularly in the United States.

Nichols, R. K., and Pannos C. Lekkas. ***Wireless Security: Models, Threats, and Solutions.*** New York: McGraw-Hill, 2002.

Geared toward professionals, this is a comprehensive guide to wireless security and discusses complete solutions for voice, data, and mobile commerce; telecom, broadband, and satellite; and emerging technologies.

Nuwere, E. ***Hacker Cracker: A Journey from the Mean Streets of Brooklyn to the Frontiers of Cyberspace.*** New York: Morrow, William, 2002.

Written by a 21-year-old cracker who is now a respected Internet security specialist, this book provides young students with a look at the Black Hat world.

Peterson, T. F. ***Nightwork: A History of the Hacks and Pranks at MIT.*** Cambridge, MA: MIT Press, 2003.

Students and adults alike will find this book interesting; as its title indicates, it gives insights into the history of the hacks and pranks at MIT in the 1960s and 1970s.

Raymond, E. S. ***The New Hacker's Dictionary.*** Cambridge, MA: MIT Press, 1996.

This book defines jargon used by hackers and programmers and discusses the writing and speaking styles of hackers. The book also provides an interesting look at computer folklore.

———. ***The Cathedral and the Bazaar: Musings on Linux and Open Source by an Accidental Revolutionary.*** Sebastopol, CA: O'Reilly and Associates, 2001.

This book, a favorite with hackers, is for anyone interested in the future of the computer industry, the dynamics of the information economy, and the particulars regarding open (freely copyable) source.

Richards, J. R. ***Transnational Criminal Organizations, Cybercrime, and Money Laundering: A Handbook for Law Enforcement Officers, Auditors, and Financial Investigators.*** Boca Raton, FL: CRC, 1998.

Written by a law enforcement professional and primarily intended for those in the same profession, the book examines the workings of organized criminals and groups transcending national borders. Topics include how criminals internationally launder money, how law enforcement officers curb such activities, and new methods and tactics to counteract across-border money laundering.

Roddell, V. ***Stay Safe in Cyberspace: Cybercrime Awareness, Prevention, and Safety for American Families.*** http://www.ccmostwanted.biz/: Cybercriminals Most Wanted, 2002.

This family reference manual discusses fundamental online and computer safety for each family member. The book would also be of interest to those with links to American law enforcement agencies and various software vendors. The book covers varied topics: fraud, scams, hoaxes, infectors, spam, identity theft, online harassment, home computer security, privacy, and parental online issues.

Schell, Bernadette H., J. L. Dodge, with Steve S. Moutsatsos. ***The Hacking of America: Who's Doing It, Why, and How.*** New York: Quorum, 2002.

This book uses psychological inventories to profile the personalities and behavioral traits of many self-admitted hackers in an attempt to answer the question: Is the vilification of hackers justified?

Schneier, B. ***Secrets and Lies: Digital Security in a Networked World.*** New York: John Wiley and Sons, 2000.

Written by an information security expert and intended for a business audience, this book presents what those in business need to know about computer security in order to survive. The book also gives insights into the digital world and the realities of the networked society.

Shimomura, T., and J. Markoff. ***Takedown: The Pursuit and Capture of Kevin Mitnick, America's Most Wanted Computer Outlaw, by the Man Who Did It.*** New York: Warner, 1996.

This book describes the capture of Kevin Mitnick by Tsutomu Shimomura. It includes some details of Shimomura's personal life and covers some of the technical, legal, and ethical questions surrounding the case.

Shinder, D. L., and Ed Tittel. ***Scene of the Cybercrime: Computer Forensics Handbook.*** Rockland, MA: Syngress, 2002.

The objective of this book is to introduce IT professionals, responsible for building systems to prevent cybercrime, to the highly structured world of law enforcement, responsible for investigating and prosecuting cybercrime. The book also helps law enforcement officers to gain an understanding of the technical aspects of cybercrime and how technology can be used to help solve such crimes.

Singh, S. ***Code Book: How to Make It, Break It, Hack It, or Crack It.*** New York: Bantam Doubleday Dell, 2002.

This book, intended for students around age 12, chronicles the history of cryptography from Roman times to the present.

Spinello, R., and Herman T. Tavani. ***Readings in CyberEthics.*** Boston: Jones and Bartlett, 2001.

This is an anthology of more than forty essays presenting conflicting points of view about new moral and ethical questions raised by computers and the Internet: free speech and content controls, intellectual property, privacy, security, and professional ethics and codes of conduct.

Spitzner, L. ***Honeypots: Tracking Hackers.*** Upper Saddle River, NJ: Pearson Education, 2002.

Written for system administrators, this book discusses attracting, observing, and tracking crackers through the use of honeypots. Advantages and disadvantages of honeypots are discussed, as are controversial legal issues surrounding their use.

Stoll, Cliffford. ***Cuckoo's Egg: Tracking a Spy through the Maze of Computer Espionage.*** New York: Pocket, 2000.

This is a reader-friendly, gripping spy thriller centering on cybercrime. Particularly appealing to young people interested in computer hacking, even for those with little computer knowledge.

Thomas, D. ***Cybercrime.*** Washington, DC: Taylor and Francis, 2000.

This book, intended for law enforcement agencies, security services, and legislators at the university level and beyond, focuses on growing concerns about using electronic communication to commit crimes. The book offers a balanced perspective on what legal issues should be noted regarding cybercrime and its impact on society.

U.S. Department of Justice. ***21st Century Guide to Cybercrime*** (CD-ROM). Washington, DC: U.S. Department of Justice, 2003.

This CD-ROM provides extensive coverage of the Justice Department's work on computer crime and intellectual property crimes and discusses the National Infrastructure Protection Center (NIPC). The topics covered in the CD-ROM are wide-ranging: searching and seizing computers in criminal investigations, legal issues, computer crime, intellectual property crime, international aspects of computer crime, privacy issues, cyberethics, and prosecuting cybercrimes.

Vacca, J. R. ***Computer Forensics: Computer Crime Scene Investigation.*** Boston: Charles River Media, 2002.

This book offers an overview of computer forensics, with topics such as seizure of data, determining the "fingerprints" of a cybercrime, and recovering from terrorist cyberattacks. The book focuses on solving cybercrimes rather than on information security per se.

Westby, J. ***International Guide to Combating Cybercrime.*** Chicago: ABA, 2003.

This book discusses the complex issues regarding the curbing of international cybercrime.

Web Sites

Hacking Sites

http://www.defcon.org/. Site of DefCon, the largest hacker gathering in the world, typically held at the end of July in Las Vegas.

http://www.2600.com. Site of the magazine *2600: The Hacker Quarterly.*

http://www.antionline.com/. A White Hat site of security professionals who are openly opposed to Black Hat activities.

http://www.hackers4hire.com/. A group of computer security professionals dedicated to helping businesses find their system flaws and correct them.

http://www.cultdeadcow.com/. Popular hacker site; home of Hacktivismo (Hacker Activists) site.

Security Sites

http://www.wired.com/. Up-to-date news on technological issues.

http://infoworld.com/security. Up-to-date news on technological and security issues, with sound features related to businesses.

http://www.infosecuritymag.com/. Security news; excellent articles for security professionals.

http://www.infosecnews.com/. Information security portal.

http://www.idg.net/. Up-to-date news related to technology and security for professionals; also has an IT job listing.

http://www.zdnet.com/. Features enterprise news on technological issues.

http://www.securityserver.com/. Features security software for purchase at a discount; also has security news items.

http://www.secmag.com/. Technology news, security applications, and solutions for businesses.

http://www.security-online.com/. Online security solutions source.

http://www.techweb.com/. Business technology network.

http://www.news.com/. Technology news; business hardware and software.

http://www.download.com/. Technology news and product reviews; the latest on gaming.

Intrusion Detection Systems

http://www.acm.org/. Site of the Association for Computing Machinery, a leading portal to computing literature.

http://www-nrg.ee.lbl.gov/. Site of the Network Research Group (NRG) of the Information and Sciences Division at Lawrence Berkeley National Laboratory in Berkeley, California.

http://www.cert.org/. Site of the CERT Coordination Center, at Carnegie Mellon University.

http://www.checkpoint.com/. Site committed to Internet security and the delivery of intelligent solutions for perimeter, internal, and Web security.

http://www.cs.purdue.edu. Site of Purdue University Computer Science Department.

http://www.networkintrusion.co.uk/. A site about network intrusion detection, hosted by security experts.

http://www.cmds.net/. Network intrusion detection solutions.

http://www.gocsi.com/. Site of the Computer Security Institute.

http://seclab.cs.ucdavis.edu/. Site of University of California at Davis Computer Security Laboratory; features papers on technological issues.

http://www.isse.gmu.edu/~csis/. Site of Center for Secure Information Systems.

http://www.cs.columbia.edu. Site of Columbia University Computer Science Department.

http://www.fstc.org/. Site of financial services technology consortium.

http://www.securitysearch.net/. Features Windows security articles.

http://www.ncs.gov/. Homeland Security National Communications System; shows the current risk of terrorist attacks.

http://www.securitywizards.com/. A site related to business-driven network security.

http://www.digital.com/. A Hewlett-Packard Development Company site, featuring business product information and technology news.

http://www.zurich.ibm.com/. Site of IBM Zurich Research Laboratory.

http://www.sans.org/. Site of the SANS Institute.

http://www.securezone.com/. A site related to network security.

http://www.communication.org/. Site of a community of Web enthusiasts.

http://www.securityfocus.com/. A site committed to security issues and vulnerabilities.

U.S. Government and International Cybercrime Sites

http://www.usdoj.gov/criminal/cybercrime/. Site of the U.S. Department of Justice.

www.crime-research.org/. Site of the Computer Crime Research Center (CCRC).

http://conventions.coe.int/Treaty/EN/CadreListeTraites.htm. Site has a complete list of the Council of Europe treaties.

Film

Hackers
Date: **1995**
Length: **107 minutes**
Cast: Jonny Lee Miller, Angelina Jolie, Fisher Stevens, and Lorraine Bracco.

This story centers on a neophyte hacker who cracks into a highly secured computer and stumbles upon an embezzling scheme masked by a computer virus with the potential to destroy the world's ecosystem.

War Games
Date: **1983**
Length: **114 minutes**
Cast: Matthew Broderick, Dabney Coleman, John Wood, and Ally Sheedy.

This film is best described as a cyberthriller. A computer hacker unwittingly taps into the Defense Department's war computer and starts a confrontation of global proportions—World War III.

Glossary

Access Controls The physical or logical safeguards preventing unauthorized access to information resources.

Anonymous Digital Cash Combined with encryption and/or anonymous remailers, digital cash allows criminals to make transactions with complete anonymity. Digital cash is a system that allows a person to pay for goods or services by transmitting a number from one computer to another. Like the serial numbers on real dollar bills, the digital cash numbers are unique.

Anonymous Remailers A remailer is a computer service that privatizes e-mail and typically contains the sender's identity. Anonymous remailers send e-mail messages that arrive in a receiver's inbox without a sender's identity.

Antivirus Software Detects viruses and notifies the user that the virus is present. This type of software keeps a database of "fingerprints," a set of characteristic bytes from known viruses, on file.

ARPANET The first transcontinental, high-speed computer network, built by the United States Defense Department as an experiment in digital communications.

Bacteria or Rabbits Viruses that do not carry a logic bomb and are therefore not as destructive as other viruses. They merely replicate, consuming resources.

BIOS The software that is built into the hardware of any PC to access the operating system on the hard drives and boot (start up) the machine.

Black Hats Hackers (more correctly called crackers) who engage in destructive computer exploits, motivated by revenge, sabotage, blackmail, or greed, that can result in harm to property and/or to people.

Black Hole A region on the Internet that is not reachable from anywhere else.

Blended Threats Complex cyberattacks combining the characteristics of computer worms and viruses.

Blue Boxing Using boxes containing electronic components to produce tones that manipulate the telephone companies' switches.

Border Gateway Protocol (BGP) One of the core routing protocols in the Internet. The BGP is used in all border routers of the tens of thousands of networks that comprise the Internet and takes care of forwarding data to the correct next hop on the path to the destination.

Buffer A portion of memory set aside to store data, often read from an input channel, in a computer program.

Buffer Overflow An error that occurs when a program writes data beyond the bounds of allocated memory, causing unexpected results.

C A computer language created in the 1970s by Dennis Ritchie.

Capture/Replay An attacker captures a whole stream of data to be able to replay it later in an attempt to repeat the effects. Thus, a bank or a stock sales transaction might be repeated to empty a bank account of a targeted person.

Channel An established communication link through which a message travels as it is transmitted between a communication source and a receiver.

Choke Points Points where security controls can be applied to protect multiple vulnerabilities along a path or a set of paths.

Cloned Cellular Phones Buying cloned cellular phones in bulk and discarding them after the crime is completed. In this context, cellular fraud is defined as the unauthorized use, tampering, or manipulation of a cellular phone or service.

Code The portion of the computer program that can be read, written, and modified by humans.

Compiler A program that converts another program from human readable source language to electronic language that can be executed on a computer.

Computer Penetrations and Looping A technique allowing cybercriminals to break into someone's computer account and issue commands from that account, posing as the account holder.

Council of Europe Convention on Cybercrime The first global legislative attempt of its kind to set standards on the definition of cybercrime and to develop policies and procedures that govern international cooperation to combat cybercrime.

Cracking Gaining unauthorized access to computer systems to commit a crime.

Crackers Those who break into others' computer systems without authorization to commit crimes. Also called network hackers or net-runners.

Crash To cause a personal computer, computer system, or network to break down or fail to operate.

CyberAngels A not-for-profit organization of White Hats assisting victims of cybercrimes, particularly of cyberstalking and cyberpornography.

Cybercrime A crime related to technology, computers, and the Internet, resulting in harm to property and/or to persons.

Cyberspace Composed of hundreds of thousands of interconnected computers, servers, routers, switches, and fiber optic cables, cyberspace allows the critical infrastructures to work. Thus, it is the "nervous system" of the global economy.

Cyberstalking Using cyberspace to control, harass, or terrorize a target to the point that he or she fears harm or death to self or to others close to the target.

Cyberterrorism Unlawful attacks and threats of attack by terrorists against computers, networks, and the information stored therein when done to intimidate or coerce a government or its people to further the perpetrator's political or social objectives.

Daemon A process running in the background that performs some service for other computer programs.

Distributed Denial-of-Service (DDoS) A cyberattack in which a cracker bombards a targeted computer with thousands or more fake requests for information, causing the computer to run out of memory and other resources and to either slow down dramatically or stop. The cracker uses more than one (typically hundreds) of previously cracked computers throughout the Internet to originate the attack. The multiple origins of the attack make it difficult to defend against it.

Driver (or Device Driver) A computer program that is intended to allow another program (typically, an operating system) to interact with a hardware device.

Eavesdropping Watching data as they travel through the Internet.

Encryption The mathematical conversion of information into a form from which the original information cannot be restored without using a special key.

Fast Exploitation The quality of a computer problem or attack being fast-acting, leaving security experts little time to analyze it, to warn the Internet community, or to protect their systems.

Finger A UNIX command providing information about users that can be used to retrieve files from a user's home directory.

Firewalls Programs used to provide additional security on networks by blocking access from the public network to certain services in the private network.

Flooding A form of cyberspace vandalism resulting in denial-of-service (DoS) to authorized users.

FTP (File Transfer Protocol) A protocol used to transfer files between systems over a network.

Gateway In computer networks this is the router (or communication node) that connects an internal or local area network to the Internet or another type of wide area network.

Hacker A person who enjoys learning the details of computer systems and how to stretch their capabilities.

Hijacking The cutting off of an authenticated, authorized connection between a sender and a receiver. The attacker then takes over the connection, "killing" the information sent by the original sender, and sending "attack data" instead.

Honeypots or Honeynets A computer or network set up to pretend that it offers some real service to the Internet, in order to lure crackers. This computer or network is then closely monitored by an expert to find out how the cracker breaks into the system and what he or she does to compromise it.

Identity Theft The malicious theft of and consequent misuse of someone else's identity (e.g., to commit crimes).

Intellectual Property A concept that treats products of the human mind similarly to physical property. Intellectual property laws grant certain kinds of exclusive rights over these products on the analogy of property rights.

Internet Piracy The use of the Internet for illegally copying or distributing software.

IP Address A numerical identifier that is divided into a part that identifies a network (like a school, a university, a government agency, or a company network) and another part designed to identify each computer in this network. The IP address is very much comparable to a street name and a house number on a nonvirtual street.

Kernel The very heart or essential component of any operating system.

Linux An operating system widely used on Internet servers and embraced by large corporations as an alternative to the Microsoft operating system.

Local Area Network (LAN) A network often contained in one or more buildings in physically close locations.

Logic Bomb Hidden code instructing a computer virus to perform some potentially destructive action when specific criteria are met.

Loop Carrier System Programmable remote computers used to integrate voice and data communications for efficient transmission over a single, sophisticated fiber optic cable; in many respects, the system serves the same function as a circuit breaker box in a home or an apartment.

Malicious Code Programs such as viruses and worms that exploit weaknesses in computer software, replicating and/or attaching themselves to other programs.

Man-in-the-Middle An attack in which the attacker intercepts data and replies to them as if they came from the intended recipient. A victim thus attacked might expose private data such as credit card or bank account information, which can later be used to defraud him or her.

MOO Acronym for MUD, Object-Oriented.

MUD A multiuser dungeon scenario used in computer gaming.

National Infrastructure Protection Center A U.S. government center for investigating threats and providing warnings regarding attacks against the nation's critical infrastructures, including telecommunications, energy, banking, water systems, government operations, and emergency services.

Net-Runners See **Crackers**.

Network Hackers See **Crackers**.

Newbies See **Scriptkiddies**.

NFS (Network File System) A method of sharing files across a local area network or through the Internet.

Packet A piece of data of fixed or variable size that is sent through a communication network like the Internet. A message is typically broken up into packets before it is sent over a network.

Patch Updated system software, created to close security gaps discovered after the software has been released.

PBX (Private Branch Exchange) A type of internal telephone switchboard.

Phreaking Using technology to make free telephone calls.

Piracy Copying protected software without authorization.

Protocol A set of rules that govern how communication between two programs have to take place to be considered valid.

Proxy Server An intermediary system to which a client program (like a Web browser) connects. This intermediary system connects to the destination on behalf of the client.

Root Servers A group of thirteen servers worldwide that are responsible for the basic level of the domain name system.

Routers A specialized computer device at the border of an Internet-connected network that stores a specialized map of the Internet and contributes to this map by informing its neighbors about what it knows about its part of the Internet.

Safe Frequency The frequency of backups done on a particular computer system at which the maximum possible system loss will be bearable.

Scriptkiddies New, relatively inexperienced crackers in the computer underground who rely on prefabricated software to do their cracking exploits.

Server A computer program that carries out some task on behalf of a user (like delivering a Web page or an e-mail). Computers on which these server applications are run are also called servers.

Sniffer Program A computer program that analyzes data on a communication network to gather intelligence (i.e., to detect a password that is transmitted over the network).

Social Engineering A deceptive process whereby crackers engineer a social situation to trick others into allowing them access to an otherwise closed network.

Spamming The sending of unsolicited e-mails for commercial purposes and sometimes with the criminal intent to defraud.

Spoofing The cyberspace appropriation of an authentic user's identity by nonauthentic users, sometimes causing critical infrastructure breakdowns.

SSH A command to remotely log into a UNIX computer.

Telnet A command to remotely log into a UNIX computer.

TFTP (Trivial File Transfer Protocol) A network protocol that allows unauthenticated transfer of files.

Torvald, Linus The creator and namesake of the Linux computer operating system.

UNIX A widely used computer operating system. It has a standardized and well-publicized set of rules and interfaces that govern the interaction of humans and programs. Therefore, it is considered to be an "open" operating system (vs. a proprietary system, where these details are not as easily accessible).

UUCP An acronym for UNIX to UNIX copy, a protocol used for the store-and-forward exchange of mail.

Virus A (usually harmful) computer program that replicates itself by embedding a copy of itself in other computer programs.

Warez Software Pirated software.

Wide Area Network A network such as the Internet, connecting physically distant locations.

War Dialers Simple personal computer programs that dial consecutive phone numbers looking for modems.

White Hat Hacker Ethic A philosophy formulated in the 1960s. It includes two key principles: (1) Access to computers—and anything that might teach individuals about the way the world works—should be free; and (2) all information should be free.

White Hats Computer hackers with good intentions who tend to hack into systems with authorization to find flaws in the computer network that could be invaded by unwanted cyberintruders.

Wizards Software tools that automate common system administration tasks.

Worm A self-replicating computer program. It is self-contained and does not need to be part of another program to propagate. A virus, in contrast, attaches itself to and becomes part of another executable program.

Zombie A computer program that awaits a signal from a cracker to bombard a particular site. On command, several zombies can simultaneously send thousands of fake requests for information to the targeted site. As the computer tries to handle these requests it soon runs out of memory and slows down dramaticcally or stops altogether.

Index

About the Authors

Bernadette H. Schell is dean of the Faculty of Business and Information Technology at Ontario's only laptop university, the University of Ontario Institute of Technology in Oshawa, Ontario, Canada. Dr. Schell is the 2000 recipient of the University Research Excellence Award from Laurentian University, where she was previously director of the School of Commerce and Administration. Dr. Schell has written numerous journal articles on industrial psychology topics and has authored four books with Quorum Books in Westport, Connecticut, on such topics as organizational and personal stress, corporate leader stress and emotional dysfunction, stalking, and computer hackers.

Clemens Martin is director of IT programs at the Faculty of Business and Information Technology and the Faculty of Engineering at the university of Ontario Institute of Technology. Before joining the University, Dr. Martin was partner and managing director of an information technology consulting company and Internet service provider based in Neuss, Germany. He was responsible for various security and consulting projects, including the implementation of Java-based health care cards for Taiwanese citizens.